TRANSNATIONAL RUPTURES

Gender in a Global/Local World

Series Editors: Jane Parpart, Pauline Gardiner Barber and Marianne H. Marchand

Gender in a Global/Local World critically explores the uneven and often contradictory ways in which global processes and local identities come together. Much has been and is being written about globalization and responses to it but rarely from a critical, historical, gendered perspective. Yet, these processes are profoundly gendered albeit in different ways in particular contexts and times. The changes in social, cultural, economic and political institutions and practices alter the conditions under which women and men make and remake their lives. New spaces have been created – economic, political, social – and previously silent voices are being heard. North-South dichotomies are being undermined as increasing numbers of people and communities are exposed to international processes through migration, travel, and communication, even as marginalization and poverty intensify for many in all parts of the world. The series features monographs and collections which explore the tensions in a 'global/local world', and includes contributions from all disciplines in recognition that no single approach can capture these complex processes.

Also in the series

Women, Migration and Citizenship
Making Local, National and Transnational Connections
Edited by Evangelia Tastsoglou and Alexandra Dobrowolsky
ISBN 0 7546 4379 4

'Innocent Women and Children'
Gender, Norms and the Protection of Civilians
R. Charli Carpenter
ISBN 0 7546 4745 5

The Gender Question in Globalization
Changing Perspectives and Practices
Edited by Tine Davids and Francien van Driel
ISBN 0 7546 3923 1

Turkey's Engagement with Global Women's Human Rights
Nüket Kardam
ISBN 0 7546 4168 6

Transnational Ruptures
Gender and Forced Migration

CATHERINE NOLIN
University of Northern British Columbia

ASHGATE

Published by
Ashgate Publishing Limited
Gower House
Croft Road
Aldershot
Hampshire GU11 3HR
England

Ashgate Publishing Company
Suite 420
101 Cherry Street
Burlington, VT 05401-4405
USA

Ashgate website: http://www.ashgate.com

British Library Cataloguing in Publication Data
Nolin, Catherine
Transnational ruptures : gender and forced migration. -
(Gender in a global/local world)
1. Political refugees - Guatemala 2. Political refugees -
Canada 3.Transnationalism 4. Guatemala - History - Civil
War, 1960-1996 - Refugees 5. Guatemala - Emigration and
immigration 6.Canada - Emigration and immigration
I.Title
325.2'1'097281'0971

Library of Congress Cataloging-in-Publication Data
Nolin, Catherine.
Transnational ruptures : gender and forced migration / by Catherine Nolin.
p. cm. -- (Gender in a global/local world)
Includes bibliographical references and index.
ISBN 0-7546-3805-7 (alk. paper)
1. Forced migration. 2. Women refugees. 3. Refugees--Guatemala. I. Title. II. Series.

HV640.N65 2006
305.9'06914--dc22

2005032385

ISBN 0 7546 3805 7

Printed and bound by Athenaeum Press Ltd,
Gateshead, Tyne & Wear.

Contents

Series Editors' Preface *ix*
Acknowledgements *xi*
List of Figures *xiii*
List of Tables *xv*
List of Abbreviations *xvii*

PART I: COMMUNITY RUPTURES AND TRANSNATIONAL MIGRATION

1 Rupture and Renewal: Guatemala-Canada Connections 3

2 Gender, Community, and Transnationalism 31

PART II: GUATEMALA TO CANADA: STATE VIOLENCE, IMMIGRATION POLICIES, AND POPULATION DYNAMICS

3 Flight into Exile: Internal Armed Conflict and Refugee Displacement 61

4 Government Policies and Refugee Dynamics: Geographies of Movement 83

PART III: SPATIALIZING GENDERED TRANSNATIONAL IDENTITIES

5 Transnational Ethnographies: Gendered Narratives of Rupture and Suture 121

6 Social Spaces and Immobility of Refugee Transnationalism 149

PART IV: CONCLUSION

7 Refugee Transnationalism 181

Bibliography *187*
Appendix One: Glossary of Immigrant Categories and Related Terms *221*
Appendix Two: Seeing More Numbers *227*

Appendix Three: *From Asylum to Control: Testimony of a Deported Taxi Driver* 235

Appendix Four: *'This is What I Want to Deliver': ANTONIO's Escape to Canada* 239

Index 241

For all my family whose love and support see me through both dark and light moments.

For Neil, Will, and baby-on-the-way – all my love.

And for the people of Guatemala within and beyond their beautiful and brutal country.

Author's Note: Portions of various chapters originally appeared in *GeoJournal* 56 (2002): 59-67. Reprinted with kind permission of Kluwer Academic Publishers. Portions of Chapter 2 originally appeared in *Policy-Relevant Research on Immigration and Settlement – Relevant for Whom? A Working Document*, a publication of the Strategic Workshop on Immigrant Women Making Place in Canadian Cities (2002). Reprinted with kind permission of Damaris Rose. Portions of Chapter 6 originally appeared in the *Canadian Journal of Latin American and Caribbean Studies* 29, 57/58 (2004): 267-288. Reprinted with kind permission of editor Victor Armony. Filóchofo political cartoon originally appeared in *Siglo Veintiuno*, 21 June (2000): http:// www.sigloxxi.com. Reprinted with kind permission of the artist Jose Manual Chacón (Filóchofo). Cover artwork kindly provided courtesy of the artist Irene Klar.

Series Editors' Preface

Transnational Ruptures: Gender and Forced Migration, by Catherine Nolin, is the ninth title to appear in the Ashgate series "Gender in a Global/Local World." The series takes advantage of critically engaged new feminist and gender studies scholarship in the turn towards the global. This turn has produced an increased concern with the (gendered) impacts of globalization and contingent international processes. All volumes in this interdisciplinary series pose alternative, gendered questions to mainstream discussion of global processes and local responses.

This volume is no exception. *Transnational Ruptures* is truly a global/local project. It contributes to a further round of transnational migration scholarship, applying a transnational optic to refugee studies in particular (its theoretical innovation) and to the landscapes of refugees from Guatemala in particular (its methodological contribution). While the refugees in the study reside primarily in Canada, comparisons are drawn with regional migrants living in other contexts, particularly the United States. The comparisons are particularly revealing of how state policies structure transnational experiences, both in contexts of origin for those who remain behind and in the new locations where immigrants reside. Gender, as well as political violence, are shown to be central organizing principles of the refugee immigrant experience.

In demonstrating the relevance of transnationalism to refugee studies, Nolin takes us well beyond the temptation to conflate place with community and community with identity, a not uncommon feature in migration studies. Instead, with a geographer's insistence on place making as a social and political process, the author charts a course through the "rupturing" and "suturing" of ties, both physical and material, social and personal, experienced by refugees whose migrations commence from political violence. Forced into exile, refugees are often unable to sustain the kinds of transnational connections to their places of origin that the new transnationalism literature describes for many immigrants. For example, remittances, now considered a definitive feature of many transnational migration flows, are less a feature of the transnational connections for the subjects in Nolin's study, a finding that directs us back to the harsh realities of racialized labour markets and the persistent "income gap" experienced by new immigrants. Further, through careful attention to the spatialization of immigrants lives, the insight that refugee social spaces are not necessarily geographic, offers significant challenge to the literature on immigrant communities which can over-read geographic proximity as "community". With this insight Nolin's work follows on from *Women Migration and Citizenship*, edited by Tastsoglou and Dobrowolsky, its predecessor in this series, to contribute further detailed examples of the gender differentiated experiences of citizenship, here provided through heart-wrenching accounts of refugee social isolation. Methodologically, Nolin's multi-scaled, multi-method, multi-sited, qualitative study, provides a model for interdisciplinary transnational studies, not only of refugees, but other immigrant populations as well. The study has significant implications for researchers and policy makers concerned with the problems and challenges confronting refugees and immigrants in an increasingly unequal yet globally connected world.

Pauline Gardiner Barber
Marianne Marchand
Jane Parpart

Acknowledgements

I have accumulated many debts during the writing of this book but it all starts with the generous financial support I received from numerous sources that funded fieldwork both in Canada and Guatemala. I wish to acknowledge the Social Sciences and Humanities Research Council of Canada (SSHRC), the International Development Research Centre (IDRC), Queen's University for several grants, fellowships and bursaries. I also thank the Alberta Métis Nation for facilitating an early research award. Transnational research, I found out the hard way, is an expensive endeavour and so support from all of these sources is gratefully acknowledged. Additionally, I have been supported more recently in so many ways at the University of Northern British Columbia (UNBC), particularly through a UNBC Office of Research publication grant.

I have so many people and organizations to thank whose contributions of valuable assistance and encouragement are woven into this book. Due to my IDRC Research Award and the UNBC publication grant, I am in the enviable position of thanking a number of people for their research assistance. After completing her Master's thesis at Queen's University in 1998, Finola Shankar trekked around Guatemala with me and offered critical assistance in the conceptualization of interview questions and translation work. I was extremely fortunate to find an excellent travel partner and writing partner in Finola and I thank her for ongoing inspiration. Graduate students Krista House, Robert Oliver, Simon Springer and Jacqui Stephens know that their contributions as research assistants are also appreciated, even if their dedicated work is not apparent here. Michael Pacey of Queen's University and Jessica McGregor of UNBC are responsible for producing the maps that are an important part of this book.

I am exceedingly fortunate to have the mentorship of Drs W. George Lovell and Audrey L. Kobayashi. I thank George for encouraging me to combine my research interests and solidarity commitments and for providing the best example of a life well-lived. He always reinforces the moral implications of my research and stressed the need always to keep a human face in front of the statistics. Audrey offered complete support during particularly difficult or discouraging times and her commitment to feminist and critical geography is an inspiration.

I appreciate all the research participants in Canada and Guatemala who shared their stories with me. I particularly thank all the participants in Guatemala who opened their homes to Finola and me with such warmth and generosity. I will never forget all the dinners, car rides, invitations to church services (Baptist, Mormon or Catholic), excursions arranged for us, and more often than not, the offer of a comfortable bed to rest on. Though not referred to by name in these acknowledgements, they are very much a part of this endeavour. Also in Guatemala, I thank Dr Linda Asturias de Barrios of *Estudio 1360* for supporting my research, *Centro de Investigaciones Regionales Mesoamérica* (CIRMA) for offering pleasant surroundings for library research, and Shannon Lockhart, the Bilingual Assistant in the Mental Health area of the *Oficina de Derechos Humanos del Arzobispado de Guatemala* (ODHAG), for meeting with us in Guatemala to share the experiences of the *Proyecto Interdiocesano de Recuperación de la Memoria Histórica* (REMHI) team. Additionally, many thanks to María Concepción Sáenz, director of *Centro de Estudio y Documentación de la Frontera Occidental de Guatemala* (CEDFOG) in Huehuetenango. Unfortunately, staff members of the Canadian Embassy in Guatemala chose to neither encourage or support my research and so their critical perspectives are largely absent.

Many friendships have seen me through the last several years as I moved through Edmonton, Calgary, Kingston, Hamilton, Halifax and Prince George. Special thanks to all of my friends across the country in the Guatemala Canada Solidarity Network (GCSN). In addition I also extend my thanks to Dr Jennifer Hyndman for advice, assistance and encouragement first from Arizona and later British Columbia, Dr Christopher H. Lutz for kind words and thoughtful consideration, and to the dynamic group of Latin Americanist geographers who met in Antigua in 2004.

I appreciate the artistic contribution of Guatemalan political cartoonist and activist Jose Manual Chacón (Filóchofo) who allowed the inclusion of one of his images in this volume as well as Canadian artist Irene Klar whose *Maternal Pattern* image graces the book's cover.

I want to also extend my thanks to the faculty, graduate students, undergraduate students and staff at Queen's University, Dalhousie University and the University of Northern British Columbia (UNBC) for ongoing interest in this project and support whenever needed. I am most fortunate to receive encouragement from my colleagues in Geography and across various programs at UNBC to organize a Geography Field School to Guatemala in 2004 and to make this project a reality. The field school experience was a highlight of my life and confirmed by commitment to complete this project.

My most sincere thanks are reserved for my amazingly supportive families – the Alberta Nolins and the Ontario, Newfoundland and Nova Scotia Hanlons. To my families and to Neil Hanlon, my husband, I carry you with me wherever I go. Neil always supports my excursions to Guatemala and memorably joined me during one fieldwork trip. Daily, Neil shows me the depths of our commitment and made my work, and all else, entirely possible. During these years of exploration, loss, violence, hope, and struggle, my most precious gift was the arrival of our son, Will, whose beautiful presence reminds me daily why we must work for change. And now with the completion of this project comes another new life in our family. How fortunate am I?!

List of Figures

Figure 1.1	Interview Locations in Canada and Guatemala	23
Figure 3.1	Sanctuary Routes to Canada	77
Figure 3.2	Filóchofo Political Cartoon: Guatemalan President Portillo Sends Family to Canada, June 2000	80
Figure 4.1	Entry of Guatemalan Permanent Residents, 1980 to 2004	90
Figure 4.2	Gender of Guatemalan Permanent Residents, 1980 to 2004	91
Figure 4.3	Age of Guatemalan Permanent Residents, 1980 to 2004	91
Figure 4.4	Age Specific Gender Ratios for Guatemalan Permanent Residents,1980 to 2004	93
Figure 4.5A	Guatemalan Population in Canada's Gateway Cities, 2001	114
Figure 4.5B	Guatemalan Population beyond Canada's Gateway Cities, 2001	115
Figure 4.6	Distribution of Guatemalan Immigrants in the United States	117

List of Tables

Table 3.1	Number of Killings and Disappearances at Guatemalan Universities by Year, 1978 to 1995	70
Table 3.2	Guatemalans Beyond Guatemala, Estimates (2001)	75
Table 4.1	Age and Gender Distribution, Guatemalan Permanent Residents, 1980 to 2004	92
Table 4.2	Guatemalan Applications for Landing Made from Abroad, by City of Application, 1980 to 1999	99
Table 4.3	Total and Percentage of Guatemalan Applications for Landing, USA vs. Elsewhere, 1980 to 1999	99
Table 4.4	Guatemalan Applications (Individuals) for Landing Made from Abroad, by City of Application (Before IRCA, Immediately After, 5 Years Later, 10 Years Later)	101
Table 4.5	Guatemalan Refugee Claims, Port of Entry, by Province, 1990 to 1999	102
Table 4.6	Guatemalan Permanent Residents, Port of Entry, by Province, 1985 to 2004	102
Table 4.7	Guatemalan Refugee Claims, Port of Entry and Inland Offices, by Province (with Number of Ports of Entry and Inland Offices) and Year, 1990 to 1999	104
Table 4.8	Guatemalan Permanent Residents, Port of Entry, by Province (with Number of Entry Ports) and Year, 1985 to 2004	105
Table 4.9	Guatemalan Refugee Claims, by Port of Entry and Inland Offices, 1990 to 1999 (Appendix Two)	228
Table 4.10	Guatemalan Permanent Residents, by Points of Entry, 1985 to 2004 (Appendix Two)	230
Table 4.11	Guatemalan and Salvadoran Refugee Claims, Acceptance Rate, 1989 to 2004	106
Table 4.12	Occupations, Guatemalan Permanent Residents, 1980 to 2004	109
Table 4.13	Guatemalan Permanent Residents, by Immigrant Class, 1980 to 2004 (Appendix Two)	233
Table 4.14	Minister's Permits Issued to Guatemalans and Other Central Americans, 1980 to 2004 (Appendix Two)	234
Table 4.15	Final Destination of Confirmed Departures, 1980 to 1998	111
Table 4.16	Guatemalan Population in Canada, by Province, 1986 to 2001	113
Table 4.17	Guatemalan Population in Canada, by City, 1986 to 2001	116

List of Abbreviations

AAG	Association of American Geographers
AI	Amnesty International
CBSA	Canada Border Services Agency
CEH	*Comisión de Esclarecimiento Histórico* (Commission for Historical Clarification)
CIC	Citizenship and Immigration Canada
CIDA	Canadian International Development Agency
CNT	*Central Nacional de Trabajadores* (National Confederation of Workers)
EGP	*Ejército Guerrillero de los Pobres* (Guerrilla Army of the Poor); one of four groups comprising the URNG
EMP	*Estado Mayor Presidencial* (Presidential General Staff); military staff attached to the presidency
FAR	*Fuerzas Armadas Rebeldes* (Rebel Armed Forces); one of four groups comprising the URNG
FRG	*Frente Republicano Guatemalteco* (Guatemalan Republican Front); political party
G-2	Army intelligence
GAM	*Grupo de Apoyo Mutuo* (Mutual Support Group)
GCN	Guatemalan Community Network (TORONTO)
GCSN	Guatemala Canada Solidarity Network
GM	*Globe and Mail* newspaper
ICCHRLA	Inter-Church Committee on Human Rights in Latin America
ICCR	Inter-Church Committee on Refugees
IMTB	Information Management and Technology Branch
INS	Immigration and Naturalisation Service (USA)
IOM	International Organization for Migrants
IRB	Immigration and Refugee Board (CANADA)
IRCA	Immigration Reform and Control Act
LCP	Live-in Caregiver Program
MRP-Ixim	*Movimiento Revolucionario Popular – Ixim* (Popular Revolutionary Movement – *Ixim*); '*Ixim*' means corn
NGO	Non-governmental organization
OAS	Organization of American States
ODHAG	*Oficina de Derechos Humanos del Arzobispado de Guatemala* (Human Rights Office of the Archdiocese of Guatemala)

ORPA	*Organización Revolucionaria del Pueblo en Armas* (Revolutionary Organization of the People in Arms); one of four groups comprising the URNG
PA	Project Accompaniment (Canadian solidarity network)
PBI	Peace Brigades International (accompaniment organization, Toronto-based Central America Project)
PGT	*Partido Guatemalteco de Trabajo* (Guatemala Workers Party); one of four groups comprising the URNG
POE	Port of Entry
REMHI	*Proyecto Interdiocesano de Recuperación de la Memoria Histórica* (Recuperation of Historical Memory Inter-diocesan Project of the ODHAG)
TS	*Toronto Star* newspaper
UN	United Nations
UNHCR	United Nations High Commissioner for Refugees
URNG	*Unidad Revolucionaria Nacional Guatemalteca* (National Revolutionary Union of Guatemala); umbrella group comprising four guerrilla factions (EGP, FAR, ORPA, PGT), founded in 1982
USAC	*Universidad de San Carlos* (San Carlos University)

PART I
Community Ruptures and Transnational Migration

Chapter 1

Rupture and Renewal: Guatemala-Canada Connections

The movement of asylum seekers and (im)migrants[1] from Guatemala to Mexico, the United States, and Canada (among other countries) has a 25 year history. State violence in the late 1970s and early 1980s led to the unprecedented flight of both indigenous and non-indigenous Guatemalans within and across national borders. The displacement of hundreds of thousands of Guatemalans led to one of the most dispersed indigenous populations in the Americas and an exiled activist population. Movement to the United States has been especially strong, with approximately one million individuals settled throughout that country. The resulting diaspora also officially includes 14,095 Guatemalans legally settled in Canada according to the 2001 Canadian census (Statistics Canada 2004a), approximately 5,000 of whom are concentrated in southwestern Ontario. Additionally, almost 3,000 women and men self-identified as Mayas (Statistics Canada 2004b). Both indigenous and non-indigenous Guatemalans fled to southwestern Ontario early on and continue to arrive there as the repercussions of state terror and violence still afflict Guatemala.

Fieldwork undertaken in Ontario, Canada and in various locations in Guatemala reveals the complex personal, cultural, and geographical aspects of exile and migration in an emerging transnational refugee landscape. With more than one million Guatemalans living and working outside their country of origin as refugees, (im)migrants, and exiles – one million of an estimated population at the time of ten million, as Lovell and Lutz (1996) speculate – there is growing interest in the social spaces these people occupy and the ways in which constructions of identity, community, and citizenship change over space and time, not only for those who negotiate their passages across borders but also for family members left behind. What do these constructions mean for the future of already established communities in Guatemala, if indeed 'communities' may be said to exist there, and the emergence of new social spaces in Canada? With a fragile peace agreement now in place in

1 Rouse (1995a, 357) argues that within much popular and academic discourse about migration, 'immigrant' suggests a process of unidirectional movement. 'Migrant,' on the other hand, suggests a process of movement back and forth, one in which individuals remain oriented to their place of origin. I agree with his statement that 'matters have rarely been that simple and they have grown steadily more complex under transnational conditions.' By using his term '(im)migrant,' ambiguity is stressed.

Guatemala, I argue that the implications of transnationalism will grow ever more significant in the re-imagining of identity, 'place making,' and citizenship in the years ahead as Guatemalans negotiate the ruptures and renewals of transnational lives.

Research Significance

Political Violence and Gender Concerns

Part of the challenge of understanding Guatemalan refugee transnationalism of the 1970s through the 1990s is the necessity to understand the political and policy contexts that refugees and immigrants fled from and entered into upon arrival in Canada. Of central concern are issues of Guatemalan political and economic violence, Canadian foreign and immigration policies, immigration status, socio-economic circumstances, and spatial concentration or dispersal of settlement – all of which factor into the vastly different experience and form of transnationalism than the more thoroughly documented American- and Mexican-destination scenarios encountered by researchers such as Fink (2003), Foxen (2002), Hagan (1994), Hamilton and Stoltz Chinchilla (2001), Loucky and Moors (2000), Popkin (1999), Rodman Ruiz (2004), and others. Whereas, the American- and Mexican-destination research highlights mobility and connections, the Canadian experience I encountered highlights immobility and rupture.

Therefore, I am interested in how political violence and new refugee spaces in Canada work together to create these particular social spaces – or spaces of social relations – which are constituted by a mix of ruptures, connections, yearning to return, denial of the past, new opportunities, concocted life stories, identity re-negotiation, and recognition. One of my main concerns in this book is to situate political violence in Guatemala as the core feature of Guatemalan transnationalism that is in turn shaped by government policies and social action. Bringing together these key components enables an examination of the destruction, alteration, and creation of multiple social spaces that are both gendered and racialized.

My second main concern is to contribute to the small but growing literature which attempts to situate gender as a central organizing principle in migration and refugee research in the Americas (Fouron and Glick Schiller 2001; Goldring 2001; Lawson 1998; Mahler 1999; Mahler and Pessar 2001; Menjívar 1999; Pessar 1999; and Pessar and Mahler 2003). This regional-specific research intersects with the work of scholars such as Willis and Yeoh (2000) and Kofman and England (1997), among others, who discuss issues at a global level, as well as the Canadian-specific work of Creese and Dowling (2001), Dyck and McLaren (2004), Hyndman (1999a), Status of Women Canada (1998), the participants of the Strategic Workshop on Immigrant Women Making Place in Canadian Cities (2002), Walton-Roberts (2004), and Waters (2002). A key development in international migration in recent years has been the 'feminization of migrant populations' or the growing number of female (im)migrants and refugees on the move, who now often out-number their male counterparts (Martin 2001). Research attention now focuses not only on the growing *number* of women on the move but also on their *changing gender roles* as more female (im)migrants participate as principal wage earners and heads of household rather than as 'dependants.'

In Martin's (2001, 3) recent study of global migration trends, she suggests that, '[o]ne of the most significant trends has been the feminisation of migration streams that had heretofore been primarily male.' The principal reason relates to continuing, and increasing, levels of global poverty and the desire of women to better their lives and those of their children. Migration, therefore, often occurs outside legal channels, leading to clandestine movement, heightened vulnerability, abuse, and exploitation. Yet women remain under-represented among refugee claimants accepted into Canada. Though the UNHCR (1999) notes that '[t]he face of refugees are overwhelmingly those of women and children, as they comprise up to 80 per cent of most refugee populations,' yet only one third of refugee claimants accepted into Canada are women (Boyd 1994, 8; Hyndman 1999a; Macklin 1996, 120).

Global/Local or a Politics of Scale?

In his recent examination of 'transnational spaces and everyday lives' David Ley (2004, 155) strongly argues for the need to move beyond the now common-place dichotomy of the global and the local where the 'global is regarded as the space of sameness, and the local with places of difference.' Ley (2004, 155) argues that in a transnational paradigm, a 're-incorporation of other scales' and 'jumping scales' in our analyses is a necessity, if we are interested in seeing how, for example, the home – one of the most localized of geographical scales – is both local and global at the same time. How do we grapple with the embodied experience of forced migration, with the accompanying connections and ruptures both across borders and within the household and immediate surroundings, without a multi-scaled social analysis? The challenge is to be mindful of the politics of scale when 'the global and the local may dissolve into closely related versions of each other' Ley (2004, 156).

Attention to *who* is (im)migrating and how this shapes and is shaped by changing gender roles comes at a time when geographers, in particular, are concentrating on the politics of scale and working to reveal the dynamics of migration and other processes at the scale of the home and the body (McDowell 1999; Teather 1999). Rich (1986 in Valentine 2001, 15) describes the body as 'the geography of the closest in;' as the 'primary location where our personal identities are constituted and social knowledges and meanings inscribed.' Feminist and critical geographers take seriously Rich's statement that 'our bodies make a difference to our experiences of place,' and work to reveal the hidden geographies of experience which are critical to our analyses of mobility and immobility.

Rachel Silvey's (2004, 5) survey of feminist migration research identifies the long-held concern in geography with the politics of scale as a major research theme and one which draws attention to the 'working of power within particular scales.' Key to this study is Silvey's (2004, 5) point that:

> Attention to the national scale as gendered and concern with the politics of scales both finer and coarser than the national scale allows for the conceptualization of relational linkages between bodies, households and the transnational sphere.

For example, in the following chapters we shall see the links between the embodied experience of political violence and terror, massive population displacement within and across borders, and attempts to maintain spatially ruptured social relations through the (im)migration process. Typically it is through qualitative, ethnographic methods that examine multi-scaled relations and processes – from the body, household, and community, to the regional, national, supra-national, and global – that the complexities of transnational lives are made known.

Why the Guatemala-Canada Concern?

Why take on this research and focus on a refugee and (im)migrant population that is less-than-numerically significant on the Canadian immigration scene? I would assert at least two good reasons. First, this is a postcolonial world – geographer Derek Gregory (2004) actually names it the 'colonial present' – in which it is necessary to think beyond the nation and to engage the NAFTA-influenced mindset that links Mexico, the United States, and Canada and thus, geographically, makes Central Americans our neighbors. As Stephens (2004, 2005) ably argues, Canadian (business) interests are exploding in Guatemala, particularly related to mining activity, with limited appreciation for the country's suffering. Though relatively few in number in Canada, their voices are growing stronger as Canada's official concerns move from issues of social justice and human rights to business and trade negotiations.

A focus on the transnational lives and place making of Guatemalan refugees and (im)migrants may illuminate the complexity of the issues facing Canada and the United States as we move towards the goal of living in healthier, more just societies in the twenty-first century. Issues of mass migration, diasporic populations, and challenges to established immigration and refugee policy from citizens of the Americas are central to contemporary political debates on the future visions of our nations. A focus on the Guatemalan population at various locations in the diaspora illuminates something of the transnational realities of many who have ventured through the difficult passage landscapes of Mexico, the United States, and Canada along with those who remained in Guatemala.

Second, as Guatemala moves through the implementation of the Peace Accords that brought a formal end to 36 years of internal armed conflict, the refugee and (im)migrant population in the United States and Canada may demand a greater role in shaping the future of Guatemala during the difficult years ahead. For example, in the early months of 2005, Guatemalan organizations in the United States are actively negotiating with the Guatemalan government in order to allow out-of-country voting in future elections (Vásquez and Escobar 2005; Vásquez and Rodríguez 2005). As well, Orozco (2003), the Inter-American Dialogue Task Force on Remittances (2004), Robinson (2004), and the International Organization for Migration – IOM (2004), among others, argue that the foreign remittances and transnational linkages cultivated and maintained throughout the years of violence will be increasingly depended upon for economic, social, and cultural sustainability in Guatemala. Economic connections may be one way in which those physically displaced from their homeland may find it possible to reclaim a place in the Guatemalan nation. Therefore, we need an understanding of the meanings and significance of communication networks and remittances in the Canadian context.[2]

Transnational Ruptures

Transnationalism is a complex process that involves, as Guarnizo and Smith (1998, 29) argue, macro- and micro- dynamics. A main concern of this book is to examine political violence in Guatemala as the core feature of Guatemalan transnationalism that is in turn shaped by government policies and social action. A triangulation of these key components enables an examination of the destruction, alteration, and creation of multiple social spaces and the ensuing reinscriptions or renegotiations of identity. But how do we begin to deal with the complexity of political violence, refugee displacement, government policies, media imagery, and new refugee spaces and identities? For geographer Michael Watts (1992a, 126), addressing such questions means manoeuvring through 'material spatial practices, perceptions, and representations [with] a geographic sensibility, the interpretive flair of the humanist and literary theorist, and the ethnographic turn of the anthropologist and social historian.' Watts, indeed, realizes that 'this is a tall order.' Like him, I do not pretend to fit this bill, but in the following chapters I take up his challenge in order to come to grips with the transnational outcomes of political violence, and the many ruptures and sutures of identity that constitute the transnational social spaces forged out of the ashes of shattered communities, whether we define those as physical entities or communities of association.

What I attempt in this book is an interrogation of notions of 'transnationalism,' 'community,' and 'identity' in the context of social disintegration in Guatemala and subsequent forced migration, displacement, and resettlement in Canada. By examining the burgeoning concept of transnationalism in relation to political violence, I set out to establish the usefulness of the concept of 'refugee transnationalism' through grounded transnational fieldwork in Guatemala and Canada. By stressing the disjuncture, ruptures, and fear that accompany the more obvious connections, points of attachment, and security offered in refuge, I want to add some complexity to the mix and differentiate a

2 As will be discussed at length later, the practice of sending remittance to one's family in Guatemala is not as significant with Guatemalan Canadians as with those living in the United States. I began this research project thinking that the issue of remittances might be a significant aspect of the research; in fact it was significant by its absence. The agency of refugees and (im)migrants to negotiate Canadian and American labour landscapes is curtailed in different ways and, in the end, restricts remittance sending from Canada and facilitates the practice from the United States.

'refugee transnationalism' from an '(im)migrant transnationalism' and to reinforce the need to see these processes through a gendered lens.

Is it appropriate, though, to distinguish a refugee transnationalism from other forms of transnationality? Seteney Shami (1996, 8) suggests that researchers such as Liisa Malkki (1997) argue against states, organizations, and scholars that 'constitute refugees differently from other kinds of deterritorialization.' Others, such as Allen White (1999), see this differentiation as central to an understanding of 'how power realizes itself through the dislocation of people in different ways.' In an era of globalization driven by neoliberalism accompanied by gendered and racialized exploitation (c.f., Nurse 2003; Watts 1997, 2004), knowledge of home country social conditions are critical to progressive understandings of new refugee and (im)migrant spaces in Canada. Social spaces are connected and ruptured by processes that hold the potential for peace, justice, and social reconstruction. Therefore, I agree with Shami that there is analytical purpose and ethical imperative to the disentanglement of the categories of all those on the move. The 'actuality of inequality, dislocation, and suffering' (Shami 1996, 8) must be inserted into an analysis in order to write against oppression, political violence, and repression.

Contradictions and Connections

As with Sarah Mahler's (1995) book *American Dreaming: Immigrant Life on the Margins*, this is not the story about which I set out to write. After steeping myself in the literature of transnationalism and migration, I came out with a wholly USA-centric notion that often celebrates the 'freedom' of transnationalism, the economic benefits to the migrants' home country (and community and family) through remittance-sending, and the ever-growing (positive) impacts of new technologies and cyber-space. Mahler found that such versions of transnationalism, so prominent in early- to mid-1990s migration literature, did not fit her research participants either, an assortment of undocumented Central American (im)migrants living 'on the margins' of Long Island. The benefits of bringing a transnational perspective to research on migration and refugee movement are clear enough, but the preliminary thinking was just not a good fit. It is too neat, tight, and often remains at the abstract level of theoretical consideration. I deliberately avoid focusing attention on the cyber-spatial, remittance-sending, freewheeling transnational migrant. My focus instead is on what Appadurai (1996, 3) calls the transnational 'ruptures' that sear through the discourse of exile, migration, place making, and identity for those with whom I spoke. As 'transnational studies' matures, others such as Wimmer and Glick Schiller (2003) and Levitt and Glick Schiller (2004), moderate the celebratory tone of early transnational studies and suggest that in the future we will see more studies which explore the varying impacts of transnationalism on places of departure, transit, and settlement. Guarnizo et al. (2003), too, suggest that results of their recent work on transnational political engagement 'help temper celebratory images of the extent and effects of transnational engagement provided by some scholars.'

Through an empirical study that is theoretically engaged, but not theoretically driven, I hope to convey the continuities and contradictions of transnational place making and identity that result from transnational ruptures. My findings reveal much about contemporary migrations and yet stress the particularities of the Guatemalan case. Everyday realities of lives across borders are messy, heart-wrenching, and guilt-ridden. After meeting with Guatemalans living in southwestern Ontario (some refugee claimants, many landed immigrants, and others now Canadian citizens), the 'sexiness' of transnationalism soon faded and the gritty details of isolation, ambiguity, loss of dignity, and constantly feeling 'out-of-place' took over. Visits with family members still in Guatemala reinforced many early analyses and added new layers, and twists, to the already 'thick' discourse on Guatemalan Canadian transnationalism that we (the participants and I) developed in the first phase of the research project. This is not to say that success or happiness finds no home in their narratives, but the process of place making is revealed to be an ongoing struggle.

In this study of Guatemalan forced migration and settlement in Ontario, I draw on theory to unsettle common notions of what 'community' means in Guatemala, the migration process, Canadian immigration studies, and the everyday lives of Guatemalan refugees and (im)migrants. By examining the consequences of political violence for Guatemalans in Canada, I reveal their place making struggles to be a gendered, political, cultural, and interpretive phenomenon. Cultural re-inventions or re-territorializations are explored to uncover the meanings attributed to historical circumstances that made these folks (im)migrants and refugees in the first place, as well as current realities that influence the renegotiation of identity. Transnational residence (or mind-set, at least) alters the meanings and practices of citizenship (central to ones' transnational self). Dual citizenship is now possible, but early refugee claimants had to make a weighty choice between one nationality and the other. Can their predicaments be instructive to a discussion of transnational citizenship?

Given the nature of migration, political asylum, immigration, and identity, there is no straightforward package of findings; instead, this is a book of contradictions. My findings are sometimes complementary, but more often contradictory, seemingly clear-cut but usually ambiguous. I think this is reasonable. The deeper one digs, the more interviews one engages in, and the frequency of chance encounters that inevitably challenge previously taken-for-granted positions all work together to make the 'fuzziness' of migration difficult to clarify. As Diane Nelson (1999, 31) so aptly reveals about Guatemala:

> It is a well-known joke that the longer a foreigner stays in Guatemala the harder it is to write about it. Whole books can come out of a three-week sojourn, whereas those who have lived there several years are gradually overcome by such a sense of complexity and contradiction that it becomes increasingly difficult to write.

I think Nelson's statement also holds true for those of us (researchers, refugees, and solidarity activists) geographically removed from, but intellectually and emotionally connected to, this Central American country. Fortunately for me, I have been able to come and go from Guatemala approximately ten times in the last twelve years, staying in touch with the changing realities through Email, the Internet, various solidarity groups, and teaching opportunities. Solidarity in Canada is strong and deep, as Kathryn Anderson (2003) so nicely demonstrates, spanning the country and rooted in local communities where least expected. Contacts with the Central America Solidarity Working Group in Kingston (Ontario), the cross-Canada Project Accompaniment (PA) network that, in 1999, transformed into the Guatemala Canada Solidarity Network (GCSN) facilitate a grounding so vital to work through the contradictions of Guatemala-Canada connections and make them comprehensible.[3]

Situating the Personal: Solidarity, Ethical Entanglements and Identity Markings

The research process involves myriad motivations, mis-steps, and marvels. How do my solidarity activities and my multiple mis-identifications as a nun/lesbian/evangelical/troubled wife/ready-marriage material/general bother imbue my questions, interactions, field notes, and final writings? My positionings, identity (and identity markings by others), and advocacy/activism roles influenced the research methodology profoundly. Tourist wanderings, Project Accompaniment activism, research, reading, talking, and listening all informed the particular shape this research endeavour took while my transnational positionings, identity markings, and continued activism encouraged ethical sensitivity in this writing.

Guatemala has not always been a fascination of mine. After one particularly discouraging course in Latin American Geography I often proclaimed that I would *never* go to that dangerous part of the world: what with all those drug lords and random violence, why would I choose to go *there*? Appreciation of historical context, cultural strength, alternative geographies or hidden transcripts was missing from my early university education and only entered my consciousness when I *did* go there for the first time in 1992. Confronted with issues I was either blind to or could easily avoid (the role of the Catholic Church, social and economic inequalities, racism, systematic human rights violations, American government and military involvement, and so forth), Guatemala shook me out of my slumber.

Upon my return home, I joined the Edmonton branch of Amnesty International. I took it as some sort of sign that at the first meeting I attended, two Guatemalan women spoke in turn of being dragged out of their houses in front of their husbands and children, of their imprisonment, rape, and torture, all because one was a teacher and another a health care promoter. It was a bitterly cold, dark November night when these women spoke of events that had happened only weeks before. A week and a

3 Project Accompaniment (PA) is a Canadian network created in 1992 at the request of Guatemalan Maya refugees in Mexico to participate in their return as international accompaniers, lobbyists, and educators. The network formally disbanded in March 1999 and at a founding meeting in Montréal was reconfigured as the Guatemala Canada Solidarity Network (GCSN) with a broader focus on social justice issues in Guatemala. See: www.gcsn.org.

half in Edmonton as refugee claimants and they had the courage to stand in front of a room of strangers and offer their testimony. The room was packed full and not a single person attempted to hide the powerful effect of their words. '*How could this happen in a sane world*?' the two women asked.

Through Amnesty International, I connected with the local group of Project Accompaniment (PA) at a time when Guatemalans in the United Nations refugee camps in Mexico requested international accompaniment for their negotiated returns. I worked both locally and nationally with the National Steering Committee from 1992 until the returns officially ended in March 1999. My early research endeavours focused on the geography of the refugee returns, and explored the links between place and identity that were central to the return negotiations and subsequent official returns (Nolin Hanlon 1999; Nolin Hanlon and Lovell 1997; 2000).

After the signing of a Peace Accord in January 1996, our network was approached by a number of Guatemalans *in Canada* seeking accompaniment for their own returns to Guatemala to witness exhumations going on in their communities or simply for first excursions back to the country after many years in Canada. It was at this point that I began to realize the multiple connections between their transnationalism and place making of home and adopted spaces. In their requests, I found an articulation of the impacts of a transnationalized identity, no longer in Guatemala, but connected and concerned with family and friends who are. This study, therefore, grew out of my long-term commitment to support social change in Guatemala, from the words of Guatemalans living in Canada, and my ongoing fascination with the relationship between place and identity.

Diane Nelson (1999, 50) wonderfully addresses the 'contact zones' of solidarity and research practice in the Guatemalan context. During our time in Guatemala, she asserts, there is always and everyday, at some level, this repellence of regular tourists, embassy officials, military advisors, and the like that gets played out in our fashionings as researchers and solidarity types. Am I different from the tourists, from all those foreigners who continue to travel to Guatemala? As Nelson puts it, 'they' take their holidays at Lake Atitlán oblivious to the brutality of the place, while 'we' only frequent such havens in order to take well-earned breaks from our research. So are we just well informed, highly educated 'terror tourists,' sickened and somehow thrilled by what we hear and read? What really is it that captures our attention and makes us return to Guatemala again and again? I know of very few people who have been to Guatemala only once. It is a well-known saying that once you go to Guatemala, you're bitten, spellbound, and keep coming back. For many, my knowledge of the country's tragic history and present conditions, partial though it is, was astonishing – '*You know more than I do about my own country and you're Canadian.*' – while for others it was a cause of some concern – '*How do you know so much about internal Guatemalan concerns?*'

Whether or not we can answer these questions, researchers and solidarity activists constantly have to distinguish between themselves and others, such as: (1) from 'everyday' *Norteamericano* tourists; (2) from Americans (always a concern for Canadians); (3) from the *evangelicos* (evangelicals) who are, according to Stoll and Garrard Burnett (1993) and Pebley et al. (2002, 15), transforming the cultural, spiritual, and physical landscape of Guatemala, seemingly overnight; and (4) from immigration authorities, among others. These questions of course mean that while I ask Guatemalans about particular kinds of transnational practices, Nelson (1999) reminds me that we are all caught up in large scale, ongoing transnational relations that shape our engagement with each other from the start.

I stress that scholars must move beyond a concern with our ability to write about lives other than our own. Our ability to comprehend fully the social interactions and life worlds of another community or culture may never be adequate, but that should not prohibit scholars from engaging in socially relevant, committed, sensitive research. I hope that the women and men interviewed for this book feel acknowledged rather than exposed by my study of their experiences and that they recognize credibility and worthiness in its completed form.

I also want to touch on several aspects of the research process that are all too often left out of our writing. Many of us confront ethical issues, questions of commitment and solidarity, as well as the identity markings of all involved. First, I will address two particular ethical entanglements that had to be worked through, and second, the transnational identity markings that attempted to 'place' me in the imaginings of participants are confronted.

Ethical Entanglements (Truth Telling and Dependency)

Ethical entanglements seem to come with the territory of qualitative, engaged research. Two examples from my research will illustrate the need constantly to re-evaluate commitments and values, and re-affirm the boundaries of our relationships. One difficult problem concerns issues of dependency and over-commitment. For example, I had not anticipated the severe isolation within which some newly arrived refugees in Canada live. JOSÉ,[4] a Guatemalan in his mid-sixties, sought asylum in Canada in December 1998 (I met him a week after he arrived) after living an undocumented existence in the United States for ten years. JOSÉ told me that during the entire time in the United States, nobody sat to chat with him or ask how he was doing. My on-going visits were a first for him and this led, I feared, to dependency on my visits and fantasies of a more meaningful relationship. A life on the run for ten years did not allow for the development of social skills such as meeting new people and going to parties. So, now in Canada, JOSÉ does not feel comfortable going out into the community, but rather he lives in isolation within his apartment. Other than my visits, he had only one or two visitors a week. JOSÉ started writing 'love letters' addressed to '*mi reina linda*' [my pretty queen] and cried when I left our meetings. His desperate behaviour escalated and I began to fear being alone with him in his apartment. These incidents led me to re-evaluate my commitments. I had to acknowledge that I could not be everything to every person I interviewed. I am

4 Pseudonyms are capitalized, as are words that participants emphasized in our interview conversations.

committed to reciprocity and ethical treatment of those with whom I worked on this project, but I learned not to promise more than I could deliver.

Another issue revolves around truth-telling and commitment to confidentiality. ANA described for me during our initial visits that she had a strong refugee case and had no trouble being accepted into Canada as a refugee claimant. While I recorded the interview during our third visit, though, ANA confessed that she had 'made up' her case of workplace intimidation (she was a member of a banana workers' union), a subsequent rape, and her desperate journey to the Canadian - American border in order to gain acceptance into Canada:

CATH [S]o you were saying your case was very strong ...

ANA *Mmhm ... I made it up myself.*

CATH You made it up? [Ana nods] Ya?

ANA *Ya, but they don't know, they don't know ... I think I was a good actor up there, ya ... I say when I came, I was working as part of the sindicato* [union] *and some people were intimidating me and some, some people shot me ... like I show my knee ... I had an operation on there, and I said they pulled* [me] *from my bicycle and RAPED me and everything... Forgive me God for this* [looks up at the ceiling]. *Like, like I want to be honest with you, this tape is going nowhere ...*

CATH No, no it's going back to you, so ya ...

ANA *And I was* [from] *a very poor family ... that was TRUE, I was the oldest, for my family part, that was true ... everything I said. But the one when they raped me, that wasn't mine, I make in my mind.*

A commitment to confidentiality is integral to working through the ethical entanglements of truth telling in qualitative research. Based on this recorded confession, ANA could be deported from the country for falsifying information in her refugee case. But without offering a firm statement of confidentiality, information such as hers would be concealed. Is there an ethical imperative to turn this information over to immigration officials? For me, certainly not. A person must identify his or her level of commitment to confidentiality *before* starting the interviewing process since researchers should not go back on this promise once illegal or unpleasant information is revealed.[5]

5 Of course there are exceptions to this rule such as when grave violations or terrorist acts are revealed. Then, perhaps, a higher ethical imperative must guide revelation of interview material for the public good.

'Las Dos Gringitas Vinieron': Transnational Identity Markings[6]

As I asked above, I wonder how mis-identification as a nun/lesbian/evangelical/troubled wife/ready marriage material/general bother imbues my questions, interactions, field notes and final writings? Who am I, how am I perceived, and how does this influence the research? These are questions that I continually asked myself, most especially during the period of research in Guatemala. How do I figure in the fantasies (and stereotypes) of others as I participate in the identificatory process myself (Nelson 1999, 54)? Of course, each person understands and reacts to my motivations differently as do I to their readings of my identity. If only briefly, I will now address some of the many ways in which my research assistant Finola Shankar and I were identified in this project in Guatemala and later in Canada.

In various parts of the country, with different families, in a period of two months, people we interviewed as well as others we met on the street, categorized Finola and I in myriad ways. First, we were both nuns roaming around the countryside greeting everyone we came across. Then we were lesbians watching a women's soccer game with a star lesbian player. One week we were evangelicals; the next week we were Mormons. On another occasion we were American *gringas* and the following week we were frightfully indulgent (with the drink) Catholics. Divergences came in the arena of 'race' as Finola was often thought to be Guatemalan, while I was often called *canche* or blonde. Finola's inclusion in the 'we' worked at times to break down barriers while for me, not really blonde, Métis, and never seeing myself as that white, I was always favourable marriage material in the eyes of the men's mothers: *You like it here, don't you*? *You'll stay, won't you*? 'Sorry, I'm married' '*Oh, that's OK, look at your light skin*!'

In other ways, my identification in Canada within solidarity circles allowed a different kind of access again. The GCSN founding meeting in Montréal, for example, brought together solidarity folks and Guatemalan exiles. A memorable moment saw us all in a circle, holding hands, in turn naming those who have been lost in our lives, those we thought of over the weekend, those who will stay with us forever. For the Guatemalans, this was followed by ¡*presente*! or ¡*viva*! – bringing the dead and disappeared into our presence. My identification in Canada was altered by these types of circumstances, by the marginal spaces that most Guatemalans occupy in Canada, and by standing in the circle with them. There was a transnational process of bringing the names of those who died in Guatemala into the social space of Montréal, in that way tying together seemingly separate places into continuous solidarity space. My identification as a 'solidarity type' allowed access to those outspoken Guatemalan exiles who might not otherwise pay me much attention.

By reflecting on mis-identifications I was subject to every day in Guatemala, I am now more conscious in my assertions of generalizability of experience, of representative cases, and the particularity of identity. By examining processes and

6 'The two little gringas came,' (TERI, in LA HAVANA, in a letter written to PEDRO, in HOPE, after our visit).

relations rather than static or solid identities (inscribed through terminology such as community, refugee, landed immigrant, returnee) it is obvious that far from homogeneous and flat (the major concern with globalizing forces of mass media and capitalism), people and 'communities' are heterogeneous, research methods are not bound or binding, my roles obviously more multiple, and my knowledge entirely partial. By focusing on relations and processes of transnationalism – through a transnational research method – we can begin to understand the connections and ruptures, continuities and contradictions. Rather than focus on any particular identity, it is my interest in the following chapters to examine the relations that continually produce such identifications.

Transnational Research

Transnational qualitative research represents a flexible alternative to structured qualitative research that facilitates my ability, influenced by my solidarity commitments, to analyze the gendered and racialized experiences of Guatemalans' violent past and transnational present. Throughout this book, I attempt to address how political violence and ensuing forced migration is both gendered and racialized, and how the geography of political violence and migration is manifest in personal, social, and spatial settings. Informed by feminist and transnational literatures, among others, I employed a multi-method, multi-sited approach to examine some of the transnational processes that contribute to community transformation and that shape the (im)migrant experience. Of particular interest is the spatialization of transnationalized identities for women and men and the processes of transnationalism that affect individuals in both Canada and Guatemala.

The optic of transnationalism employed here offers a fresh perspective on refugee and (im)migration studies. By linking place of origin, processes of (im)migration and flight, and place of exile, transnational research seeks a clear understanding of how ethnicity, cultural change, and connections among space, place, and identity are rooted in two interconnected places (Glick Schiller et al. 1995). A transnational perspective also allows for attention to be focused on the tremendous contradictions that transnationals face in their everyday experiences through such dimensions as 'race,' class, and gender (Rouse 1995b), by allowing a comparison of two places, and by showing how the construction of 'race,' class, and gender in the two places are interconnected.

Rather than employing a transnational communities approach, advocated by Portes (1996a, b) and Portes et al. (1999a, 1999b), among others, the experiences of Guatemalans in Canada require an exploration of the use of social relations at the household level (connecting Canada and Guatemala), with limited neighbourhood and community interactions, as the primary means of coping in exile. In contrast to most of the literature on Guatemalan (im)migrants and refugees in Mexican and American contexts, which focuses on the collective orientation of return negotiations and transnational community connections, respectively, this research employs a transnational refugee approach that focuses on the *individual* as an active agent in transnational social relations.

Siting Transnational Research: Multi-Method, Multi-Sited Research

Multi-method research is an attempt, McKendrick (1999, 41) tells us, 'to combine research methods to address a particular research question' in the most effective manner. Multi-method research is an opportunity for generality and specificity within one research project that offers breadth and depth of understanding. A diverse range of questions can therefore come together to explore varying perspectives on a given issue or research topic.

Though transnationalism is a growing area of research in migration studies, the practice of conducting interviews transnationally has yet to receive significant attention, even in the geographical literature influenced by transnational studies. A notable exception is the work of Jennifer Hyndman (1999b, 2000). For example, work on the interconnection of space and the power politics that imbue it with meaning now receives significant attention through multi-method projects (Pred and Watts 1992; Sibley 1995; Watts 1992b), yet far less attention is paid to multi-*sited* research as a means of investigating those spaces

My multiple-method approach incorporates examination of immigration and refugee policy decisions, analysis of relevant immigration and refugee statistics, participant observation, and transnational interviewing. Rather than strictly following the methods of one approach, I let the requirements of the research problematic guide the selection of research design. If it is truly the research participants' experiences and meaning-making that critical research is about, and that I am interested in sharing, then the research design had to accommodate this perspective.

A transnational perspective, along with the critical ethnographic methods employed, I argue, allow the richness, nuance, and ever-changing aspects of each persons' identity and cultural connectedness to be given top priority. Rather than looking for generalizable rules of cultural continuity and change, I explored the 'particularities' of the research participants' lives (Abu-Lughod 1991). I chose a critical ethnographic approach, along with interview conversations, for the practical advantages of understanding the life in exile and (im)migration for Guatemalans more sensitively than possible with other approaches. As Hagan (1994, xvii) reveals in her work with Mayas in Houston, 'with this approach one is permitted to examine social action in a more complete form – as it unfolds and as it is understood by the actors themselves.'

Scholarship in cultural and feminist geography demands reflection by the researcher with the aim of producing 'more inclusive methods sensitive to the power relations of fieldwork' (England 1994, 80; Women and Geography Study Group 1997). This approach led to an examination of both extraordinary events as well as the everyday experiences of the participants as they are situated in the broader Canadian and Guatemalan contexts within which they move. Relevant statistical analysis provides the contextual fabric on which to layer and weave participants' words shared during the more intimate phase of the research. As Jessor et al. (1996, 6) state, 'joint reliance on qualitative and quantitative procedures, producing kinds of information that are complementary and converging, can now be seen as a powerful strategy for enriching the understanding of social life.'

In addition to exploring the transnational contexts of Guatemala-Canada connections, interview conversations in Canada and Guatemala allow for Chapter 5's presentation of three carefully constructed, and 'honestly' (Barone 1992, 142) reproduced, *transnational ethnographies*, which make room for voices all-too-often silenced in migration research (Lawson 2000; McDowell 1992). Prioritizing participants' understanding and 'meaning-making' (Geertz 1973) of their experiences enables an attempt to overcome some of the silencing that Perera (1993) sees as the hallmark of the 'Guatemalan tragedy.'

Transnational Interviewing and Ethnographies of the Particular

Geographers and other social scientists interested in the situatedness and interconnectedness of lived experience are concerned with the issues of in-depth interviewing, field site choice, and ethical research practices. Though interviewing is a more popular technique in geography than previously (Halfacree and Boyle 1993; McDowell 1992; Miles and Crush 1993; Nast 1994; Winchester 1996), only in the past several years are they the subject of debate in the pages of the major geographic journals (Bailey, White, and Pain 1999; Baxter and Eyles 1997, 1999; Crang 2002; Valentine 1999; Wiles et al. 2005). Deciding *whom* to interview, as well as deciding *when* and *where* to conduct interviews, raises problems that have not been addressed at length in the geographic literature.

As anthropologist Clifford Geertz (1973, 416 in Nelson 1999, 33) stresses, there is 'not a very generalizable recipe' for appropriate methodology. This point seems fitting for transnational interviewing and therefore I will instead highlight the pros and cons and potential ethical concerns. For example, multi-*sited* (more than two field locations) transnational research is exceedingly difficult for a single researcher. Given the realities of research funding, community to community transnational research is far more typical in that it requires less travel and fewer expenses.

So, how to get around what Geertz (1988, 144) calls the 'un-get-roundable fact that all ethnographic descriptions are homemade, that they are the describer's descriptions, not those of the described'? Perhaps there is no getting around this fact, but by drawing upon collaborative, sensitive, critical ethnographic methods I attempt to be explicit about the nature of reflexivity and subjectivity that shape my findings and analysis. Additionally, I also follow Abu-Lughod's (1991, 149) suggestion to experiment with narrative 'ethnographies of the particular' or what I call *transnational ethnographies* in a continuing tradition of fieldwork-based writing. Validity becomes the goal, then, rather than generalizability and replicability. Validity means the integrity and value of the research that Ristock and Pennel (1996, 50) argue is 'achieved through accountability both to the participants and those who will be affected by the outcome.'

Interview Conversations and Transnational Ethnographies

When situated within the larger debates on qualitative research, the concern in academic circles regarding *testimonio* (testimony) or in-depth interviews (some would say 'interview conversations') seems to revolve around issues of representation, validity, credibility, and 'objectivity.' If the researcher is interested in a journalistic endeavour of fact-finding rather than exploring the human dimensions of coping and meaning-making, then perhaps *testimonio* and in-depth interviewing are not the appropriate methods of inquiry. On the other hand, in-depth interviewing can be an excellent tool if the researcher is flexible enough to allow for some inconsistency, repetition, exaggeration, or omission in order to understand the subject of their research project in more depth. If the point of research or investigation is to come to understand participant's understandings of particular events or processes, then one must listen to the participants. When the limitations of *testimonio* and in-depth interviewing are understood and acknowledged, then the identified shortcomings can be dealt with through supplementation with secondary material such as newspapers, journalistic accounts, and other written material. In this way, statements are contextualized without compromising their integrity.

In reference to the ethnographies of the particular, rigor, subjectivity, and particularity can function to weave together memories, interpretations, and layered meaning without bending to somewhat misplaced notions of 'objectivity,' generalizability, and replicability. Instead of concern with subjectivity and over-immersion in the research situation, which geographers Baxter and Eyles (1997, 509) suggest can 'threaten the credibility of findings,' I strongly argue that the use of *transnational ethnographies* requires sensitivity, honesty, immersion, and at times, solidarity. These qualities do not detract from scholarly research but open researchers to meaning-making and strategic choices of participants. When used as one element in a multiple-methods approach, new realities surface that might otherwise have been missed.

With Geertz's viewpoint in mind, I sought those participants who were willing to discuss their lives with me. There is any number of criteria that could be established for participant selection but, fundamentally, I am interested in the varied experience of particular situations. As questions of validity (in the traditional sense) and replicability are increasingly seen as misplaced concerns in qualitative research (Jessor et al. 1996; Wolcott 1990), I suggest that a focus on the quality of each representation is more beneficial than a forced systematic approach to selection. If it is truly the research participants' experiences and meaning-making that critical qualitative research is about, and that I am interested in sharing, then research design, implementation, and presentation must accommodate this perspective.

'Field' Questions and Multi-Sited Research

Given mass migration and population dynamics, commitment to fieldwork potentially requires commitment to more than one field site. Van der Veer (1997), for example, argues that when people live in more than one place, research will have to be done in more than one place. It is standard practice for migration studies fieldwork to take place in 'place of destination' or in 'communities of origin,' and rarely in both. (Im)migrants and their stories are not always followed to their places of destination, which would illuminate much more about their migratory lives than simply investigating the effects of migration on the home community. The same can be argued for a singular focus on 'settlement and adjustment' studies with little or no regard for the interconnectedness of social spaces in migration landscapes.

Following the desire for appropriate fieldwork methodologies, Gupta and Ferguson (1997a) seek to redefine the meaning of the anthropological commitment to 'the field' in an era of globalization and rapid change. Researchers, for decades committed to knowledge gained at the community level, now confront lives that resist singular geographical locations, instead sustaining what Zelinsky and Lee (1998) call 'translocal' or 'heterolocal' orientations, and therefore must re-think field site choice. Key to addressing the affects of migration on populations on the move are the not-so-straightforward processes that facilitate ongoing place making practices. These processes are shaped by dialectical relationships between (im)migrants and refugees and immigration/migration policy; by dynamics of place (Sack 1997); by memory and imagination; as well as power relations that mediate cultural difference and social space.

In an effort to grapple with the certain complexities, it becomes necessary to expand common-sense notions of the 'field' and co-ordinate research projects accordingly. If we begin, as Gupta and Ferguson (1997b) urge, with an understanding of interconnected space and power dynamics that shape it into discrete places rather than taking bounded space/place as given, then it makes sense that the organization of transnational research will highlight flash points of connection and rupture, continuity and contradiction. As individuals and groups migrate, form new social relations in exile, and maintain connections with home communities, researchers are challenged to think through multi-sited, transnational interviewing methods.

The Social Fields

As many ethnographic studies have informed us, it is important to study the everyday lives and symbolic practices of daily existence. But extraordinary events of displacement are disrupting sedentarist notions of community studies, of rootedness, of belonging, and of direct links between place and identity (Malkki 1997). The most straightforward methodology for organizing my research would have involved two community studies, one at both ends of a transnational network. Instead, the focus is on the extraordinary events of political violence, flight, exile, and return that serve as guideposts in the lives of many Guatemalans in Canada. By examining the transnational social spaces of these extraordinary events, the discourse of rupture, connections, isolation, and continually feeling 'out-of-place' is given priority. In this way, the impact on families physically separated is dealt with. Rather than a concern for discussion of the everyday activities that shape adaptation and adjustment to 'Canadian life,' the psychic, social, and geographical spaces of Guatemalan transnationalism are explored.

Influenced by Gupta and Ferguson (1997b), then, I did not focus on a discrete 'Guatemalan community' in Canada but rather on the social fields of relations organized by Guatemalans in one region of Canada that extended to a network of towns in the region and to their families in Guatemala. These social fields are historicized and contextualized in Chapters Three through Six in which I explore some of the ruptures, contradictions, and continuities that are made evident when the 'field' is rethought and multi-sited, transnational research is conducted.

Transnational interviewing grew out of my interest in understanding: (1) refuge-seeking and (im)migration as a multi-dimensional process; (2) transnationalization of identities; and (3) place making dynamics under conditions of forced migration and immigration. Curiosity about the transnational experiences of (im)migrants and refugees began during previous research (Nolin Hanlon 1999; Nolin Hanlon and Lovell 1997; 2000), when refugee representatives from the UN-run Mexican refugee camps spoke of the dual forces of desire and fear of returning to Guatemala. Maya refugees in Canada spoke to Ronald Wright (1993, 75-76) of their sense of Canada, like the refugee camps, as a 'waiting place' rather than a new 'home.' One refugee put it this way:

> We have to wait, but the thought of returning to our country is always with us. For us the story isn't over, for us being here is only a step. We know we must go back eventually – either because things have changed or, if they haven't, so that we can help them change.

This same sentiment can be heard expressed by many refugees around the world, but according to Burns (1993, 4-6), who has participated in ethnographic research with the Maya in exile in Florida, there are fundamental differences when grappling with Maya experiences:

> The Kanjobal [Q'anjob'al] and other Guatemalan Maya who have come to Florida are a different kind of refugee from those normally encountered ... They are living in exile, a group of people who have been forced into a diaspora stretching from southern Mexico to Canada ... It is difficult for those of us whose families have lived in the New World only a few generations to appreciate the Maya attachment to their lands and homes. The Maya continue to live on lands their ancestors inhabited three thousand years ago.

Do these statements, delivered closer in time to their departure from Guatemala, still hold true in the late 1990s and early years of the new millennium? Have their responses to an adopted country and concrete settlement practices changed over time? How do Guatemalans explain their connections and social relations in Canada? Are responses different for refugees who fled the country from responses from (im)migrants who have arrived in Canada for other purposes?

Questions such as these indicate that I am interested in Guatemalan-Canadian connections. Due to this interest, I met with both Maya and Ladino (those who identify with a non-indigenous culture in Guatemala) participants in order to understand the experiences of flight and (im)migration to Canada versus movement to the United States. Most studies in the United States focus on Maya refugees. I am most interested in getting at the varied experiences of Guatemalan movement to, and transnational relations forged, in Canada. Attention, therefore, is paid to refugees, (im)migrants, Mayas, Ladinos, student leaders, union members, teachers, guerrilla sympathizers, and those with ties to specialized military forces.

I did not try to force a 'community' label onto the networks, fragments, and ruptures, though I did encounter attempts at community organizing. My evasion of a 'community study' in Canada echoes the work of Wright (1993, 81), whose findings led him to assert that:

> [T]hey are no more a community than their country is a nation. I found fragments, small networks of individuals trusting only the ties of blood and friendship. They are wary of each other, believing, rightly or wrongly, that some of their compatriots may be *orejas* – 'ears' – who watch and listen and report.

Participation in 'Guatemalan activities' in many Canadian locations, and certainly discussions in interview conversations, cemented Wright's statements. In October 1997, for example, the Guatemalan Community Network (GCN) in Toronto organized a high-profile speaking event for Jennifer Harbury, an American lawyer seeking answers for her husband Comandante Everardo's disappearance in Guatemala years earlier. Annoyed with the GCN's scheduled event, and perhaps the organizers themselves, other Guatemalans in Toronto registered their displeasure by organizing a rival event for the same evening. In the end, therefore, I argue that a focus on the social fields of relations and processes of place making, rather than a 'community study' approach, allows the connections *and* ruptures to emerge through the interview conversations. This dynamic is discussed further in Chapters Five and Six.

To that end, I identified five towns and small cities in southwestern Ontario with Guatemalan populations ranging from a handful to 300.[7] At my suggestion, and by agreement of participants, pseudonyms are used for all local place names in Canada and Guatemala. The selection of the Guatemalans in southwestern Ontario was determined by evidence of a concentration of Guatemalan refugees and (im)migrants and a willingness of key collaborators to participate in the study as well as a history of settlement in this region. The key participants in Guatemala were then determined by family and friendship linkages with Guatemalans living in Canada. There were,

---

7 I chose not to focus on Toronto, the Ontario city with the largest Guatemalan population, as Alan Simmons and Jean Turner (1997) commenced a large study with Guatemalans and Salvadorans in Toronto shortly before I was to begin fieldwork. Since research with Guatemalans in Canada is limited, I instead chose to focus on a nearby region that served as an entry point for many Central American refugees in the late 1970s and early 1980s. That entry point continues to be an important location, with refugee claimants entering there from many African countries, Iran, and Afghanistan. The proximity to the Canadian-American border served to pique my interest to the issues of 'illegal' or undocumented migration, border crossings and enforcement, the sanctuary movement, and seasonal migration.

therefore, many 'field sites' in Guatemala depending on the origin of the participant in Canada. Figure 1.1 identifies interview regions in both Canada and Guatemala. Regional areas are identified rather than individual cities and towns in order to provide contextual information but hinder participant identification.

The Participants

In 1999, I conducted repeat interviews with Guatemalans living in southwestern Ontario, Canada, along with those family members (and sometimes with friends) who remained in Guatemala and are part of the social field of relations. The participants in the interview conversations in Guatemala were family members of those I met with in Ontario, sometimes mothers, fathers, sisters, brothers, in-laws, nieces, nephews or some combination thereof. I met with family members in Guatemala only if the participant in Canada was supportive of that arrangement.

Meeting Participants

Through my association and long-term participation in Project Accompaniment (PA), a number of individuals and organizations assisted me when I chose to focus on southwestern Ontario. Due to this prior connection and initial contacts in Toronto, I built on a solid foundation and used extensively the snowball sampling technique in order to bring more participants into the study. This technique allows existing networks of family, friends, and interviewees to guide future participant choice. In this way, confidence and trust are built up over time and individuals who might not otherwise participate can be incorporated into the study.

In the Canadian context, association with PA and the GCSN and maintaining a relatively long history with Guatemalan solidarity proved critical for gaining the confidence and trust of participants and non-governmental organization (NGO) members. Since I did not conduct my research extensively or exclusively in Guatemala, it became readily apparent that I would only gain entry to families in Guatemala through their family members in Canada. Because most participants contacted family members in Guatemala before I arrived in the summer of 1999, once we met there was an implicit faith that I was *buena gente* (a 'good person') and did not have ties to intelligence gathering organizations nor immigration officials.[8] Trust was not automatic, but knowledge that I knew their family members in Canada and spent time with them before traveling to Guatemala meant that people participated quite willingly, without much hesitation.

I met participants in a number of ways before introductions began to gather momentum. I was fortunate to meet with a few key individuals and groups in the

8 Misconceptions of research motivations have stood in the way of more than one research project in Guatemala. Rumors of connections to the *la migra* forced Patricia Foxen (2002) to abandon her first research site and relocate to another community when she started asking locals about transmigration to HOPE, USA.

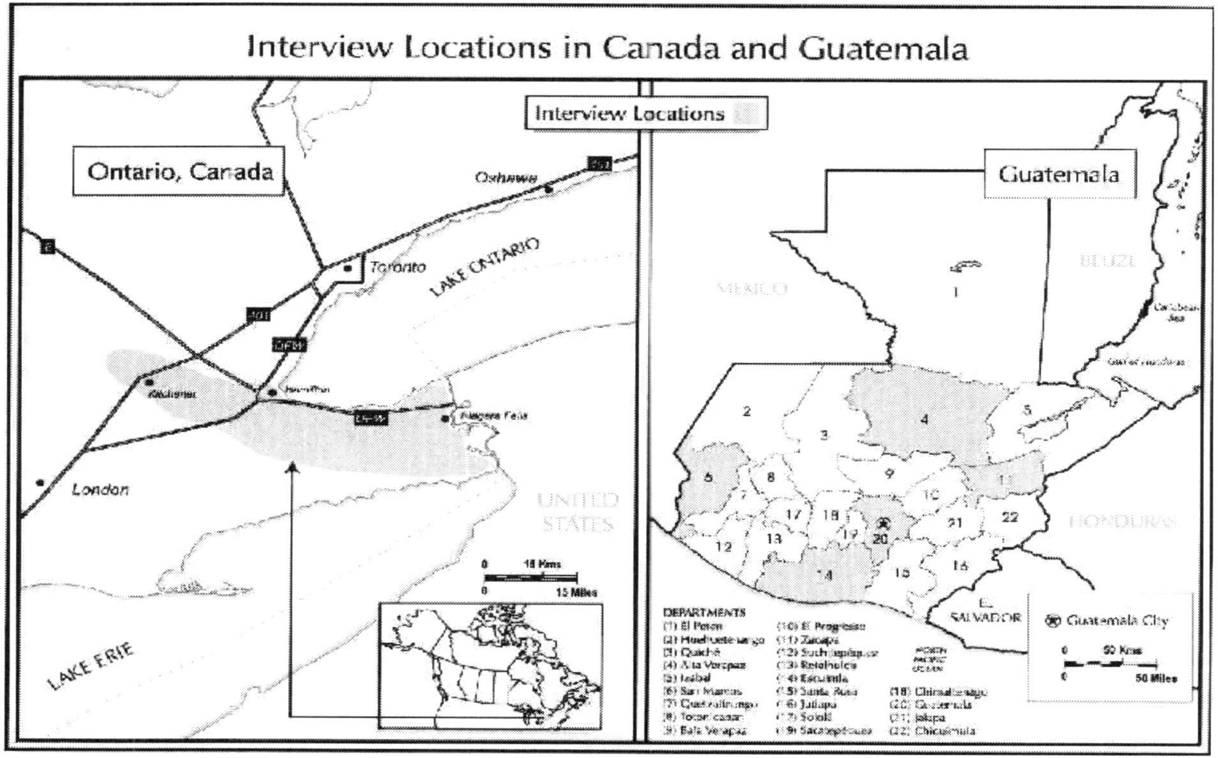

Figure 1.1 Interview locations in Canada and Guatemala

region before approaching any Guatemalans. CAROLE and SISTERS BETH and JOAN run two refugee transition houses in southwestern Ontario, CASA LIBERTAD and CASA NUEVA.[9] They know most of the Central Americans in my region of study and have paved the way for early trust and understanding. CAROLE, SISTER BETH, and SISTER JOAN have worked with refugees in southwestern Ontario for many years and have a strong reputation for their compassion and spiritual guidance. These women are key figures in the refugee arrival services offered in the region. Together they have received the majority of refugee claimants at this point along the Canada-USA border and accompany refugees under deportation orders to waiting border officials.

Most Guatemalans who made refugee claims in this region of Ontario passed through one of these transition houses, if for only one night. Many continue to return and volunteer their time at the houses, maintaining strong ties with the house of first refuge. Spanish-language Catholic mass offered each Sunday by SISTERS BETH and JOAN in CASA LIBERTAD draws Guatemalans (and other Central Americans) back on a regular basis. Their confidence in the project led to many introductions, most importantly to recently arrived refugees who might otherwise have not spoken with me.

Second, contacts developed through the founding meeting of the GCSN in Montréal greatly facilitated meetings with prospective participants. Importantly, people whom I met at this event are more active in solidarity circles than those I met through the refugee transition houses. Diversity is key to documenting the varied arrival and transnational practices of Guatemalans in Canada. It means going beyond the vocal political refugees who are spokespeople for Guatemalan solidarity organizations in Canada. Though these individuals' stories are obviously quite instructive, so too are the stories of refugees who have chosen a quieter existence in exile and stories of (im)migrants who chose to move to Canada.

Finally, I made contacts through the PA network in Ontario. Participation in solidarity and community events (such as the annual Miss Latina pageant in one small town) allowed me to discuss the research with potential participants in a relaxed, non-threatening atmosphere.

Fieldwork Reciprocity

Fieldwork reciprocity is vital to an engaged qualitative research project, most especially when participants are those often identified as 'living on the margins.' Everyday activities such as driving participants to language classes, welfare offices, the hospital, pharmacies, friend's houses, and between refugee transition houses are concrete activities that reflect my concern for people who graciously allowed me into their homes. At times, I was serving as translator for doctor's appointments and official documents. My research experience was useful in collecting material

---

9 Pseudonyms. The uses of real names for the refugee transition houses or the people who work there undoubtedly would identify the locations of the participants.

for participants' refugee claims, funding grants, educational interests, and current country situation reports on Guatemala.

Participants and Pseudonyms

Twenty-five interview conversations were conducted with Ladinos and Mayas, women and men, in order to identify 19 individuals willing and able to participate in repeat interviews over the course of several months. The participants are diverse: government-sponsored refugees; refugee claimants; landed immigrants; Canadian citizens; entire families; single women and men; and couples. Their diversity reflects the Guatemalan population in Canada. Backgrounds in Guatemala (those with military connections, some with ties to guerrilla forces, others with unions) are as varied as were their reasons for leaving Guatemala (direct threats to life, escape after torture, threats to family members, sickness).

The majority of participants were Ladino, reflecting the population composition in Canada, and there was almost equal representation by gender (eight women and eleven men). I chose not to include children specifically as research participants, but some joined in with their parents during the in-depth interview conversation sessions. I made this decision in response to the ethical concerns of obtaining informed consent from children. Other than for children, though, age was not a determining factor in participant selection.

Because the problematic of this study deals with the issue of transnational existences and transnational social relations between Guatemalans in Canada and their families in Central America, I chose to include those people who maintain some sort of contact as well as those who do not. There are powerful reasons for *not* or being *unable* to maintain contact, as came to light during the initial 25 interview conversations.

Research participants were contacted by telephone approximately a week prior to the actual interviews and were provided with information about the research so that they were prepared when the actual interview conversations took place. I asked participants if they were interested in having the interviews take place in their homes; so that discussion could be more open, rather than in an unfamiliar environment. Interviews early on in the process were conducted in one of the refugee transition houses, but most chose to meet in their own houses or apartments. Through the 25 interview conversations, I learned of the participants' reasons for leaving Guatemala, how and why Canada came to be their destination, whether or not they maintain contact with Guatemala, and if they do keep in touch, how this is done. Concrete practices were also explored, among them employment status, social status, and patterns of return along with the more imaginative, remembered experience of life in Guatemala and the role of violence in their departure.

Due to the violent conditions under which Guatemalans, like other Central Americans, have come to Canada, I met with the research participants on a number of occasions in order to provide the time and space needed for trust and confidence to be established. I have found that on-going meetings with participants are necessary given the nature of refugee life and early settlement experiences in Canada. Given early concerns that I was connected with Citizenship and Immigration Canada (CIC), some participants' stories have changed and shifted from our early conversations. Once people realized I was who I said I was, a few confessed to lying early on about themselves. Therefore, even after a recorded interview, I kept in semi-regular touch with all participants as our relationships evolved and changed over time. These interviews, then, are the result of between one and five meetings ahead of time with each person, usually requiring at least two blocks of time. For example, an initial meeting was arranged to explain the research project and explore the ways in which they might participate, to find out their concerns about the research, to establish their level of interest for continuing with either moderate or more in-depth participation, and to go through the basic information questions.

My promise of confidentiality and anonymity was more difficult to fulfill than I had imagined. Because so many participants knew one another, it became clear for some people that their friends might be participating. In those cases, I made it clear that I would not discuss any details about our conversations or recorded interviews. Most people were comfortable with this arrangement and, as far as I know, there were no incidents of 'leaked' information. In most cases, we did not sign a consent form. Rather, we discussed the voluntary nature of the interview conversations and that they could withdraw from the research at any time.

Most participants chose to use pseudonyms in place of real personal names and geographic locations. While, for the most part, anonymity offered relief, others wondered what all the fuss was about. For example, JUAN and JOSÉ suggested that their names are common enough to offer anonymity and therefore pseudonyms were unnecessary. MIGUEL's high profile in Guatemala and the circumstances of his departure made anonymity impossible, but certain details of his case are concealed to protect those who assisted in his escape from Guatemala. Pseudonyms, therefore, are used in most cases but real names and certain place locations are revealed at participants' request.

Research participants were offered the option of proceeding with the interview conversation in either English or Spanish. Fiona Smith (1996) discusses the challenges and implications of conducting research in a foreign language and then proceeding with the writing process in the researcher's 'home' language. Smith suggests that the processes of writing and representation apparently become more problematic, but that it can be turned into a positive engagement both between languages and participants. Representation of other people's worlds in our own reconstructions is problematic no matter how empowering the research methodology, Smith (1996, 163) argues; but 'if the research is in a foreign language or a foreign culture it becomes a more complex but perhaps more overt operation of representation.'

The advantages of tape-recorded interviews are many. West (1996, 340) suggests that recorded interviews offer a remedy to intuition and faulty recollection, and increases the precision of observations and the range of things that can be observed. But circumstances do not always allow for the intrusion of technology. Ten of the 19 interview conversations were recorded while nine were not. If it seemed appropriate,

I asked participants if they were comfortable with the use of a tape recorder. Often during initial meetings it became clear that a tape recorder should be nowhere in sight. In these cases, more common in Guatemala, I wrote sketch notes during the interview and later I followed up with intense field notes. If the tape recorder did not pose a problem, I took notes instead on body language and contextual information. While working with research assistant Finola Shankar, time was set aside immediately after interview conversations, as suggested by Emerson et al. (1995), to record the more contextual information that could not be obtained while in their presence.

Most interview conversations in Canada were transcribed and returned to the participants for their review, comments, and approval. I also returned the tape itself to interviewees after transcription was complete. No participants requested adjustments to the text. Willson (1986, 267) indicates that even when interviewing with a non-literate population (a situation for some participants in Guatemala) where such a policy is not possible, the informant must be made aware of how his or her memories will be used. The lack of security (both perceived and real) of the postal system in Guatemala meant that some requests were made not to return the transcripts and especially not the tapes. Therefore, in Guatemala I did not return transcripts or the tapes. Few interviews were recorded anyway but, in the end, security outweighed the ethical imperative to return transcripts.

Participants: Guatemalan Dimension

The process of data collection and use of collaborative, sensitive, and critical ethnographic methods that I used in Canada were also employed in Guatemala. Finola and I set up a base in the colonial city of Antigua Guatemala and over a period of two months ventured to six locations around the country to meet with families. We met with approximately 25 individuals who are family of those interviewed in southwestern Ontario. All but two interviews were conducted in Spanish (the other two in English), as no family members' first language was one of the many indigenous languages of Guatemala. Two additional individuals were interviewed after their deportations from Canada after approximately ten years of residency. Questions such as the following guided the unstructured, open-ended conversations:

- What impact did the departure of the family to Canada have on the family?
- What role did violence play in the departure of the family member to Canada?
- What social relations and social processes have developed in order to facilitate and maintain such transnational linkages?
- Which way does money flow in the social fields that connect families (to or from Canada)?
- What are the cultural impacts of bi-national (or multi-national) families?

Our normal pattern of meeting began with a phone call (except in one case when the family did not have a phone) from Antigua a week or two before our planned meeting. We organized our travels around weekends to avoid the work week during which we might miss many members of the family. Instead, we usually arrived in the new city or town on a Thursday or Friday and stayed until Monday or Tuesday. Often we spent all day Saturday meeting with family members before arranging a more formal interview conversation for Sunday. While we sought out small *pensiones* for weekend accommodation, families often asked us to spend the weekend in their homes. Informal, extended visits engendered more personal communication and allowed many more topics to be broached than possible in short, hour-long 'interviews.' 'Interview conversations' took on real meaning in our two or three-day intensive visits. Because we met with people on their family days rather than through the work week, we met with extended family members and often we were invited around to various family and neighbouring homes.

Inevitably, commonalities and contradictions emerged in the transnational narratives as each family member spoke of personal experiences of similar events. One event may be (and usually was) interpreted in myriad ways. Interviews with various family members in Guatemala and Canada usually clarified differing perspectives on the same event. For example, the impact of a family member's departure – a shared reality – might be seen as a devastating blow or a liberatory opportunity, temporary or permanent. A transnational perspective allows different perspectives to inform the examination of the social field that binds those at home with those who are away.

Since members of the family are separated, one drawback is that people cannot be interviewed again together. Gill Valentine (1999) discusses the benefits of interviewing couples together and apart and makes an interesting case for attempting to do both as interviewees reveal and withhold information depending on the circumstances. In my case, all participants were interviewed separately from their family members out of the country, while some couples were interviewed together in Canada and relatives in Guatemala usually spoke together in our meetings. I did not see this as a problem as the couples experienced the pain of exile together and appeared to share common perspectives on causes and outcomes of their problems in Guatemala and present situation in Canada. But, additional separate interviews would have been useful to differentiate more clearly the gendered experience of (im)migration and exile with all couples.

Returning to Canada

Part of my commitment to reciprocity was to follow-up with participants in southwestern Ontario upon my return from Guatemala. I met all those I could contact (eight) and we discussed events that had transpired since our last meetings as well as my visits with their families. I passed on photos that I took of each visit and any letters that families asked me to forward on. These follow-up visits proved to be a useful wrap-up for loose ends and allowed participants to hear the progress made in the research project.

Chapters to Follow

This book has opened with a number of introductions: to the connections between Guatemala and Canada, to the research approach, my positionings, and to the participants. Chapter Two situates the specifics of transnational reality of forced migration from Guatemala to Canada within a discussion of the basic theoretical concepts of this study: transnationalism, migration, gender, and community.

The rest of the book is structured into three further parts. Part II 'Guatemala to Canada' is composed of Chapters 3 and 4, which offer an examination of the spatialization of the refugee exodus through the circumstances that caused people to flee Guatemala and document the Canadian government's policies towards their arrival and taking up residence in this country. In order to identify the spatial distribution and concentrations of Guatemalans in Canada, official geographies are established through the citizenship, immigration, and refugee records compiled via Statistics Canada, CIC, the Immigration and Refugee Board (IRB), the Information Management and Technology Branch (IMTB) of the Canadian International Development Agency (CIDA), and through the newly formed Canada Border Services Agency (CBSA). Where did the individuals enter Canada? Where did they make refugee claims or immigration requests? Is Canada a third country resettlement location or first country of asylum? Analysis of data obtained through these sources provides a broad vista from which to examine the individual *transnational ethnographies* and interview conversations.

Exploration of the undocumented reality or 'speculative geographies' that elude official reckoning was restricted for two main reasons. First, and foremost, this issue was not pursued vigorously in order to ease concerns of participants; and second, 'going underground' is seen as an urban phenomenon (as in Vancouver, Toronto, and Montréal), not a rural, small town, or small city issue. Though not examined formally, the topic of 'illegal' migration and 'going underground' is part of the discourse on Central American migration; it is acknowledged but not systematically pursued.

Data gathered from relevant federal government documents (such as parliamentary sub-committees, CIC, and IRB research reports), NGO participation, and newspaper sources enabled a contextual analysis of country conditions upon Guatemalan arrival to Canada, a multicultural society of official inclusion built on policies of exclusion.

If Parts I and II offer historical context, discussion of immigration policy, and reflections on the *spatialization* of refugee exodus, Part III, involves rather more intimate expressions of living a transnational existence. Interview conversations make up the core of Chapters 5 and 6. The scale of analysis shifts to individual articulations of the rupture of 'community' and sense of self as well as points of attachment in Canada and Guatemala that suture together a new sense of belonging. I conclude, in Part IV, with an evaluation of the notion of 'refugee transnationalism,' and argue for the need to examine forced migration through a gendered lens, in addition to the contemporary concerns to poverty, unemployment, and continued isolation for many Guatemalan women and men in Canada.

Chapter 2

Gender, Community, and Transnationalism

In this study of struggle and place making in Ontario and Guatemala, I draw on theory to question common-place notions of what 'community' means in Guatemala, throughout the (im)migration process, and in the everyday lives of Guatemalan women and men in Canada. Reconfigured communities, renegotiated places, and newly imagined identities continue to emerge from the political violence in Guatemala and subsequent refugee flight and (im)migration. Though community studies are the centrepiece of Guatemalan studies, I attempt to bring in work in geography, anthropology, and sociology on transnationalism and place making in order to make sense of contemporary realities. Additionally, until recently, much community research in Guatemala and migration research in general has been gender blind. My goals for this chapter are two-fold. First, I discuss the central role of gender in community and migration studies and situate this specific discussion in the broader context of global and local concerns of gender and migration studies. Second, I outline the changing nature of 'community' in the context of forced migration and transnational migration, from a place-bound reality to one that is trans-local and trans-national. The literatures of gendered migration, community studies, and transnationalism are central to my examination of the varying experiences of women and men before, during, and after the internal armed conflict.

Some parallels exist between Guatemalan transnationalism in the Canadian and American contexts, particularly regarding the role of state violence in initiating refugee flight as identified by Popkin (1999), *Prensa Libre* (2000), Stoltz Chinchilla and Hamilton (1999), and Hamilton and Stoltz Chinchilla (2001). On the other hand, particularities of the Guatemalan Canadian population urge a new reading of Guatemalan transnationalism. Single generation refugee flight, as individuals or family units, encompasses much of contemporary Guatemalan migration to Canada rather than multi-generational labour migration that grew out of the original refugee experience to the United States as documented by Burns (1993), Fink (2003), Foxen (2000, 2002), Hagan (1994), Hamilton and Stoltz Chinchilla (2001), Loucky and Moors (2000), and Rodman Ruiz (2002), or the collective experiences of Mexican refuge revealed in the work of Montejo (1999a, 1999b), Nolin Hanlon (1999), and Nolin Hanlon and Lovell (1997).

Throughout this chapter, in addition to a discussion of gender and migration, it will be clear that a conceptual shift is in the works, from a focus on 'community'

– the foundation of cultural studies in Guatemala – to that of place-based identities and multi-scaled, cross-border social relations. I am particularly interested in the spatialization of transnationalized identities and how this process affects those in both Canada and Guatemala. The journey through the literatures of gender and migration, community studies in Guatemala, place making and identity in geography, and transnationalism will lay the groundwork for an extended engagement with the many individuals and families who shared their joys and pains of place making and identity renegotiations in Canada and Guatemala.

Gender Structures the Migration Process

Gender structures the migration process and therefore I was compelled to conduct research that treats gender as a central organizing principle in migration. Migration affects women and men differently depending on the context (social, political, cultural) of the migration decision, the migration journey itself, as well as the settlement experience. When gendered migration is situated transnationally, the differing experiences of women and men in the home and adopted country context are made visible. Not only does gender differentiate physical movements across borders, but gender relations also are reaffirmed, negotiated, and reconfigured in their transnational contexts. Gendered processes also lead to differences in people's interactions with settlement and other service delivery institutions. They may also lead to divergent interests in return migration.

Recognition of the necessity of a gender lens to examine migration, settlement, and integration urged Tastsoglou et al. (2005, 91) to state that 'research that does not accord serious attention to immigrants as gendered subjects is fundamentally flawed.' As many researchers note, though, until recently, women were statistically invisible in migration data and are the 'absent centres' ignored in policy, research, and action. Boyd (1986, 1994), Hyndman (1999a), and Macklin (1996, 2003) have shown that it makes a difference to one's understanding of immigration policy if a gendered perspective is taken rather than a non-gendered one. Jan Ryan (2002) explains that Western migration literature traditionally focuses on the male experience. Ryan (2002, 105) indicates that literature on 'female migration as a collective movement is sparse, despite the fact that that women now make up the majority of migrants in the many migration systems, especially those favouring family reunification or specifically targeting women as workers.'

Attention in migration research is turning to the transnationalization of migrants' lives or the ways in which immigrants, migrants, and refugees negotiate the multiple realities of places of origin and places of migration or settlement. A transnational optic enables researchers to explore both the causes and effects of migration, how lives change throughout the process of migration, the conditions that affect those who migrate and those who remain behind, and the ways in which gender relations are transformed by policies, actions, and movements. Few researchers situate gender as the central organizing concept of their research even though gender is seen as an important area of investigation in transnationalism and migration studies. Additionally, most studies of migration and gender are limited to either the sending or receiving communities and not both.

A focus on transnational contexts allows gendered migration processes in the Americas to be situated in a global political-economic context. For example: (1) the intensification of export-led production in third world countries implicates female and male workers differently, often precipitating international migration experiences to countries such as Canada; (2) changes in the role of women in society. For example, women are increasingly pursuing educational opportunities in third world countries, working outside the home, and participating in civil society; (3) changing immigration policies and intensified border patrols in first world countries must be analyzed for their gendered impacts on migrants and their families; (4) how Canada's positioning in the changing geo-political scene is affecting migration streams and refugee acceptance rates; and (5) the imperatives of gendered labour migration draw female and male migrants to different countries, sectors and work sites. Notably, among migrants from the Caribbean to Canada and the United States, females outnumber males and a large percentage of recent migration has been female-initiated (CIC 1999a).

To understand the texture of migrant lives, researchers must explore categories that are meaningful to women and men. For example, Guatemalan women tend to put more emphasis on the many barriers to integration in Canada (such as underemployment and limited childcare opportunities) and their strong sense of isolation, while Guatemalan men tend to stress the limitations of ethnic solidarity and employment contacts but emphasize opportunities for learning new skills (in Chapter Five). An expanding literature exists on how female and male migrants differ in regard to their desires to return 'home' permanently. Luin Goldring's (1998) U.S.-based work indicates that men's nostalgia for pre-migration gender roles and ideologies makes them regard return more favourably. And finally, a central finding from focus groups conducted in the Greater Vancouver area by Creese et al. (1999) and in-depth interviews by Waters (2003) is immigrant women's contradictory experience of independence from former gender roles in the household. While some find new freedoms and greater equality as women in Canada, others find greater restriction on their movement and participation in everyday society. This latter finding is particularly clear in the cases of mothers of young children and elderly women who experience the loss of extended female networks.

Gendered Migration to Canada

Analysis of recent Citizenship and Immigration Canada data (CIC 2004a) offers a sketch of gendered migration in the contemporary Canadian context. Generally, at least since 1980, females and males are almost equally represented in the incoming immigrant population. Since 2000, though, the percentage of female and male immigrants to Canada is consistent at 51 per cent and 49 per cent, respectively, regardless of the fluctuating overall numbers. However, once the various programs, categories, and relationships are examined, a clearer picture emerges of the gendered dimensions of migration to Canada, from negotiations of CIC categorizations ('dependant,' 'principal applicant,' 'business class,' 'investor,' and 'Live-in Caregiver') to settlement patterns across the country.

Three examples will serve to highlight gendered findings in the recent CIC (2004a) data. First, in the Family Class category, the gender ratio for children is evenly distributed among females and males, but fairly skewed to females in the case of 'dependants,' fiancé(e)s, and parent/grandparent category. This finding is consistent with a UNHCR (2001, 2; 2005a, 5) statement that 'women tend to be over-represented in the age category of 60 and over, reflecting a longer life expectancy of women compared to men.'

A second finding indicates that for 'economic immigrants,' male immigrants comprise a significantly higher proportion of the principal applicants than female immigrants in the categories of 'skilled workers' (72 per cent vs. 28 per cent), 'entrepreneurs' (86 per cent vs. 14 per cent), 'self-employed' (80 per cent vs. 20 per cent), and 'investors' (87 per cent vs. 13 per cent). Additionally, the Live-in Caregiver Program (LCP) is one avenue through which women migrate independently to Canada. In 2004, female migrants comprise more than 97 per cent of the principal applicants accepted through this program (CIC 2004a, 13). This program, though, arguably ensures women's 'de-skilling' as participants need the equivalent of Grade 12 as well as six months of formal training related to the care-giving position they are seeking yet does not offer them employment commensurate with their qualifications (Bakan and Stasiulis 1997; Pratt 1997).

Gendered Migration: What Do We Know?

Oxman-Martinez et al. (2001, 304-305) argue that Canadian immigration policies have differential, gendered impacts, but that the rights of female migrants are not effectively protected. They cite the Live-in Caregiver Program (LCP) and fiancé(e) visas as those areas of immigration policy that are prone to placing women in vulnerable positions in relation to the state as well as within the domestic sphere. These programs provide women with legal immigration documents to enter Canada, but the authors argue that women frequently must relinquish possession of those documents to human traffickers and others who force them to work and subject them to violence. Migrant activists call for the replacement of the LCP and fiancé(e) visa system with the granting of visas to independent women workers (Oxman-Martinez et al. 2001, 309).

Geographers Geraldine Pratt and Brenda Yeoh (2003, 160) further the discussion of gender and labour migration, arguing that bringing women's labour into view leads to increased attention on the influence of gender on transnational experiences. Pratt and Yeoh (2003, 160-161) also note that women are more likely to send a higher proportion of their earned incomes back to their home countries, resulting in the tendency of women 'to resettle more fully than men, to live less mobile transnational existences' and see transnationalism as an opportunity to balance gender relations.

Pratt and Yeoh's (2003, 162) example from Singapore highlights the oft-dashed gender balancing hopes:

> 'Going transnational' has done little to trouble the gendered division of household labour, or destabilize the gendered inequalities of the patriarchal state. Instead, traversing transnational space seems to be a hegemonically masculinised enterprise where men and women remain complicit in the reproduction of patriarchy beyond national borders.

Geographer Victoria Lawson (2000, 175) suggests that gender must be taken into account in discussions of migration and transnationalism. She argues that gender blind analyses of migration limit our understanding and therefore gender must be examined as a process 'that is played out through the gendered households, communities, labor markets and projects of neoliberal restructuring through which migrants move.' Drawing upon her research in Latin America, Lawson (1998, 40) demonstrates marked gender differences in migration that highlight the need for greater attention to the role of intrahousehold dynamics in both migration and labour force participation. Lawson (1998, 42) argues that 'intrahousehold hierarchies of gender and generation can help to explain the mobility of women and men.'

Anthropologist Sarah Mahler (2001, 586) also argues that migration and migration research are gendered processes. Mahler (1999) states that women have long been excluded from migration research and gender issues, in many ways, remain at the level of adding gender as a variable to already established research endeavours. Only recently have scholars begun to demonstrate that gender influences all aspects of migration, including settlement patterns and relations between women and men. Mahler (2001) illustrates the influence of gender on migration through a case study with Salvadoran refugees and (im)migrants in Long Island (USA). Among the estimated one million Salvadorans who fled the country's civil war, men fled beyond the country's borders in significant numbers. Women were often spared recruitment and thus far fewer women fled the country. However, Mahler (2001, 593) points out that many women who did leave El Salvador faced a difficult undocumented journey, including frequent incidents of rape and robbery. Based on earlier field work in El Salvador, Mahler (1999, 707) also argues that a main influence of gender on post-conflict migration is the pressure to emigrate, as 'boys experienced more pressure from the relatives and friends to emigrate than girls do.' Furthermore, men who leave the community often sponsor boys to enter the new country before returning home themselves.

So, what is the connection between gender, geography, and power? Sarah Mahler and Patricia Pessar (2001, 445) introduce a model of 'gendered geographies of power' in order to effectively study gender across transnational space. Mahler and Pessar (2001, 445) state that gender operates 'simultaneously on multiple *spatial* and *social* scales (e.g., the body, the family, the state) across transnational terrains.' Pratt and Yeoh's (2003) work confirms their sense that transnational actions can reaffirm asymmetrical gender relations. Pessar and Mahler's (2003, 812, 815-816) later work aims to bring gender into 'an even tighter transnational focus' by concentrating on three key elements: geographical scales, social locations, and power geometries.'

Power geometries, in this case, is a concept used to explain the degree of agency that people exert in their unequally positioned social locations.

Gendered Migration: What Do We Need to Know?

To build up an adequate understanding of the texture of migrant lives, researchers must be aware of gender differences and explore categories that are meaningful both to women and men. We need to know much more about the gendered experience of both forced and voluntary migration in the Canadian and international context. (Im)migrants are often involved in both transnational social relations and local support networks. But, to what extent and how does immigration policy influence the depth or shallowness of these relations? We need to evaluate the content, intensity, and importance of transnational ties and local networks as well as the interests served through these ties. And, we need to examine the various transnational actors – individuals, families, communities, and governments.

Before grappling with the social support networks developed by (im)migrant women in Canada it is necessary to identify how gender structures the migration process. In order to assess the strengths and weaknesses in formal and informal mechanisms of social support, we need a clear picture of migration processes in general and gendered migration to Canada, in particular.

Transnational, cross-country, and place-specific comparative studies with female and male (im)migrants and refugees are needed to address general conceptual issues about ways of understanding migration to Canada in a global context. Migration research needs to go beyond notions of uni-directional movement to be sensitive to the multiple realities within which (im)migrants operate. Several avenues are open to scholars with a keen interest in gendered issues of migration. In the following section, I locate myself in the broader work of feminist geographers and others who see the many connections between gender, 'race,' and place.

Feminist Research

The Guatemalan refugee and (im)migrant population in Canada is stratified by gender, 'race,' class, location, political consciousness, and other factors, all of which are best explored through strategies of feminist qualitative research. Feminist geographers recognize the numerous axes of difference that must be accounted for in any examination of social life and employ strategies to reveal the unequal relations that perpetuate difference through power dynamics. With its predisposition to address concrete social change, Linda McDowell (1999, 248) argues that feminist geography has an important task ahead, which is 'to uncover the variations in … gender power relations, the ways in which they are maintained and the ways in which they might be undermined.'

The specific aim of feminist geography, McDowell (1999, 12) contends, is 'to investigate, make visible and challenge the relationships between gender divisions and spatial divisions, to uncover their mutual constitution and problematize their apparent naturalness.' The challenge, Kobayashi (1990) argues, is to expose the ways in which unequal power relations operate to reinforce racialized and gendered geographies. Contemporary anti-racist feminist research such as Kobayashi and Peake (2000) and Peake and Ray (2001) challenges essentialist notions of 'race,' exposes gendered experiences of place, questions the ways in which we conduct research and fieldwork, and incorporates the perspectives of research participants into research design, fieldwork, and writing. It therefore explores theoretical insights that call for critical reflection of assumptions, commitments, and practices (Hyndman 2000).

Fundamental to addressing issues of 'race' and racism in contemporary critical analysis are the notions of 'race' and 'gender' as social constructions rather than 'natural' or biological divisions among humans (Jackson 1987; Kobayashi and Peake 1994). Kobayashi (1994, 77) argues that racism and sexism maintain power by building on 'naturalistic assumptions' of essential qualities based on 'race' or 'sex' as though they were pre-given, 'simple, natural traits.' Despite the recognition of diversity and plurality of social experiences, McDowell (1999, 11) comments that 'the belief that a distinctive version of femininity for women and masculinity for men is appropriate remains extremely powerful.' Strategies of feminist research to overcome ideas of 'essentialness,' Desbiens (1999, 184) points out, include 'plurilocality, dispersion, difference, diversity,' considerations that guide research goals and methodologies. Through her work in feminist geography, Rose (1993) contends that the grounds of geographical knowledge, too, are shifting, unstable, uncertain, and contested.

Academic engagement with people 'on the margins' comes, one hopes, from an ethical and moral commitment to work for social change, to change public consciousness about an issue, or to influence public policy. Linda Green (1998) advocates that researchers, feminist and otherwise, should not perpetuate the silence of so many 'research subjects' through 'studied silence,' rather, we must talk and write of what we have seen and heard as listeners, observers, and witnesses. Researchers become participants through the acts of witnessing and listening. As participants, a colleague and myself have noted, we are compelled to speak out *and* provide space in our work for *multiple voices* despite the unequal relations that shape our engagement with those with whom we collaborate (Nolin Hanlon and Shankar 2000).

By employing a progressive politics of analysis and writing, through anti-racist feminist research, not only is there the possibility of political solidarity but, as Hodgson (1999, 215) suggests, theoretical advantage. Increasingly, Kobayashi (1994, 73) observes, feminist scholars are 'unabashedly forward in using their work to engage the political … by helping to bring about social transformation.' Hodgson (1999, 215) indicates, as do other feminist scholars, that 'there is no neutral.… [T]o be neutral is to side with the structures of domination, be they global capitalism, imperialism, or patriarchy.' As feminist researchers employ methodologies that address the gendered experience of political violence and (im)migration, the varying experiences of war, violence, community, memory, and survival are articulated.

All research is political in that, at minimum, our values, intentions, and worldviews underlie our work. In my case, these are overt and exposed in the research design. Smith (1992) also indicates that collaborative, immersed research is a moral act in which we engage in meaningful relationships with the participants. Kirby and McKenna (1989, 105) stress, though, that it is a 'rare researcher who can do full justice to a research question if there is *no* experiential basis from which to begin' (emphasis in original). Therefore, all participants in this study were made aware of my advocacy roles in addition to my academic position. In order to transcend, or at least acknowledge, our ethnic and cultural differences during the phase of in-depth interview conversations, it was important to come to an understanding of the disconnections that exist between us as well as the connections that bring us together.

Silvey and Lawson (1999) note that feminist geographers such as Fincher (1993, 1997), Kofman and England (1997), and Lawson (1998) work to analyze gender differences in migration processes best informed, it is argued, through culturally and historically embedded qualitative research that focuses on agency, power relations, and dynamics of decision-making at the individual and family level. I bring a feminist perspective to the research of Guatemalan refugees and (im)migrants in Canada – both women and men – which is perhaps more in line with the writing of Central American feminists and women struggling for change in Latin America (Radcliffe and Westwood 1993). Repeatedly, concerns expressed by these women focus on their communities and families rather than for their individual struggles (Green 1999; Schirmer 1993). I attempt to explore the experiences of both women and men in order to reveal the significance of the gender dimension of life in exile and social relations that connect Canada and Guatemala.

Renato Rosaldo (1989, 201) argues that there is a great need to move the social science inquiry of 'culture' away from old conceptions of static, monolithic cultures presented to us by 'objective' observers, towards celebrations of diversity, narrative, emotion, and the 'unavoidability of subjectivity.' Since Rosaldo made these comments, some sixteen years ago, there has been a proliferation of feminist geographic scholarship on these very points, found particularly in the pages of the journal *Gender, Place and Culture* and edited collections by Jones III et al. (1997), the Women and Geography Study Group (1997), and Sharp et al. (2004), among others. I am mindful, as well, of the researchers and ethnographers who have gone before me. Many anthropologists, including La Farge (1947), Oakes (1969), and Tax and Redfield (see Rubinstein 1991), have been concerned with critical 'contemporary' feminist research concerns such as 'reflexivity' and 'situating one's voice' long before what Lovell (2000, 151) calls the 'postmodern soul searching' of anthropologists and geographers. For example, when introducing his classic ethnography of Santa Eulalia in Guatemala, Oliver La Farge (1947, v-vi) acknowledged:

> There will be found [in this book] a good deal of subjectivity, even opinionated, writing.... [E]thnology is an inexact science, inseparable from subjective, qualitative observations. The opinions and biases of the observer, therefore, are essential data which should be

frankly presented. The colorless objectivity affected by many ethnologists is a deception and a suppression of data.

Therefore, I see some of the more recent feminist and postmodern concern with reflexivity and subjectivity in fieldwork – such as Behar (1996), Guba (1990), Nelson (1999), Ristock and Pennell (1996), Watanabe (1995), and Valentine (1998) – as vital to the creation of valid and credible ethnographies, but not without precedent.

'Community' Within and Beyond Guatemala

Increasingly important in geography, anthropology, and other disciplines interested in population dynamics in the Americas is the need to connect theoretically issues of community, place, (im)migration, violence, and constructions of identity. From the foundational work of Sol Tax and the Chicago School of Anthropology in the 1930s to more current research in Guatemala, community studies have focussed on the *municipio*, or 'township,' as the basic unit of analysis of cultural continuity and change. Structures of power within and outside Guatemala, however, have irrevocably altered traditional notions of what constitutes a community through economic marginalization, state terror, and genocide. Maya and activist communities are changing and, consequently, so too are the types of community studies being carried out, specifically with reference to new Guatemalan 'communities' and networks in Mexico, the United States, and Canada.

As Guatemalans re-work and re-build their lives – at times across national borders – the challenge for researchers is to conceptualize theoretical and methodological frameworks that advance appropriate and 'sensitive research' (Renzetti and Lee 1993). Displaced lives get played out locally; therefore, in addition to speaking of spaces of movement, Pratt and Hanson (1994, 25) suggest a focus on the 'geography of placement' is vital. Liz Bondi (1993, 84) concurs, arguing that 'the emphasis on where, on position, on location … allows questions of identity to be thought of in different ways.' In order to move forward in conceptualizing place-informed identity in a rapidly changing world, therefore, inquiry into the contexts of movement and placement must be stressed.

It is important to focus on 'community' in Guatemalan studies as key to exploring the relations among place, identity, and cultural change. The use of a transnational migration perspective must be brought to the study of communities in Guatemala and beyond in order to have the theoretical and conceptual tools to grapple with the changing realities for the indigenous and non-indigenous populations. This perspective challenges the unilinear, static, rather rigid assumptions of traditional migration and community studies and opens research to the richness and complexity of the contemporary Guatemalan diaspora. In this era of 'globalization,' researchers interested in 'Guatemalan reality' are challenged to look beyond the local, tightly bounded geography of the *municipio* to include the 'new kind of social spaces' (Rouse 1991, 8) that are created by transnational (im)migrants and refugees.

Community Studies in Guatemala

A community studies approach in anthropology was pioneered and developed in Mesoamerica (Chambers and Young 1979; Diskin 1995; Hawkins 1983, 328; Nutini 1996). This approach has continued to hold its position as the main avenue for studies with the Guatemalan Maya population as it has long been argued that community studies in Guatemala have not been so much the study of community as such – meaning the terrain or the geographical particularities – as a distinct methodological approach (Arensberg 1954). Clearly, many studies with the Maya of Guatemala continue to be informed by single or individual community studies.

The vast majority of community studies have been carried out in rural areas north and west of the capital, Guatemala City. The rugged topography of highland Guatemala seems to have facilitated the conceptualization of the 'community' as a bounded unit, which is seen as an appropriate and manageable category of analysis. Given the isolation and extreme difficulty of travel between mountain populations, researchers note that each grouping of people takes on particular characteristics. White (1991, xiii) argues that this is also particularly true with island societies, where 'geography offers spatial boundaries that frequently do become a basis for group definition.'

The focus on the community as the main unit for ethnographic inquiry has often been criticized, as Diskin (1995, 164) suggests when he writes: 'The village community as the frame of reference for study allows too many important phenomena to go unobserved and unanalyzed.' Yet the 'community' continues to dominate conceptualizations within Mesoamerican studies. Why has a community studies approach endured through the years? I contend that its persistence is due to the method's resonance with the lives of those living in Guatemala and those who study with them; that is, an acceptance of the centrality of indigenous identity that is constructed within and reinforced by local geography (Nolin Hanlon 1999). Studies of single communities have been invaluable to our understanding of Maya and Ladino cultures and change over time and space.

When we listen to the voices of the Maya, to their myths and legends, to their worldviews, it is evident that the Maya maintain a strong association of traditional identity with the *municipio*. Burns (1989a), for example, argues that many Mayas, when questioned about their identity, will most often relate the answer to their place of birth. *Soy Cobañero* ('I hail from Cobán'), rather than *Soy Maya* ('I am Maya') or for that matter, *Soy Guatemalteco* ('I am Guatemalan').[1] Early anthropological, and a few geographical, studies identify this connection with 'place,' Hanks (1990) indicates, when Maya peoples conveyed their worldviews as an articulation of their

1 This may change to varying degrees as the indigenous population embarks on what has been labelled as a 'Maya renaissance.' Additionally, local place-based identities may be influenced by the signing of the *Accord on the Rights of the Indigenous Population*, discussion of a Maya university, and the pursuit of pan-Maya identification (Burns 1993; Fischer 1996; C. Smith 1991; Warren 1998).

perceptions of themselves and their place in the world. This same connection is noted by C. Smith (1990a) who emphasizes that Maya identity is rooted in 'place' rather than in a general sense of 'Indianness.' Even more forcefully, Wilson (1993, 1995a) articulates this connection with the term 'anchored communities,' a term that he uses to illuminate the cornerstone of community identity, which is location or local geography.

Less rich is research beyond the highland Maya but it nevertheless points to the difficult realities of Ladino *campesino* populations as well as Maya groups resident in the eastern region of the country. Throughout the 1940s and 1950s, researchers in Guatemala began to incorporate both Maya and Ladino community residents into broader, more complex understandings of cultural continuity and change. 'Race relation' studies such as those of Gillin (1945, 1948, 1951) and Tumin (1952) were based in mixed communities hosting 'parallel cultures' while Méndez-Dominguez (1961) later explored social stratification within Ladino communities. Metz's (1998) research picks up on the sparse literature on non-highland indigenous communities with the Ch'orti' of eastern Guatemala to challenge taken-for-granted notions of community and Maya nationalism, as does Rodman Ruiz (2002, 2004).

The meaning of community has not remained static throughout the years of conquest, state violence, and 'modernization.' As Guatemalans grapple with their changing conceptualizations of what a community can and will be in Guatemala and beyond, it becomes necessary for this study to break out of the community mould and illuminate newer realities.

Few community studies were carried out in the early- and mid-1980s as violence and counterinsurgency took hold of the Guatemalan countryside. Manz (1988, 2-3) points out that heightened violence during this period impeded long-term fieldwork in a single community and proved 'highly unsafe for both researchers and informants.' Structures of power within and outside of Guatemala irrevocably altered traditional notions of what constitutes a Maya community through economic marginalization, state terror, and genocide. Diskin (1995, 164) highlights the devastating outcome of 'state violence [that] has destroyed the notion of community enshrined in the classic anthropological literature.' Maya communities have been thrown into the process of rapid and fundamental change and, consequently, so too are the type of community studies being carried out with the Guatemalan Maya. Following contemporary realities, in addition to transnational migration studies, for example, we see Bastos and Camus (1994) focus their research on the 'community' of displaced peoples in the capital, Sanford (2003) focuses on community processes of healing, grieving, and active remembering through the exhumation process, Taylor (2005) grapples with post-conflict highland community development challenges, and Manz (2004) revisits Santa María Tzeja to reconnect with this community of returned refugees who struggle forward.

A brief sketch of Guatemala's horrific years of violence will illuminate the changing make-up of community and community studies that have followed. A fuller examination of the historical context of political violence is offered in Chapter

Three. For our purposes in this chapter, I am restricting comment to the impacts of political violence on 'community studies' in Guatemala.

Political Violence and 'Community'

Ten years of social reform between 1944 and 1954 ended with a military coup from which Guatemala has yet to recover as a modern nation. Armed confrontation between government security forces and guerrilla insurgents was sporadic in the 1960s, calmed somewhat in the 1970s, and reached hitherto unknown levels in the late 1970s and early 1980s through what Melville (2005) calls the 'U.S. holocaust against the Guatemalan civilian population.' Findings of the *Proyecto Interdiocesano de Recuperación de la Memoria Historica* / Recuperation of Historical Memory Inter-diocesan Project (REMHI 1998) and the *Comisión para el Esclarecimiento Histórico/* Commission for Historical Clarification (CEH 1999a) or 'Truth Commission' shatter any attempt to deny systematic human rights violations and genocidal military and para-military activity in the 1970s and 1980s which was funded and supported by various American administrations and religious organizations.[2] Responsibility, but thus far not accountability, extends far beyond those on the ground in Guatemala to the intellectual authors of these crimes against humanity and their supporters.

Testimonios collected for historical clarification reveals much that was hidden and unacknowledged by state forces in Guatemala and underreported by various news sources and human rights organizations.[3] Thorough documentation charts the escalating urban terror of the late 1970s, when individual targeting of 'communities' of activists, teachers, professors, students, and union members was commonplace in Guatemala City and other urban locations. The brutal so-called counterinsurgency programme of the early 1980s then focussed military and other government security forces' activity towards Maya life spaces in the rural highlands.

On the outcome of 36 years of internal armed conflict, many researchers have attempted to come to grips with the social, economic, political, and cultural upheaval found most intensely, though not exclusively, in the countryside. The Guatemalan refugee crisis, Manz (1995a, 154) argues, must be situated 'within a discussion of terror,' a discussion that grapples with the 'violation of this last sanctuary for Indians:

2 This, of course, does not stop official military denial. Shortly after the release of the CEH report, Ex-President General Ríos Montt argued 'I never ordered a massacre!' (quoted in Barrios 1999) while almost half of the registered human rights violations took place during his tenure in 1982. Progress is slow. More recently, the Berger administration offered an official apology for one specific case of human rights violations, that of the murder of anthropologist Myrna Mack (visually documented by McDonald 2004), and committed to compensation for survivors of the government-directed Plan de Sánchez massacre, one massacre among hundreds, under order by the Inter-American Human Rights Court (Seijo 2005).

3 The findings of the Commission documented more victims than previously estimated. In past years, scholars and activists spoke of approximately 100,000 to 150,000 deaths due to the violence. Here, *testimonios* corroborated journalistic accounts and other human rights investigations and then went further to reveal information too painful to disclose previously.

the community.' Manz's (1988, 1) early, courageous efforts in the regions of conflict used the community studies approach to 'understand change at the community level ... and the impact of military penetration on the patterns of everyday life.' Manz's research combines the localized focus on the communities in question within a broader analysis of actions at the national level.

Parallels between community life in the country and new anthropological and advocacy approaches are opening up researchers and activists to a nuanced understanding of what is going on in the country. For example, outrage and fear pulled together ten anthropologists, a geographer, and a political scientist in the publication of *Harvest of Violence* (Carmack 1988) – an edited collection – where researchers wrote of the impact of military violence on the individual communities they knew so well in the rural countryside. Suddenly, in order to make sense of mainly rural communities, researchers found it necessary to deal with and write about issues of terror, killing, and violence, issues that were not well developed in the literature.[4] Here, community by community, analysis of the infliction of differing levels of violence illustrates a geographical diversity to the so-called counterinsurgency, better called genocide, and community responses and resistances to it.

The height of the internal armed conflict ruptured so many individual lives, so many community ties, that contemporary research in the highlands of Guatemala cannot be approached without understanding the 'culture of fear' (Green 1994, 235) that has transformed the lives of the Maya. The call to place the discussion of Guatemalan realities within a discussion of terror has been carried through with subsequent work with the Maya and other displaced peoples. For example, anthropologists Green (1995, 1999), Nordstrom and Robben (1995), Sanford (2003), and others working in Guatemala addressed the sensitive nature of working in conflict and post-conflict situations in their recent publications.

Contemporary research projects in highland and urban communities require sensitivity to the extremely violent conditions under which most key informants and participants have lived their lives. As Warren (1993), Manz (1995a, 1995b), Oglesby (1995), Falla (1994), Wilson (1993; 1995a), and other field researchers in Guatemala have discovered, this is a challenge that must be dealt with on many levels and requires commitment not only to the study, but to the individuals and communities with whom they interact.

In Ricardo Falla's (1994) account of massacres in the Ixcán and the Communities of Populations in Resistance (CPRs), he asks the question of why anyone would write about massacres and terror. Falla answers his own question when he suggests the need for research as praxis – reflective and active – that can situate researchers as agents of social change. Research on and writing about violence in field sites, Scheper-Hughes (1992, 28) asserts, can be a way to act in solidarity and 'write

4 Since the publication of Carmack's (1988) *Harvest of Violence*, several works offer methodological and theoretical suggestions for dealing with terror and violence in field settings. See, Green (1999), Manz (1995b), and Nordstrom and Robben (1995), and Scheper-Hughes and Bourgois (2004).

against terror;' to do otherwise, she states, is an 'act of indifference.' Ruth Behar (1996, 177) pulls out all the stops and emphatically argues: 'Call it sentimental, call it Victorian and nineteenth century, but I say that anthropology that doesn't break your heart just isn't worth doing anymore.'

In addition to murder and massacres, the world witnessed massive internal displacement of well over one million people – mainly Maya – and subsequent (im)migrant and refugee movement to Canada, Mexico (Casillas and Castillo 1994; Nolin Hanlon 1999; Salvadó 1988; Stepputat 1989, 1994a), and the United States. The result of counterinsurgency activity within the country directly links with the movement of refugees and (im)migrants north to Mexico, the United States, and Canada and the development of a Guatemalan diaspora. Jonas (1996a, b) estimates that approximately one million Guatemalans are in the United States for economic, political, and social reasons. In terms of official figures, Popkin (2003, 354) reports that according to the 2000 US Census, 372,487 Guatemalans are resident in the United States, while Suro (2002, 14) adapts those official figures to 534,951. It is unequivocally the case that state policies dictated the murder of individuals and communities, leaving 'devastation and fear where the literature once described self-regulated communities' (Diskin 1995, 165).

Transnational Community Studies

Now, with a large population of Guatemalans living and working outside of their country of origin as refugees, (im)migrants, interest in transnational community studies is high. Maya and non-indigenous refugee and (im)migrant communities are evident from the hustle of Mexico City (Bottinelli et al. 1990), to the streets of Los Angeles (Kohpahl 1995; Hamilton and Stoltz Chinchilla 2001; Loucky 1988, 1996; Popkin 1999; Stoltz Chinchilla and Hamilton 1999; and Vlach 1992), San Francisco (Córdova 1996), Tucson (Woodward 1989), and Houston (Hagan 1994; Rodríguez 1987; Rodríguez and Hagan 2000), to the vegetable fields, citrus groves, and golf courses of south Florida (Burns 1989a, 1989b, 1989c, 1993; Wellmeier 1994), to the plastic factories of 'Hope' (Foxen 2002), domestic services of Washington, DC (Repak 1994; 1995), and the chicken farms and poultry factories of North Carolina (Fink 2003; Fink and Dunn 2000). More than 12 years ago, the Q'anjob'al Maya refugee community in Los Angeles alone was estimated to be 6,000 strong (Tedlock 1993, 169), while Popkin's (2003, 355) more recent estimate is between 4,000 and 10,000 Maya.

Compared to the research underway in the United States with the Guatemalan Maya and non-Maya populations, an undeniable dearth of research on Guatemalan refugees and (im)migrants in Canada is evident, and indeed on all Central American populations for that matter. Limited research on Guatemalan refugees and (im)migrants has focused on their invisibility in the city (Wright 1987), participation in language programs (Brown 1997), and integration possibilities in Toronto (Meredith 1992) as well as Guatemalan women's settlement networks in Montréal (Jacob and Lévy 1994; Rose, et al. 1998). More often their participation is worked into research on 'Latin Americans' in Canada, which can brush over the complexities of each cultural group and conflate common language with 'community' (e.g. Bernhard 1997, Corter 1998, and Israelite 1998). Recent collaborative work of the Toronto-based Latin American Research Group (LARG) (Bernhard, Goldring, and Landolt 2005) provides a hopeful avenue of enquiry. No Canadian studies to date explore Guatemalan or Central American transnationality, though Simmons and Turner (1997) incorporated links with home community as one component of their ongoing research project with Guatemalans and Salvadorans in Toronto.

Given the violent assault on community in Guatemala, newer conceptualizations of meaningful community association and identity are needed, as indicated by the innovative research by Wellmeier, Hagan, and others. As Wilson (1993, 1995a, 20) argues, war and Catholic conversion shifted the emphasis on identity from community to wider forms of association such as ethnicity and class. It is well documented that Guatemalan Maya identities continue to be rooted in the local geography of residence and its surrounding lands. Displacement of thousands of indigenous peoples during the internal armed conflict, though, has led to peoples 'out of place,' that is, out of 'their place' in the world and subsequent attempts at the rebuilding of civil society (Nolin Hanlon 1997).

Changing the 'Field'

Anthropologists and geographers alike are now arguing that even with the changing contexts of displaced lives there need not be a denial of the importance of place in the construction of identity and community cohesiveness (Appadurai 1991; Gupta and Ferguson 1992; 1997b; Lavie and Swedenburg 1996; Marden 1997). Instead, it can be argued that as (im)migrants and refugees re-establish themselves in new locations, their identities may shift, layer, expand, and weave the experiences of displacement in a more complex, place-informed and place-based identity.

Given contemporary realities of mass displacement and population movements (forced and otherwise), anthropologists Gupta and Ferguson (1997a) have sought to redefine the meaning of the anthropological commitment to 'the field' in an era of globalization and rapid change. Social scientists, for decades committed to knowledge gained at the community level, now confront 'issues that resist geographic localization' – such as transnational movement – and must re-think 'field site choice' and a shift from commitment to the *local* to a commitment to 'social, cultural, and political *location*' (Gupta and Ferguson 1997a, 5). Appadurai (1991, 191 and 196) poses the problem as follows:

> As groups migrate, regroup in new locations, reconstruct their histories, and reconfigure their ethnic projects, the *ethno* in ethnography takes on a slippery, non-localized quality ... the task of ethnography now becomes the unravelling of a conundrum: what is the nature of locality, as a lived experience, in a globalized, deterritorialized world?

By way of an answer to the questions posed above, Ortner (1997) proposes that researchers concentrate their efforts on tracing how 'community in the sense of locality is transformed into community as a state of mind' when individuals are no longer bound geographically to their home communities but maintain emotional, financial, and cultural ties to them. Roseberry and O'Brien (1991, 10) advocate that community, and other social forms such as gender, ethnicity, and household must not be taken as fixed units but as 'changing results of social and political processes' operating in particular social fields. By focussing on processes that operate in particular places rather than on the fixity of the place itself, Roseberry and O'Brien see new opportunities for greater understanding. Feminist and socialist geographers such as McDowell (1999), Mitchell (2000), and Rose (1993) continue to draw attention to ways in which unequal power relations and social struggles affect multiple and shifting senses of place.

Salovesh (1983) suggests that the notion of *elastic cultural boundary* might be an alternative conceptualization worth consideration when decisions are made regarding 'where' Mesoamerican research can or should be conducted. Salovesh suggests that instead of rigid adherence to geopolitical lines when exploring cultural connections, researchers need to identify the type of social relations and cultural events that take place within and beyond national borders. For example, if life ways and social relations of Guatemalans in Houston are 'Mayan' or 'Guatemalan,' then the cultural boundary of their community extends far beyond the borders of the Republic of Guatemala.

At the most obvious and everyday level, a community 'exists on the ground – as a neighbourhood or formal institution,' but it also exists 'in the hearts and minds of the people who constitute it' (Markowitz 1993, 225). Since I am interested in how communities are maintained and transformed in Guatemala – through conquest, state terror, and exile – then it is to the realm of the hearts and minds and stories of the community members that I turn my attention. In the following section, I propose a potential avenue for continued studies with the Guatemalans living in Guatemala and beyond, one that grapples with the realities of their diasporic locations given the centrality of 'place' in constructions of identity, acknowledges the importance of collaboration with Guatemalan individuals and communities or networks, and identifies the necessity for continued qualitative research.

Transnationalism

In the past decade, the emerging field of transnational studies has presented 'transnationalism' as a useful conceptual tool to deal with the current period of globalization characterized by what Appadurai (1996) identifies as the twin forces of mass migration and electronic mediation. Key to most transnational studies is the desire to bring a dialectical approach to the study of the dynamics of globalization and bring together the study of 'structure, cultural process, and human agency' (Basch et al. 1994). Through such a prism, the agency of people and their multiple roles are given primacy as a way to access the complexity of transformation and population dynamics.

The scope of work that has emerged in the past few years is enormous, leading to both celebration and scepticism. The literature is fraught with studies employing the terms 'transnational' and 'transnationalism' with little consistency or commonality of meanings and, therefore, it is important to outline the various streams of scholarship that are identified by Glick Schiller (1997) and Mahler (1998). Since the categories offered by these two scholars differ slightly, we will discuss them in turn. Glick Schiller (1997) identifies the streams as: (1) *transnational cultural studies* in which concepts of unboundedness (Basch et al. 1994), postnation/transnation (Appadurai 1996), and cultural hybridity (Bhabha 1994) are explored in largely abstract, theoretical terms; (2) *transnational migration studies*, which are grounded in empirical research on the myriad effects of population movement and 'double consciousness' (Glick Schiller et al. 1992a, 1992b; Mahler 1995; Rouse 1991, 1992; Smith and Guarnizo 1998); and (3) *transnational communities studies* that focus on bi-national households and communities as well as the transnational social relations that sustain them (Goldring 1998; Levitt 1998, 1999a; Loucky 1996; Portes 1996a, 1996b; R.C. Smith 1998).

Mahler's (1998) delineation of transnational studies tends to distinguish between the two streams of *transnationalism from below* and *transnationalism as transmigration*. Transnationalism from below, Mahler indicates, is generated by transnational activities and practices such as social movements and grassroots politics (M.P. Smith 1994) that transnational actors employ to 'resist and disrupt' the workings of 'transnationalism from above,' or those structural entities and processes that influence the reconfiguration to global capital (e.g. International Monetary Fund, World Bank, nations, and so forth). Transnationalism as transmigration encompasses both the (im)migration process itself and the impacted communities, influenced by the theoretical explorations of transnational cultural studies. Since I am more concerned with the latter category, the following discussion will focus on that transnationalism that flows from population movement and cultural processes.

Though interest in migration and home community connections is not new to social scientists, a 1990 workshop on transnational migration and the United States (Glick Schiller et al. 1992a) is widely recognized as the 'birthplace' of the field of transnational migration studies. Glick Schiller et al. (1992a, 1992b) and Basch et al. (1994) explore the dynamic interactions between home and host countries and reveal the social, economic, political, and cultural fields that span borders and boundaries. Transmigrants are described by Glick Schiller et al. (1992b, 1) as social actors who, while clearly influenced and constrained by political and economic hegemonies of both home and host countries, are actively involved in developing and maintaining multiple, layered, fluid identities and relations which span the borders of several societies. Glick Schiller et al. (1992b) presented a new conceptual and analytical framework for understanding migration, outlined in the introductory chapter, which sought to examine relations between displacement and ethnic identity and must be situated economically and politically within the changing global capitalist system and arenas of political conflict, best attempted in an ethnographic context that is historically-informed. This work was followed by *Nations Unbound* (1994) in which the case studies include analysis of transmigrant communities developing between the United States and Haiti, St. Vincent and the Grenadines, and the Philippines.

Due to mass migration and rapidly changing cultural processes, scholars of transnational studies often challenge the analytical fixation on the nation-state; instead, they use transnationalism to 'illuminate the specificities of the contemporary moment' (Rouse 1995b, 358) by situating contemporary changes within broader transformations in the character of global capitalism (Rouse 1995b, 357). For example, many anthropologically-informed studies highlight the ways in which millions of people are living lives that challenge the established ideologies of citizenship and national allegiance (Kearney 1998, 1999; Laguerre 1998; Rouse 1995b, 358). The 'internationalization of business and capital' has opened up the world to increased levels of migration and to 'transnational changes in identity, tradition, and family' (Small 1997, 204). It is here, within the human dimensions and consequences of the globalizing forces of late capitalism, that the concept of transnationalism has sparked interest on the part of researchers of migration and refugee movement.

Like most researchers, I take my working definition of transnationalism from Basch et al. (1994, 7). They suggest that transnationalism deals with 'the *processes* by which immigrants and refugees forge and maintain multi-stranded social relations that link together their places of origin and places of settlement.' They 'call these processes transnationalism to emphasize that many immigrants today build social fields that cross geographic, cultural, and political borders' (Basch et al. 1994, 27). Mahler (1998) suggests that two key points underpin their definition and most of the studies of transnationalism that followed: first, the reconfiguration of population movement in this period of globalization is changing the organization of power and identity at various scales; and second, that a reorientation of analytical paradigms and conceptual tools of inquiry acknowledge the new entanglements at these local, regional, national, and global scales.

Many contributors to the new scholarly trend towards transnationalism see it as an effort to reconfigure thinking on population movement so that it will 'reflect current transformations in the way in which time and space is experienced and represented' (Glick Schiller et al. 1995, 49). Whereas global processes are largely decentred from specific national territories and take place in global space, Kearney (1995, 548) suggests that 'transnational processes are anchored in and transcend one or more nation-states.' James Clifford (1997, 246) states that 'separate places become effectively a single community through transnational movements' and so 'to study each location separately would obscure as much as it revealed.' Therefore, those of us interested in the study of refugee and (im)migrant experiences have the task of explaining the place-based life experience within a rapidly changing, globalized world that is largely dealt with through transnational practices. To me this means that migration researchers must explore the social and cultural landscapes at the level of transnational social fields in order to begin to understand the 'new social spaces' of those we study.

The subject of Central American, specifically Guatemalan, migration encompasses a broad range of experiences that challenge traditional approaches to migration studies. In their work on Guatemalan and Salvadoran experiences in the United States, California in particular, Hamilton and Stoltz Chinchilla (1991, 75) suggest that 'the lines of demarcation between dimensions of economic, political, temporary, permanent, circulatory, voluntary, involuntary, and so forth are rarely clear-cut, and this complexity is now being recognized in theoretical analysis.' Issues of place and identity have never been straightforward, but given the increasing intensity of movement across national borders acknowledged in recent literature (Córdova 1996; Hamilton and Stoltz Chinchilla 1991, 1996; Jonas 1996a, 1996b; Loucky 1996; Bailey et al. 1998) and the development of transnational social fields, the shifting nature of migrant identities both within and across borders and boundaries is becoming more evident.[5] These arrangements and processes, Rouse (1995a, 354) explains, stress transnational, multi-local existence rather than any 'single, bounded, and contiguous locale as the principal setting in which [people] organize their lives and orchestrate their actions.'[6]

By linking places of origin, processes of migration and flight, and place of exile, researchers can embark on an alternative way of conceptualizing population movement in order to attain a more nuanced understanding of ethnicity, cultural change, and connections between space, place, and identity (Glick Schiller et al. 1995; Wellmeier 1994). A transnational perspective allows for attention to be focussed on the striking contradictions that transnationals face in their everyday experiences through such dimensions as 'race,' class, and gender. In her work with Maya refugee groups in Florida, Wellmeier (1994) asserts that communities of consciousness are created through transnational networks that link 'sending communities' in Guatemala with refugee groups in Canada and the United States. 'Communities of association' facilitate resistance to absorption into the host culture and maintain a connection with a Maya culture no longer constrained by geography or national borders.[7]

5 The contemporary processes of movement for the Maya in particular are seen by Wilson (1995b) as being but the most recent process influencing Maya identity transformation and community adaptation.

6 The publication of *Global Migrants, Local Lives* (1995), researched by Katy Gardner about globalization and growing frequency of migration from rural Bangladesh, has been criticized for its presentation as a classic 'community study' in the rural countryside. Migrants and their stories were not followed to their places of destination, which critics contend would illuminate much more about migratory patterns than simply investigating the effects of migration on the home community. Van der Veer (1997), for example, argues that when people live in more than one place, research will also have to be done in more than one place.

7 Conceptually for Wellmeier (1994, 263), 'communities of consciousness' are the transnational realities developed by those refugees and (im)migrants, along with their family members in Guatemala, who believe in 'continuity of Maya spirituality, the symbolic nature of the struggle for a pan-Maya unity, the global scope of the indigenous identity movement, the face-to-face quality of the reconstructed community, and the fluidity of the process of identity formation.' 'Communities of association,' though, are those groups of individuals who actively pursue the goals of the 'communities of consciousness.'

Transnational refugee and (im)migrant networks, a 'transnational public sphere' in the language of Appadurai (1991), negotiate new spaces of social relations (with other migrants and non-migrants in settlement context) and create extended parameters for imagining meaningful places which force us as researchers to reconceptualize fundamentally the politics of community, identity, and culture. It is not only those who are displaced or who live in exile who experience displacement; those people who remain(ed) find 'the nature of their relation to their place forever changed and any illusion of a natural or essential connection between the place and of the culture are broken' (Appadurai 1991). This is particularly true for those displaced *within* Guatemala, but it is applicable also to those with family members who are displaced beyond the national borders. Those individuals who remained in Guatemala, who receive remittances or communications from relatives in the United States and Canada, see that their displaced / deterritorialized family remain Guatemalan in some way, even in a place geographically distant from 'their place' in the world.

Other important contributions to the development of a transnational perspective include an articulation of the concept of deterritorialization by Appadurai (1990; 1991) and Basch et al. (1994). One of the central forces of the modern world is the process of deterritorialization: 'the loosening of bonds between people, wealth, and territories [that] fundamentally alters the basis of cultural reproduction' (Appadurai 1990, 193). One can speak of a 'deterritorialized nation-state' that allows, and at times facilitates, the 'nation's people living anywhere in the world and still not living outside of the state' (Basch et al. 1994, 269), by claiming their dispersed population as 'citizens.' Basch et al. (1994, 3) suggest that for countries such as Haiti, the Philippines, and St. Vincent, a deterritorialized nation-state becomes operational through a renewed nation-building process in the home country context when a significant portion of the population lives beyond its physical borders. These nations are 'engaged in constructing an ideology that envisions migrants as loyal citizens of their ancestral nation-state.'

At this point in the history of the Guatemalan diaspora, and for many of the world's displaced and diasporic populations, deterritorialization in this sense is *not* a reality. I see this as being fundamentally different in the Guatemalan context, where the nation has consciously constructed a racialized ideology about its indigenous population, its refugee population, and opponents to an authoritarian order as apart, separate, and distinct from the nation-building process. Maya groups, according to Carol Smith (1991) and others, were socially constructed as being 'less than human' and not really citizens of the 'modern' nation. One of the root causes of the refugee situation, and of Guatemala's woes in general, is that the state has *never* been able to incorporate the indigenous population into its vision of the 'nation' (Grandin 2000). Deterritorialization of everyday life is a reality, as the Maya and those working for change have been physically denied their 'place' in the nation, but Guatemala itself cannot be studied as a deterritorialized nation-state. Therefore, reference will be made in the Guatemalan context to the process of deterritorialization but not to the deterritorialized nation-state.

Rouse (1991, 13) argues that a transnational perspective illuminates the inadequacy of conceptualizing (im)migration as a movement between two distinct communities. Rather, he articulates the space of 'transnational migratory circuits,' created by Mexican (im)migrants between their home communities in the state of Michoacán and their places of migration in Redwood City, CA. These circuits function through the 'continuous circulation of people, money, goods, and information,' meaning that 'various settlements have become so closely woven together that, in an important sense, they have come to constitute a single community spread across various sites.' Only further studies will reveal if a focus on 'communities' or 'circuits' is appropriate.

The kinds of social life people create in a transnational context have received growing attention in recent years, with studies of diasporas, borders, and other de-territorialized settings in which people practice culture. Individual articles, edited collections (Smith and Guarnizo 1998), and special journal issues (Goldring and Adler Hellman 2004; Mitchell 1997a, 1997b; Portes et al. 1999a, 1999b) emphasize the transnational dimensions of (im)migrant and refugee experiences as do large scale, interdisciplinary research projects (Vertovec 1999).

Geography and Transnationalism

Geographers conducting their research with a transnational lens, at their core, are interested in what Waters (2002, 117) identifies as 'the enduring relations between spatial distance and social relations' in transnational settings. Though geographers' engagement with transnationalism is in its infancy I would argue that their contributions through attention to issues of scale, agency, social structures, and spatial distance are critical to the development of transnational studies. Starting with a challenge posted by Mitchell (1997b, 101) in a special issue of *Antipode* to bring geography back into transnational studies on several different scales, the work of geographers on issues of (im)migration, and to a less extent refugee movement, are influenced by, and shape our understandings of, what it means to 'turn transnational' (Bailey 2001, 413). Geographers employing a transnational perspective, used most often along with appropriate research frameworks as critical ethnographic methods, allow the richness, nuance, and ever-changing aspects of each refugee, (im)migrant, and home community members' identity and cultural connectedness to be given top priority. Such ethnographic research methods are often used to delve into the contradictions, complexities, and uncertainty of transnational lives in the United States and Canada.

All the authors in the *Antipode* forum – Mitchell (1997b), Hilbert (1997), Hyndman (1997), and Vasile (1997) – emphasize the importance of a transnational perspective for theorizing accelerated cross-border flows and rightly indicate that it had been used at an abstract level of discussion of spaces of movement and left out the real contextualization of movements. Though not explicitly stated, the call seems to be for engaged, fieldwork-based, socially relevant social science research to contextualize the then highly theoretical work on transnationalism and globalization. To some extent, geographers have taken on the challenge but exceedingly few studies of transnational migration actually conduct transnational, multi-sited, multi-nation research. Exceptions include Hyndman (1997), Ley and Kobayashi (2005), Miyares et al. (2003), Walton-Roberts (2003), and Wong (2003).

From a 'transnational feminist perspective,' Hyndman (1997, 173) argues for a 'transnational geopolitics of mobility that is attentive to material and historical locations of struggle;' she stresses that 'borders are more porous to humanitarian aid flow from Europe to Africa than to displaced people for whom such aid is intended.' Conclusions drawn by Hilbert (1997) in her article on Zapatismo and the struggle over Mexican modernity are perhaps more appropriate for the discussion of Guatemalan transnationalism. Hilbert (1997, 142) suggests that Zapatistas in Chiapas have 'demonstrated the necessity of destabilizing the concept of a bounded, autonomous community,' and have replaced such a concept with an 'articulation of the connections between local, national, and international communities.' Guatemalan (im)migrants and refugees, like Zapatistas, are confronted with border realities that divide and separate, yet they maintain the same continuity of community by destabilizing the static notions of place.

Bailey's (2001) extensive overview of scholars' engagement with international migration, examined from a transnational perspective, focuses particularly on research exploring migrants' contributions to daily life in emerging transnational communities, while a review by Yeoh et al. (2003) identify geography's contributions to studies of transnational identities and transnational morphologies which are shaped by social processes and agencies across various scales. These reviews will not be repeated here, but I would like to draw particular attention to three overlapping streams of geographical research that have emerged in recent years which highlight the distinctly different possibilities for transnational connections depending on several factors such as the (im)migrant group under investigation, the country/region/city of settlement, the individual researcher's own orientation and expectations, the scale of analysis, and the methods employed to draw out people's experiences of living in transnational social spaces.

First, the Canadian-based work of Kelly (2003) with Filipinos in Toronto, Ley and Kobayashi (2005) with returned Hong Kong migrants from Vancouver, and Walton-Roberts (2003) with Vancouver residents from the Punjab region of India, all stress aspects of mobility and connections. Their work identifies the relative ease of transnational social and economic connections, the significance of remittance commitment to the country of origin, and corporeal mobility between locations via air travel – all of which illustrates how everyday relations are shaped transnationally and how particular (im)migrant groups benefit from transnational possibilities.

Second, Hiebert and Ley (2003, 4) note that 'transnational ties have been obscured in the past in the Canadian literature on ethnicity that has been based on assimilation or multicultural frameworks ... which presupposed a model of immigrant containment within national borders.' But, recently, Canadian geographers such as Hiebert and Ley (2003), Ley (2004), Ley and Kobayashi (2005), participants of the

Strategic Workshop on Immigrant Women Making Place in Canadian Cities (2002), Waters (2002, 2003), and Wong (2003) are drawing attention to the ways in which transnationalism may or may not be used as a strategy of settlement and integration among and within various (im)migrant groups. For example, Ley and Kobayashi (2005, 111) identify the role of return migration within transnationalism as a strategic and deliberate choice over the lifecourse for middle-class Hong Kong returnees from Canada who view their 'strategic switching' of bases within an 'extended but unified social field' as key to family success. At the household level, Waters (2002, 2003) explores Hong Kong and Taiwanese transnationalism in Vancouver, which establishes spatially split 'Astronaut' families as a strategy for business and personal success. Waters (2003) stresses that though these business and professional families use transnationalism to optimize financial opportunities, it would be misleading to focus on their 'hypermobility' at the expense of their 'settlement' in Vancouver. The so-called 'satellite' children and sometimes the female partner remain in Canada while the husband/father travels between the two countries. Therefore, segments of the family undergo settlement experiences under trying circumstances.

The third stream of geographical research, mainly among Central Americans, in Canada and the United States, also focus on the 'emerging spaces of transnational social fields' (Bailey et al. 2002, 125) yet identifies what Miyares et al. (2003) call a 'truncated transnationalism' or one in which immobility, insecurity, and relative poverty are stressed. Across several publications, the research team of Bailey, Mountz, Miyares, and Wright (i.e., Bailey et al. 2002; Miyares et al. 2003; Mountz et al. 2002) explore how the legal provision of Temporary Protective Status (TPS) for Salvadorans in New Jersey is 'neither protective nor temporary' and 'in fact, damages immigrants, their families, and the host society' (Mountz et al. 2002, 352). Rather than establishing protection for the expected integration of this vulnerable population, the TPS legal provision creates a sense of 'permanent temporariness' (Bailey et al. 2002, 138) which leads to a 'state of structural and behavioural limbo' (Miyares et al. 2003, 75) which dis-enables the vibrantly mobile transnationalism seen among other (im)migrant groups. Mountz et al. (2003, 352) stresses that immigration scholarship needs to pay attention to 'critical transnational geographies that theorize the state and the effects of its power in immigrant communities at multiple scales.' Certainly, this attempt, partially based on previous research (Nolin 2004), seeks to address this call.

The possibilities and expectations of Transnational Studies – including and beyond geography – are clear, but what about the doubts raised by critics of this newer approach to migration studies? First, most early studies of transnationalism as 'transnationalism from below' have a tendency to examine transnational practices as liberatory forms of resistance, subversion, and counter-hegemony. Through further studies, these celebratory and somewhat utopian (Guarnizo and Smith 1998, 4) visions may become less so and instead seek to identify the broader range of outcomes for refugees and (im)migrants. Second, studies tend to focus on snapshots of the migration process and are criticized for lack of historicity. In the rush to be cutting edge, the danger of forgetting the past is very real. Third, as mentioned earlier, lack of consensus with terminology leads to confusion over meanings and needs to be rectified. Fourth, the common charges are 'so what's new about all this?' and 'will these processes be replicated beyond the first generation?' Mahler (1998) suggests that comparisons will be possible over different cultural groups, locations, and age groups as further studies are carried out and as long as researchers are asking similar questions. The research agenda she lays out stands as the clearest way forward for improved collaborative and comparative research.

To Mahler's concerns I will add one of my own. I am particularly concerned with the possibilities offered by this 'optic' for dealing with refugee issues. As mobility is identified as a key feature of transnationalism, it must be recognized that the agency and life choices of the 33 million uprooted people worldwide are quite different from those of (im)migrants.[8] As with all people on the move, refugees undoubtedly maintain a 'double consciousness' but the transnational social fields that they forge and maintain are decidedly different from labour migrants, international entrepreneurs, and transnational political activists. For refugees, bodily mobility might be short-lived, uni-directional, and violence-ridden. They may move quickly and then remain stuck 'out of place' for much longer than expected. As with other transnationals, refugee processes are not a new phenomena but by bringing in a newer optic, researchers may get at the layered, complex experience in ways not possible with standard research practices.

Place Making

We are, according to Sack (1997), all geographical beings who negotiate multiple locations and positions. It is the task here to understand how refugees and (im)migrants, as geographical beings, participate in the dynamics of place and processes of transnationalism that occur in a series of places. Refugees, (im)migrants, exiles, and other transnationals are living lives that 'challenge bounded categories in a world that is still built on nation-states and "race" placing' (Basch et al. 1994, 268). Globalization, transnationalism, and the reconstruction of meanings of places are happening within a world that is already unevenly developed, both socially and geographically. Given geography's commitment to the concepts of space and place, transnationalism has implications for its theory and methods. The processes of globalization, the reconfiguration of capital, and ongoing civil strife that have triggered the mass movement of world populations have enormous local implications. Geography is well suited to deal with the consequent complexities, but in order to

8 The US Committee for Refugees (2005) indicates in the *World Refugee Survey* that as of 31 December 2004 there are approximately 33 million uprooted people worldwide, including more than 11.5 million refugees outside their home countries and 21.3 million people displaced within their own country. The United Nations High Commissioner for Refugees (UNHCR) (2005a, 2005b), on the other hand, states figures of slightly more than 19.2 million 'persons of concern' at the end of 2004, an increase of 2.2 million people from the previous year, including refugees, asylum seekers, returnees, and internally displaced persons.

move forward effectively with this, notions such as place, identity, and community must be sharpened and refined.

How are understandings of locality and community formed and lived (Gupta and Ferguson 1997b, 6)? Since locality, community, and sense of belonging are not given or natural, Gupta and Ferguson (1997b, 6) suggest a turn toward a 'focus on social and political processes of place making … of embodied practices that shape identities and enable resistances.' It is important to stress that, even though this research project explores the transnationality of Guatemalan lives, their everyday experiences of living outside of their country still take place in specific places within specific countries. Their lives may span borders, but their realities continue to be mediated by the nations, regions, communities, and homes within which they function.

Anthropologists, sociologists, and geographers who are at the forefront of globalization and transnational studies generally agree that movement and changing contexts do not deny the importance of place in the construction of identity (Appadurai 1986, 1990, 1991; Gupta and Ferguson 1992; 1997b; Kearney 1995; Keith and Pile 1993; Malkki 1992, 1997). Observing that more and more people of the world are living in a 'generalized state of homelessness' (Said 1979, 18), chronically mobile, and routinely displaced, Malkki (1992, 38) forcefully states that 'deterritorialization and identity are intimately linked' and if we only consider place of birth, we would be blind to the richness of the multiplicity of attachments that people develop with and to places by living in, remembering, imagining, and recreating them. Diasporas and transnational social fields always leave a 'trail of collective memory about another place and time and create new maps of desire and of attachment' (Breckenridge and Appadurai 1989, i). Globalization and what Harvey (1989) calls the postmodern 'speed-up' have not made space irrelevant; space has instead been *reinscribed* with new meaning.

Much social science research and conventional studies of migration tend toward an unproblematized view of space, place, and culture. Too often unproblematic assumptions of space and identity suggest a direct link between place and identity and give primacy to the 'authentic local' over the 'inauthentic global.' But what about border people, refugees, exiles, migrants, and transnationals – those people who can no longer be conceptualized as automatically and naturally anchored in space (as if they ever were)? We need to pay particular attention to the way spaces and places are made, imagined, contested, and enforced in Guatemala and Canada. This will require attention to the role of the nation-state in its place making project carried out through the production of difference (for Guatemala, this is played out in the Maya-Ladino divide). It will also require attention to those resistances that attempt to re-write the nation (Bhabha 1990) in Guatemala, to claim certain places as their own, and to reinscribe Maya, peasant, student, and unionist space.

Gupta and Ferguson (1992) suggest that we need to explore the *production* of cultural difference within an increasingly interconnected global system of cultural, economic, and political relations. This approach is stressed over one that would take cultural *difference* as a starting point. This could prove highly appropriate when attempting to understand how identity reconstruction takes place through the processes of transnationalism and inscribing of transnationalized identities. Gupta and Ferguson (1992, 6) suggest the need to 'go beyond culture' as a spatially localized phenomenon and see the not-so-straightforward link between place and identity. We can *rethink* cultural difference through *connection* if we view spaces as having always been *interconnected*, rather than naturally *disconnected*, as is expressed most vividly on ethnographic maps of world cultures: 'your culture is in this space, mine is in this other space.' Transnational refugee and (im)migrant social fields reinscribe place and create a 'new kind of social space' (Rouse 1991) that forces us as researchers to reconceptualize fundamentally the politics of community, identity, culture, and so forth.

In response to the realization of shifting identities and cultures that accompany the mass movement of populations, Clifford (1988, 275) asks: 'What does it mean, at the end of the twentieth century, to speak ... of a "native land"? What processes rather than essences are involved in present experiences of cultural identity?' These types of questions regarding changes in culture and identity are not necessarily new; in the context of globalization, however, and given the special character of the present conditions of massive displacement, quickening population movement, and improved technology and communication, they allow us to question the ways in which identities and culture are now 'differently territorialized' (Gupta and Ferguson 1992, 9).

Spaces and places, more specifically, are mediated by unequal power relations which define who belongs and who may be excluded – or, in the Guatemalan context, eliminated. Places and spaces are constituted by connections and movement (Massey 1991) but also maintained and altered by boundaries that are both spatial and social (McDowell 1999, 4). Transnational worlds are open through the workings of globalization (Appadurai 1996); ideas, money, goods, communications, and so forth, are jettisoned about the world – crossing borders and all sense of time – all the while a reality of national borders restricts the movement of individual people on a daily basis.[9] When researching transnational social fields, then, I suggest that it is imperative that both the real and imagined borders that divide the sending and receiving countries are remembered and incorporated in order to ground the discussion.

For a geography of transnational social spaces to embrace the richness and complexity of the contemporary Guatemalan diaspora, an engagement with the 'individual realities' (Behar 1996, 26) of refugee and (im)migrant lives must be central. Transnational culture and social relations are played out through individual lives, in particular places at particular times. Through a grounded, socially relevant, transnational approach researchers can be sensitive to the multiple realities within and between communities in Guatemala and beyond and explore the ongoing re-workings and re-imaginings of community. The key questions that shape the

9 Hyndman (1997) examines this problematic in the context of UNHCR activities in Africa.

following text, therefore, are: (1) what are the social, cultural, and political processes that facilitate and maintain identity in the context of exile, transnationalism, and globalization; and (2) under these sorts of conditions, how are spatial meanings worked, reworked, and fought over (Watts 1992b), and how is space reinscribed and what sorts of differences are produced through these processes in the 'disputed field of the nation' (Fox 1990, 7).

Notions of community and straightforward connections to place underwent and continue to undergo radical reconfiguration in Guatemala given the context of political violence, state terror, disappearance, and mass population displacement. On-the-ground realities are challenging academic practice and theoretical assumptions that tie identity to a bounded sense of local geography. Understandings of violence-induced change and contemporary diasporic realities require a refocus from a confined 'community studies' approach to one that explores the ways in which social life is organized through primary social relations and weak ties shaped by processes of racialization, gender, and transnationalism. In the following chapters, I link population dynamics of Guatemalan refugees and (im)migrants to practices of state violence in Guatemala and immigration/refugee policy in Canada to explore the spatializing of transnational identities and social relations.

PART II
Guatemala to Canada: State Violence, Immigration Policies, and Population Dynamics

Chapter 3

Flight into Exile: Internal Armed Conflict and Refugee Displacement

This chapter provides a basic historical overview of Guatemalan political violence of the late 1970s into the early years of the new millennium. Though much is left out of such an overview, key points that relate to refugee and (im)migrant movement to Canada are highlighted. It should be clear that transnational refugees must deal with at least two national contexts, though usually more (Mexico and USA, for example), in their journeys to safety. Therefore, the internal conflict and Guatemala's indigenous/Ladino divide (often referred to as the 'two nations' within one) are discussed before proceeding to an examination of select findings of the REMHI (1998) and CEH (1999a, 1999b) reports. I then move to examine Kobrak's (1999a) findings regarding repression experienced by intellectuals and leaders in Guatemala as well as the *Guatemalan Military Archive* (1983-1985), better known as the *Death Squad Dossier*, obtained by the National Security Archive's (1999) Kate Doyle. These recent findings are then connected to the Canadian dimension of Guatemalan refugee flight.

Guatemala's Two 'Nations' and the Internal Armed Conflict

How does a country come to be equated with such levels of cruelty, brutality, and inhumanity as Guatemala? What thinking informs the intellectual authors of what the CEH (1999b) identifies as the 'multiple acts of savagery and atrocious acts' against men, women, and children that were seen to 'degrade the perpetrators and those who inspired, ordered or tolerated these actions'? Key to answering such questions is an understanding of the links between nation, 'race,' class, ethnicity, and gender that tie contemporary circumstances with Guatemala's nation-building past (Grandin 2000). What follows, then, is a discussion of some of these links in an attempt to clarify the foundation of much of the military and elite discourse of these violent decades.

Theories of nationalism emphasize the socially constructed nature of nations at various times and places (Alonso 1994; Duany 1996) and the possibility for many 'nations' to function within one 'state' variably defined as either a 'multination state' or a 'multicultural nation-state' (Gurr 2000; Kymlicka 2004). Guatemala's pursuit of national development functioned on dividing, rather than uniting, its working population and resulted, Carol Smith (1990a) argues, in the country's contemporary ethnic and class divisions. Smith (1990b, 150) goes on to suggest that these divisions were 'created by the way in which Guatemalan elites tried to create a Guatemalan nation.' At the beginning of the twentieth century, Guatemala was already a coercive state divided into two nations, Ladino and Maya. The existence of two unequal 'nations' within Guatemala led to a cruel war between the 'world's most ruthless military dictatorship and one of the world's most brutalized native populations' (C. Smith 1990b, 170). Crucial to comprehending this violent history is the fact that the powerful 'nation' that controls the Guatemalan state never attempted to incorporate the indigenous population into its 'imagined national community' (Anderson 1991; Stepputat 1994b, 13), nor allow popular protest from within activist Ladino and union circles (Levenson-Estrada 1994), but rather 'broke down powerful collective movements into individual survival strategies, and extracted leaders from their communities' (Grandin 2004).

Fundamental to all this repression and conflict is the notion of 'race' as a social construction rather than a natural or biological division among humans (Jackson 1987; Kobayashi and Peake 1994). This distinction is extremely important to understanding the two categories that separate Guatemalan society: *indígena* (indigenous) or Maya and Ladino (non-indigenous or identification with Western culture) or *mestizo* ('mixed blood'). These terms tend to be regarded as 'racial,' and Guatemalans describe the two as *razas* ('races'). Burns (1999, 135) notes that Mayas explain how 'their identity is essential to their very bodies' and how their culture is 'embodied in their physical as well as social lives.' In practice, however, the categories often refer more to cultural circumstance than biological inheritance, as people are able to move along the 'racial' continuum based on situational needs, desires, and motivations.

Beatriz Manz (2004, 36) rightly notes that the boundaries between the two groups often blur but were far clearer during the colonial period, whereas today the distinction between Mayas and Ladinos is 'complex, ambiguous, and not always easy to identify.' C. Smith (1990a, 3) explains the ever-changing social classification system in Guatemala, which is based on 'ideologies of race, class, language, and culture ... which take on different meanings over time.' Most of Guatemala's contemporary non-indigenous peoples, or Ladino, are descendants of the Maya, as are the contemporary indigenous Maya peoples. Therefore what has distinguished indigenous and non-indigenous peoples over time has not necessarily been biological difference, but a system of social classification based on a *belief* in biological difference. Guatemalan society is racialized by power relations that are mediated through social practices. Because of these practices, it is possible for Maya to identify themselves, and be identified by others, as Ladinos, as phenotypical characteristics do not necessarily prevent this process, though it often entails a move from one's home community to shed the social 'stigmatization' of indigenous identity. The ability to identify as Ladino rather than 'Indian,' C. Smith (1990a) argues, has been due to the desire of the elite, powerful Ladino to have the majority of the population identify with an image of the nation as 'modern' and 'whiter.'

The link between 'race' and class – that Guatemala's upper elite is mainly 'white' rather than *mestizo*, while many Ladino often share the same lower class position as

Mayas – tends to reinforce the *understood* 'racial' hierarchy. Throughout Guatemalan history, geographical marginalization, or spatial segregation, of indigenous and non-indigenous peoples reinforced attempted nationalist movements of modernization (the former in mostly rural, highland country, the latter mostly in urban areas). The geographical marginalization of the Maya is entrenched further by economic marginalization resulting from the excessive inequality in regard to land ownership (de Villa and Lovell 1999; WOLA 2003a)

The constructed nationalism of the ruling Ladino minority was also forged and maintained through strategic foreign alliances. As C. Smith (1990b) puts it:

> [T]he path chosen in Guatemala did not just build on past [colonial] social relations, but created new ones: relations that put the elite, together with their foreign backers, in an unchallenged position of power, that elevated the Ladino into a new power position in the coffee zone as plantation agents; and that virtually enslaved those who remained categorized as Indian - at the same time preserving them as a separate and resistant culture.

As in other Latin American countries, the Guatemalan state, in the words of Radcliffe and Westwood (1996, 23) 'acted as an apparatus of discipline and productive power intervening materially and violently in a variety of sites to reinforce their idea of the nation.' The state has been built on the concept of European superiority in every aspect from religion, social values and customs, to intellect, reasoning, and worldviews. This is the perpetuated myth that created the reality of the 1970s, 1980s, and 1990s – decades of repression and human rights abuses directed toward the indigenous Maya population. This myth was such a powerful force that Carmack (1988) and Galeano (1992), among others, state that ethnocide and genocide became the basic cultural policy of the state. ANTONIO, a Maya refugee from San Marcos, now in SUMMERLAND, Ontario, describes his experience this way:

> *Where I came from they had killed many of* [my] *countrymen. The bodies of some had been seen, and others were not seen. They made us suffer, they took them away because we are Indians and there the Ladinos or rather the rich have taken us* [away] … *furthermore because we also studied the bible and because we are a little ignorant we wanted a little and to learn we only went to the church ... but the church of the poor because there are also churches of the rich and they think that that is why they came to take us.*

Resistance to the nationalist ideology of the Guatemalan state forced thousands of Guatemalans into exile in Canada and other countries – a nationalist ideology that continued to provide a space for the ancient Maya of the Classical Period in the nation's imagined history, all the while driving the contemporary Maya from their land in a continued attempt to *unwrite* them from the nation (Bhabha 1990). Eloquently expressed by Montejo (2005) and Warren (1998), the contemporary 'Maya Movement' in Guatemala is resisting assimilation and silencing on the national scene and instead is becoming what Diane Nelson (1996, 288) calls 'Maya hackers,' its members are 'decoding and reprogramming such binary oppositions as those between past and future, traditional and modern, being rooted in geography and being mobile.' These Maya hackers are 'creating spaces for themselves inside the state' (Nelson 1996, 294) by 'sharing information and creating networks' (Nelson 1996, 293) that span the Americas and connect those in exile with those who remained during the violence.

Maya cultural activists, along with many others who worked through the Peace Process, pushed for the establishment of the CEH, better known as the Truth Commission, to investigate human rights violations that occurred during the internal armed conflict. Resistance to the repressive 'politico-military structures' (Schirmer 1999) that grew out of the fundamentally racist nationalist ideology is now most visible in the pages of two historic documents – *Guatemala: Nunca Más / Guatemala: Never Again* (REMHI 1998) and *Guatemala: Memoria del Silencio / Guatemala: Memory of Silence* (CEH 1999a) – presented to the Guatemalan people in 1998 and 1999, and echoed in protest marches and vigils that accompanied their presentations. The two reports reveal much that was hidden and unacknowledged by state forces in Guatemala and underreported by various news sources and human rights organizations. Through the *testimonios* of thousands of Guatemalans, decades of denial by the government and state forces of state-sponsored terrorism and campaigns of repression can be refuted and challenged.

During the difficult process of social investigation, Canadian lawyer and CEH member, Albert Kohl, returned to Canada to take testimonies from exiles who see their efforts as part of the process of creating a new Guatemala (CEH Canada 1998). Through this particular transnational action, some refugees and (im)migrants in Canada, together with those negotiating for change within Guatemala, are attempting to *rewrite* the nation in order to re-inscribe identities and places into a 'new,' pluricultural, multilingual Guatemala of the future. But, of course, it is not as clear-cut as that and the collection of *testimonios* in Canada was not entirely successful, as many Guatemalans in Canada were not comfortable with the prospect of providing *testimonio* to unknown lawyers and volunteers, even when equipped with guarantees of confidentiality and anonymity.

None of the participants who I met with in southwestern Ontario indicated that they provided testimony to the CEH. Their responses to my query ranged from a lack of knowledge about the possibility of providing testimony to grave concerns that the information potentially might fall into the 'wrong hands' within Guatemala. MIGUEL, a union leader now in Canada, offers perhaps the clearest sense of a continued concern over speaking out and lack of 'safe spaces' of community support:

> *I think it was quite difficult ...* [silence for a few seconds] *... we have, all of us, and I think that all those who come for political reasons, we have something to say that what happened to us ... the reality. But I think that presenting a testimony here somehow was kind of difficult ... because you say, "Well, even though people came with credentials, in this case with the United Nations, right," and I think that some of the people give the testimony but in other cases ... you ask me, "Miguel, did you provide your testimony?" I didn't. You know, somehow I was feeling, "What is going to happen with this information?" Once again, I don't think we ... we ... I was thinking of my family. What is going to happen, right? And after I talk with, like for example, the daughter of my friend ANTONIA who is*

> *herself a survivor of ... when she was captured she was only 14 years old in Guatemala she was raped and tortured and when I said to her, "Well listen this is what's happening." And she said, "I don't believe them." You know why? Because the psychosis what we lived was really nothing that we make up, you know, it's nothing that we make it up ... it was a reality and very hard. And some of us react in different ways. But somehow I don't feel like it was something serious, even though how with all the official ... I think there were a lot of Guatemalans that we didn't present our testimony unfortunately because maybe, in my case, I didn't feel comfortable.*

At the very least, individuals expressed concern that simply they did not know how their information would be used by the CEH. Paradoxically, the security offered by exile in Canada did not allow for the development of 'safe spaces' within which to speak out. Rather, isolation in Canada often perpetuated a silence quite at odds with the burgeoning movement within Guatemala to provide testimony. Let us now turn to the findings of REMHI and the CEH.

Genocide and State-Sponsored Terrorism: Findings of REMHI and CEH

> We are gathering the memories of the people because we want to contribute to the construction of a different country.... Discovering the truth is painful, but it is without doubt a healthy and liberating action ...
>
> Monseñor Juan Gerardi Condera, *Presentation of REMHI report*, 24 April 1998.

In 1995, approximately two years before the government of Guatemala and the URNG (*Unidad Revolucionaria Nacional Guatemalteca*) – the umbrella organization of the guerrilla forces – signed a 'firm and lasting' Peace Accord, members of the Archbishop's Office for Human Rights in Guatemala (ODHAG) began the process of collecting *testimonios* of human rights violations. This process was initiated to organize material for the future United Nations-sponsored *Comisión para el Esclarecimiento Histórico* / Commission for Historical Clarification (CEH) and to provide protected spaces within various dioceses throughout the country for those who chose to come forward with information.[1] Members of the REMHI team, including Carlos Beristain (1998), immediately recognized the significance of memory and the necessity to give voice to memories in order to understand the experience of state-violence and war. Shannon Lockhart (1999), a member of the ODHAG mental health unit, argues that the social reconstruction of Guatemala lies in knowing the

1 The REMHI team understood the limitations of what a United Nations-sponsored CEH could do in one year, therefore, they undertook a three-year Catholic church-sponsored investigation that began *before* the signing of final Peace Accord and approached the project as part of a national healing process (Gidley et al. 1999). REMHI trained 600 interviewers and human rights promoters (mostly indigenous) with the collaboration of more than 200 parishes during a period when speaking about the violence was considered by many to be a political act. After 'official' peace was proclaimed in Guatemala, information in the REMHI database was turned over to the coordinators of the CEH and provided a model for their own work.

truth, of having your truth heard and respected. This reconstruction, she asserts, is necessary for social healing and recovery to succeed and is fostered in ongoing training of mental health workers, and distribution and community discussion of the final report titled, *Guatemala: Nunca Más /Guatemala: Never Again* (REMHI 1998) which was released on 24 April 1998.

The REMHI (1998) report, *Guatemala: Nunca Más*, was presented to the Guatemalan people by Monseñor Juan Gerardi Conedera, the Auxiliary Bishop of the Archdiocese of Guatemala and driving force behind the project, on 24 April 1998. Two days after his presentation of the landmark human rights report, Monseñor Gerardi was bludgeoned to death by blows to the head with concrete blocks as he was entering his house in the evening. Despite the lack of progress in the investigation and outrageous government theories (ranging from common crime to a crime of passion to a dog attack), most people in the country believe that Monseñor Gerardi was killed for political reasons related to the REMHI report (Goldman 1999; Melgar 2000). As the REMHI project was not bound to the same restrictions as the official Commission for Historical Clarification (CEH), names of those responsible for crimes were listed when known. At a presentation during the early days of his exile in Canada, Judge Henry Monroy (1999), the second of many judges appointed to the case over the years, argues that the 'dark forces in power sent a clear signal about certain attitudes and activities … about whether they are deemed permissible or not. Monseñor Gerardi's activities were not deemed permissible.' Clearly, speaking the truth of the people and naming those responsible for acts of violence and genocide are still powerful acts of courage in Guatemala. Monseñor Gerardi's murder remains unsolved.

Ten months after the presentation of REMHI, on 25 February 1999, Guatemalans received the much anticipated report of the United Nations-sponsored CEH (1999a), *Guatemala: Memoria del Silencio / Guatemala: Memory of Silence*, which detailed in 3,600 pages war-time atrocities and decades-long American support of the Guatemalan army. Using the recently released report and database of the CEH (1999a), I highlight statistics that help to contextualize the refugee movement to Canada and elsewhere.

Spaces of Terror and Assault

More than 6,000 *testimonios* collected by REMHI were turned over to the CEH for their United Nations-sponsored investigation. Commissioner Christian Tomuschat, in his presentation of the CEH (1999a, Prologue) report, argues that 'despite the shock the Nation could suffer upon seeing itself reflected in the mirror of the past, it was nevertheless necessary to know the truth and make it public.' The mandate of the CEH (1999b, Prologue) was neither to neither judge nor prosecute, but to 'place on record Guatemala's recent, bloody past.'[2] The CEH received thousands

2 Prosecutions could only proceed if the CEH concluded that acts of genocide occurred during the years of violence. This indeed was a conclusion of the CEH commissioners who

of *testimonios* from various human rights organizations within Guatemala and even supported the collection of information from Guatemalans now living in Canada (CEH Canada 1998). Within a short time-frame (six months extended to one year) and limited budget, over 14,000 *testimonios* were collected and analyzed by the CEH in 1998 and 1999 (CEH 1999b).

The CEH registered 42,275 victims, of whom 23,671 were victims of arbitrary execution and 6,159 were victims of forced disappearance. Eighty-three per cent of identified victims were indigenous Mayas and 17 per cent were Ladino. Approximately 25 per cent are women and 75 per cent are men (CEH 1999a, Cap 2/Vol 3, Item 38) and while both women and men were subjected to all forms of violations, it is important that the types of violation are differentiated by gender. For example, men outnumbered women approximately four to one in the categories of arbitrary executions, torture, forced disappearance, detention, and the category of 'other,' while women and men were found in equal numbers in the statistics of death by forced disappearance. Women, though, experienced 99 per cent of the reported sexual violations.

When the *testimonios* collected by the CEH are combined with other studies of political violence in Guatemala (Ball et al. 1999; Kobrak 1999b; REMHI 1998), we can now state categorically that over 200,000 individuals were killed or disappeared as a result of the 'fratricidal confrontation' between 1962 and 1996. Overwhelmingly, the military and other state forces such as civil patrols, state police, military commissioners, and the like are implicated in 93 per cent of the human rights violations and acts of violence, while responsibility for three per cent goes to the guerrilla forces, leaving four per cent as unknown or unresolved cases. Going further than all expectations, the CEH reported that state forces were also responsible for 626 massacres and acts of genocide against the Mayan peoples during the years of 1981 and 1983.[3]

Through an in-depth study of three communities (Kobrak 1999b), the Commission identified a fairly consistent chronology of political violence, with regional variation, against the Maya population and those accused of supporting subversion against the State. Thorough documentation by the CEH and other researchers now charts escalating urban terror in the late 1970s when individual targeting of 'communities' of activists, teachers, professors, students (Kobrak 1999a), and union members (Levenson-Estrada 1994; Reed and Brandow 1996) was routine practice in Guatemala City and other urban locations (CEH 1999a, 1999b; *Guatemalan Military Archive 1983-1985*; *National Security Archive 1999*; REMHI 1998).

---

stated that 'acts committed with the intent to destroy, in whole or in part, numerous groups of Mayans were not isolated acts or excesses committed by soldiers who were out of control' (CEH 1999b *Conclusions and Recommendations,* Item 120) and therefore 'the CEH concludes that agents of the State of Guatemala, within the framework of counterinsurgency operations carried out between 1981 and 1983, committed acts of genocide against groups of Mayan people' (CEH 1999b *Conclusions and Recommendations,* Item 122).

3 Guerrilla forces are responsible for 32 massacres (CEH 1999a, b).

Generally, a pattern developed of selective violence in the countryside and smaller urban centres in the late 1970s and very early 1980s, when community leaders, such as catechists, Maya priests, development promoters, cooperativists, political authorities, union leaders, professors, and students, were targeted for detention, torture, disappearance, and death. At this stage, men were the main victims as they held most positions of authority and led most community organizing.

The next stage functioned in 1981 through 1983 and took on the general character of 'scorched earth tactics,' in which no distinctions were made during massacres and mass killings. The brutal so-called counterinsurgency programme of this period then focused military and other government security forces' activities toward organized groups throughout the country and indigenous Maya life spaces in the highland region of the country (Carmack 1988; Falla 1994; Green 1999; Manz 1988, 2004). Here, men, women, and children were all victims, and rape began to accompany collective violence and forced detentions.

Almost half (48 per cent) of all registered violations took place in 1982 alone, at the time when General Efraín Ríos Montt was in power (CEH 1999a, Cap 2/Vol 2, Item 865).[4] Many scholars, human rights organizations, and solidarity activists now attempt to come to grips with the resulting social, economic, political, and cultural upheaval throughout the country but found most intensely in the rural countryside.

In a highly anticipated publication, Thomas Melville (2005) also documents the American Embassy's supportive role toward various Guatemalan military and high-profile government figures during these brutal years and the lengths to which the staff went to present a positive spin on events to the international press. Melville (2005, 597) categorizes the attempts of then Ambassador Frederic Chapin to 'imply that the kidnappings, tortures, dismemberments, murders, and massacres that plagued the country were somehow the work for common criminals' as 'ludicrous.' The spin became too much even for Chapin. Melville (2005, 598) recounts one revealing, but all too infrequent, moment which sees Ambassador Chapin break down after Maryknoll priest Ron Hennessey confronts him in his office in late 1983 over his unwavering support of the Guatemalan government:

> The Ambassador looked at the priest for a few moments, breathing deeply, and then suddenly put his head in his hands. "What can I do? What can I do?" he repeated. "The

---

4 Fears that the present will repeat the past were reinforced when former dictator General Efraín Ríos Montt, called 'The General' and 'Our Maximum Leader' by supporters, re-surfaced on the political scene during the 1999 election season as a key figure in the right-wing FRG (*Frente Republicano Guatemalteco* / Guatemalan Republican Front) party of 'generals, evangelicals, and mafia leaders' (GCSN 2000, 1). Elections in November (first-round) and December (second round) 1999 saw Ríos Montt elected as President of Congress and as the strategic ally and strong man behind then-elected President Alfonso Portillo Cabrera (Associated Press 1999; Lovell 1999). Playing on fears of escalating crime, the FRG's campaign slogan '*Seguridad, Bienestar, Justicia*' / 'Security, Wellbeing, Justice' and 'Portillo president - Ríos Montt to power' hark back to Ríos Montt's iron fist of the early 1980s (Barrios 1999).

Guatemalan military is a bunch of animals! They're just animals, and that's all they are! They are not human! You cannot deal with them as rational human beings! What am I supposed to do?".... He [Hennessey] was pleased to see that Frederic Chapin was neither ignorant of, nor indifferent to what was going on around him. Here was the highest official of the U.S. government in Guatemala admitting that the Reagan administration had been propping up a series of killers – those whom the White House and State Department had continuously insisted were "advocates of human rights" and "leading Guatemala down the road to democracy" – who were, in reality, animals and irrational human beings. At this, Hennessey knew implicitly that Mr. Chapin was not going to last long as the front man for the Reagan Administration in Guatemala.

Spaces of Loss: Death, Disappearance, and Departure of Leaders

Urban violence and repression against the student and labour movements decimated their ranks through death, disappearance, and flight. Urban violence is particularly significant for this study, and its claim that transnational processes link the spaces of loss in Guatemala with experiences of refuge in Canada. The spaces of loss are still deeply felt in Guatemala as a new generation of student, labour, and community groups struggle to cope with the many challenges they face in building a 'new Guatemala' without experienced leadership.

Paul Kobrak (1999a, 5) documents the 'deliberate and sustained violence committed by state forces against students and intellectuals' at the University of San Carlos (USAC) in the years 1944 to 1996. As a centre of political opposition since the CIA-backed coup in 1954, USAC students and faculty viewed the campus as a site of revolutionary ideology and practice. By the late 1970s, the military government labeled USAC as a 'center of subversion' not only due to student activism but also in response to the many ties that guerrilla groups – such as the PGT Communist Party, the Rebel Armed Forces (FAR), the Guerrilla Army of the Poor (EGP), and the Revolutionary Organization of the People in Arms (ORPA) – maintained on the city campus.

State forces unleashed a wave of violence in 1980 against USAC, killing over 125 students and professors in that one year alone and kidnapping, torturing, and releasing many more (Kobrak 1999a, 70). Between 1980 and 1983, 80 university professors or administrators were killed or disappeared in Guatemala – 77 of them from USAC (Kobrak 1999a, 88). By the end of 1983, most of the country's progressive faculty were dead or, as with other survivors, had gone into exile. Few options existed so, in addition to exile, some survivors chose to go underground while others joined armed insurgency groups in the countryside. One source of Kobrak's (1999a) suggests that 70 per cent of the teaching staff at USAC's Labor Orientation School (with strong links to the labour movement) was killed or forced into exile.

Table 3.1 charts the number of killings and disappearances at Guatemalan universities, by year, between 1978 and 1995. I include this chart to demonstrate the intense repression experienced by the university sector and related opposition groups (most of whom maintained strong ties with university members and workers). In Chapter 4, I examine the documentation of deaths and disappearances in conjunction with the Citizenship and Immigration (CIC) data on the number of students, usually survivors of attacks or threats, entering Canada. In this way, a clearer picture emerges of state directed violence against progressive Guatemalan intellectuals and how Canada acted as a kind of safety valve.

Table 3.1 Number of Killings and Disappearances at Guatemalan Universities by Year, 1978 to 1995

YEAR	TOTAL	YEAR	TOTAL
1978	10	1988	8
1979	11	1989	20
1980	127	1990	11
1981	52	1991	10
1982	46	1992	13
1983	21	1993	8
1984	40	1994	3
1985	33	1995	5
1986	8		
1987	7	**TOTAL**	**433**

*Adapted from Kobrak (1999a, 121).

Kobrak (1999a) notes that state terror obviously affected the mental health of survivors in Guatemala City where selective repression created a 'culture of death' among the opposition groups and university students. As MIGUEL reveals in our interview, '*the psychosis of terror is always with you*,' leaving many survivors in exile traumatized for years to come. Many kidnappings took place 'in the middle of the day, in the middle of the city' (Kobrak 1999a, 105), leaving students, faculty members, and labour movement participants feeling that they could be killed or disappear at any time. As MIGUEL comments, '*that was the certainty, when you knew that death was maybe traveling close to you, when you were traveling on the bus or when you were walking.*'

Research by Levenson-Estrada (1994) and Reed and Brandow (1996) documents the struggles of the labour movement and offers insight to the findings of the CEH and REMHI. In addition to these sources, the U.S.-based *National Security Archive 1999* recently made available declassified American government documents that shed more light on the American role in Guatemala's 'dirty war.' Unearthed secret memos, in a short few sentences, capture the brutality directed at the labour movement. For example, Document 16, a declassified secret American Defense Intelligence Agency (1979) summary of November 1979, indicates an increasing level of violence against political opposition and labour groups in Guatemala City:

> Violent acts against political and labor personalities have increased since the October 1978 crisis. Government actions in dealing with that issue resulted in the dismantling of most public sector labor groups (1).

Another recently released document by the National Security Archive, the *Guatemalan Military Archive* (1983-1985), also referred to as the *Death Squad Dossier* (National Security Archive 1999), identifies 183 targeted victims of Guatemalan security forces in the years 1983 to 1985, many of whom were university students either affiliated with an opposition group or members of the student executive body. This chilling document, the first of its kind to come to light, includes the names, photographs, and summary information about each victim, including opposition group membership, the date of kidnap, how the kidnap operation functioned along with the final outcome. For some, this meant capture and torture for a month or more before release or death, which is coldly noted by the number 300.

Of the 183 victims, 13 women are listed with various ties to opposition groups such as PGT (7), ORPA (4), and FAR (2) while no group affiliation is noted for eleven women (for example, they lived in raided safe houses). Only 18 of the 159 men listed do not have direct affiliations with the main opposition groups, but rather are members of the student movement or members of various unions. Men with group affiliation include: PGT (87); ORPA (25); FAR (16); EGP (8); MRP (3); Frente Guerrillero (1); and CNT (1).

Within months of the *Death Squad Dossier's* release, two prominent and direct Canadian links became public. The first case involves Julio César Pereira Vasquez, then living in Calgary, identified as Victim Number 73 in the dossier, who returned to Guatemala in August 1999 with the assistance of GAM to give testimony before the Ministerio Público. The *Dossier* (National Security Archive 1999, 21) states in Spanish (my English translation is added below):

73. JULIO CÉSAR PEREIRA VASQUEZ
(s) LUIS
Miembro del PGT-CC
22-02-84: Puesto al tiro por (s) Claudia y capturado en la Avenida Petapa, entre 6a. y 7a. Calles, Zona 12
26-02-84: Quedó libre para contactos
21-03-84: Se asiló en la Embajada de Francia, con su familia

73. JULIO CÉSAR PEREIRA VASQUEZ
(alias) LUIS
Member of the PGT-CC
22-02-84: Set up by (alias) Claudia
and captured on Petapa Avenue, between
6th and 7th Streets, Zone 12
26-02-84: Set free for contacts
21-03-84: Sought exile in the French Embassy, with his family

At a conference with the Guatemalan press during my fieldwork, Pereira, a former member of the PGT, confessed that after repeated torture in a clandestine prison, he decided his survival rested on collaboration with his captors (*el Periódico* 1999).

To that end, he participated in the abduction of Sergio Saúl Linares Morales (Case 74 in the *Dossier*), who was executed seven days later, and Alma Lucrecia Osorio Bobadilla (Case 34), whose case remains unresolved. Within four days of capture, freedom was Pereira's reward, after which he sought asylum at the Venezuelan consulate and, contrary to evidence in the *Dossier*, from Caracas final asylum was granted to his family by Canada.

The second case involves Wendy Méndez, a 25-year-old Guatemalan Canadian woman who, until recently, lived in Vancouver. In December 1999, Méndez revealed to the Canadian press and CBC radio that she identified her 'disappeared' mother's name and photograph in the military's document (Dafoe 1999). Luz Haydee Méndez Calderón, a 35-year-old wife and mother, was tortured and abducted from her house in Guatemala City in front of her children. The military's information indicates that Méndez Calderón was in charge of the PGT's international affairs and party propaganda. The brief entries in the chilling document do not reveal, Méndez divulged, that the G-2 military unit arrived at the house looking for Méndez's Calderón's husband, Marco Antonio Santizo Velásquez, a USAC professor, who was tipped off and fled the country (Dafoe 1999). The Dossier does not reveal Méndez Calderón's ultimate fate, only that she was transferred to a U-4 unit almost two months after her abduction. Santizo Velásquez made his way to Vancouver and brought his children to live in Canada two years later.[5] The *Dossier* (National Security Archive 1999) states:

83-1. LUZ HAYDEE MENDEZ CALDERON
(s) CHAVE
Nombre falso: SOFIA ESTRADA
Miembro del Secretariado del PGT-CC
Encargada de asuntos internationales y Propaganda del partido.
Cuando (s) JULIAN venía de México, lle Gaba a dar a la casa de (s) Chave.
Su esposo MARCO ANTONIO SANTIZO VALAS-QUEZ (s) TITO ó CABALLON, es el responsable de la Oficina donde se reúne la
DN. en la Zona 10, 4 to. Nivel del Edi-
ficio Rodriguez.
1968, estuvo en Rusia.
08-03-84: Fue capturada en la 3a. Ave-
nida 22-16 Zona 19, Colonia San Francisco.

02-05-84 PASÓ A U-4

83-1. LUZ HAYDEE MENDEZ CALDERON
(s) CHAVE

5 In Spring 1999, Méndez returned to Guatemala to co-found the group HIJOS (*Los Hijos por la Identidad y la Justicia contra el Olvido y el Silencio* / Children for Truth and Justice, Against Forgetting and Silence) with 30 other children of the disappeared to demand that those who tortured and murdered their parents be brought to justice (Sandoval 1999).

False name: SOFIA ESTRADA
Member of the Secretariat of the PGT-CC
In charge of international affairs and
party propaganda.
When (s) JULIAN came from Mexico,
He gave up the house of (s) Chave.
Her husband, MARCO ANTONIO SANTIZO VALAS-QUEZ (s) TITO ó CABALLON, is in charge of the office where the DN. met up
in Zone 10, 4th floor of the Rodriquez
Building.
1968, was in Russia.
08-03-84: Captured on 3rd Avenue
22-16 Zone 19, San Francisco
neighbourhood.

[Hand written note follows]:

02-05-84 HANDED OVER TO U-4

With Méndez Calderón's case in mind, I examined the document for any further explicit link to Canadian exile and found mention of one person, ALVARO RENE SOSA RAMOS, captured on 11 March 1984. Listed as number 87, the summary information for SOSA RAMOS indicates that he escaped a death squad two days after his capture and fled to the Belgian Embassy. A single note records that he left for Canada eight days after his escape, on 21 March 1984. The *Dossier* (National Security Archive 1999, 25) states in Spanish (English translation added):

87. ALVARO RENE SOSA RAMOS
(t) Tte. JOEL, RICHARD

Responsable de la Estructura Militar del Frente Urbano de las FAR
11-03-84: Capturado en los campos del Roo
sevelt, Zona 11
13-03-84: SE ESCAPO Y ENTRO A LA EMBAJADA DE BELGICA. SALIÓ PARA CANADÁ 21-03-84

87. ALVARO RENE SOSA RAMOS
(alias) JOEL, RICHARD

Responsible for the Military Structure of the Urban Front of FAR
11-03-84: Captured in the
Roosevelt neighbourhood, Zone 11 (Guatemala City)

Hand written notes follow:

13-03-84: HE ESCAPED AND ENTERED THE BELGIAN EMBASSY. LEFT FOR CANADA 21-03-84

In both urban and rural terrorized spaces, Guatemalans witnessed government sanctioned violence, the killings and disappearances of tens of thousands of people, and in the final stage, the massive displacement of more than a million indigenous and non-indigenous people within the country, and at least a million people beyond the borders (Loucky and Moors 2000; Montejo 1999a, 1999b; Nolin Hanlon and Lovell 2000). This assault meant the immediate creation of new cultural geographies and the erasure of others. Various refugee scenarios are evident as individuals, families, and whole communities reacted in myriad ways to the terror and violence that peaked in the early 1980s but continued in new forms through the 1990s and into the early years of the 2000s. The displacement of thousands of Guatemalans due to their indigenous identity and/or supposed 'subversive' behaviour led to one of the most dispersed indigenous populations in the Americas and an exiled activist population.

Surely there are other survivors from this list of 183 kidnap victims who found refuge in Canada. Two former PGT members now living in THOMASBURG confided that many of their colleagues and friends were among those listed in the *Dossier* (ISAIAH and LILLIAN). But until they or their family members come forward publicly there is little possibility of confirming this statement.

Situating Canada (1980s to early 2000s)

In addition to Mexico and the United States, Canada became a key destination in the northward movement of political refugees, undocumented migrants, and (im)migrants from Guatemala (see Table 3.2). The largest movement of Guatemalans to Canada took place in the late 1980s and early 1990s. As they arrived in Canada, Maya peoples and others particularly targeted by the military forces encountered a country dealing with a contested multiculturalism policy and rather inflexible policies dealing with immigrant and refugee populations. The 1980s saw a significant alteration in immigrant and refuge seeking populations, as source countries shifted from their historical base in Europe to countries such as Iran, Guatemala, El Salvador, and Vietnam. This period stands as a critical moment in Canadian immigration history, when officials and civil society once again negotiated the limits of an understood 'open-arm' refugee policy.

The geographical spaces of movement varied over time to incorporate both official and contested spaces of refuge before living Canadian geographies could be forged. The passage north often begins with the terrifying, frequently undocumented, 1000-kilometre odyssey to the United States' border with Mexico and continues through safe communities and dangerous landscapes within the United States or replays itself in repeated attempts to elude *la migra* (the United States Border Patrol).

Table 3.2 Guatemalans Beyond Guatemala, Estimates (2001)

COUNTRY OF ASYLUM	GUATEMALANS
USA	1,000,000 +
MEXICO	100,000 - 200,000
CANADA[6]	14,095*

*Plus refugee claimants still in process.
Sources: Jonas (1996a), Pessar (2001, 467), Statistics Canada (2004a), and US Committee for Refugees and Immigrants (1993).

For others, the long migration route continues overland past the American-Canadian border before safe haven is achieved. And for others still, safe passage is secured through the Canadian Embassy in Guatemala City or Mexico City.

Canadian government responses both to the potential and concrete arrivals of Guatemalan refugees took two sharp turns that must be examined. The cross-trajectories of Guatemalan and Salvadoran refugee arrivals and complete Canadian immigration and refugee policy reversals were most evident during 1984 and 1987. These years stand as critical moments of Canadian government policy change and refugee response that created changed geographies of movement and settlement.

First, in response to growing concerns over 'illegal' immigration to Canada in 1984, Immigration Minister John Roberts argued for the necessity of a travel visa requirement for Guatemalans. The measure was taken to ensure that assistance went 'to those most in need rather than those seeking only personal gain,' even though approximately 70 per cent were expected to be legitimate cases. Numbers of those seeking asylum in Canada were quite low, as well, with approximately 200 in 1982 and 453 in 1983 (Montgomery 1984). Minister Roberts couched the requirement within a statement of 'relaxed rules' that allowed Guatemalans with family members already in Canada to be sponsored under eased criteria and for deportations against Guatemalans to be postponed for at least one year. Paradoxically, by ceasing deportations the Canadian government recognized the dire circumstances in Guatemala but still chose to impose the visa requirement that effectively blocked those most desperate from fleeing (CP 1984).

The geographical implications of the policy change are clear. Where once refugees could board a plane to seek refuge in Canada, the visa requirement cut off this route and forced refugees into the much more difficult and potentially dangerous overland route through the United States in order to make their claims at border crossings.

6 Among few others, Samuel Dunn's (2000, Chapter Two) ethnographic work with Guatemalan men in Toronto highlights the often overlooked dimension of undocumented migration and settlement in Canada. For example, ALFRED, one of Dunn's participants, comments that *'the last census – which of course is not real because there are many people who are afraid to answer the census. Even though they say that it is confidential, you never know so they prefer not to answer. But according to that census there are 12,000[sic] Guatemalans in Canada, legally. You can add those who are afraid to answer, those who are illegal.'*

Ironically, if Guatemalans reached the Canadian border on their own, Canadian officials recognized the majority of claimants as refugees with little hesitation. But in order to reach Canada, Guatemalan refugees had to travel the dangerous passage through the United States, at a time when the Reagan administration adamantly supported the Salvadoran and Guatemalan governments and downplayed or outrightly rejected reports of massive human rights violations. Instead, the State Department labeled Central American refugees as 'economic migrants,' denied refugee status to virtually all asylum seekers, and ordered the deportation of thousands (Coutin 1993; Cunningham 1995).

In response to what they consider immoral American policy, Crittenden (1988) identified more than 200 American churches – Catholic, Presbyterian, Quaker, Methodist – and several Jewish congregations who declared themselves as sanctuaries, hideouts from American immigration authorities. In addition to the Sanctuary Movement's clandestine work of bringing Guatemalan and Salvadoran refugees safely across the Mexican-American border through the 'Underground Railroad,' members also pursued a legal 'Overground Railroad' by escorting refugees to Canadian consulates to apply for refugee status in Canada (Elbow 1992). The latter option was not always available and, therefore, a Canadian branch of the 'Underground Railroad' was pursued when all other avenues were exhausted (see Figure 3.1).

The Canadian government's willingness to accept Central American refugees threatened with American deportation prompted the organization of an Ottawa-based group called North Star Railroad (Ferguson 1985). North Star became the Canadian legal alternative to the 'illegal' Sanctuary Movement in the United States wherein Guatemalan and Salvadoran refugees enter Canada through formal legal channels. Immigration and refugee law in Canada allowed a public, legal route for refugees, as opposed to the clandestine Sanctuary Movement operation in the USA. North Star's role became one of tackling asylum case paperwork and finding sponsors for 'illegal refugees' channelled through the Underground Railroad to the Canadian border by the sanctuary workers.

The year 1987 stands as another benchmark in Canada's complete policy reversals in dealing with Guatemalan and other Central American refugees claiming asylum at our borders. In late 1986 and early 1987, the American government imposed tighter immigration laws required by the Immigration Reform and Control Act (IRCA) to deal with 'illegal aliens' – most directly meaning Guatemalans and Salvadorans – and began deportations. At this time, Canadian officials continued to state that they would *not* deport people to these countries even if their refugee claims were not accepted. Canada's policy position changed in February 1987 once Guatemalans and Salvadorans started arriving at the border in large numbers. The Canadian government took *all* countries off the B1 non-deportation list and indicated that deportations would ensue for anyone whose claim of asylum was denied.

Policy action (or even discussion of policy change) in both Canada and the United States soon created a panic mentality among Guatemalans and Salvadorans in the United States and flight to the Canadian border. In response to these unwelcome

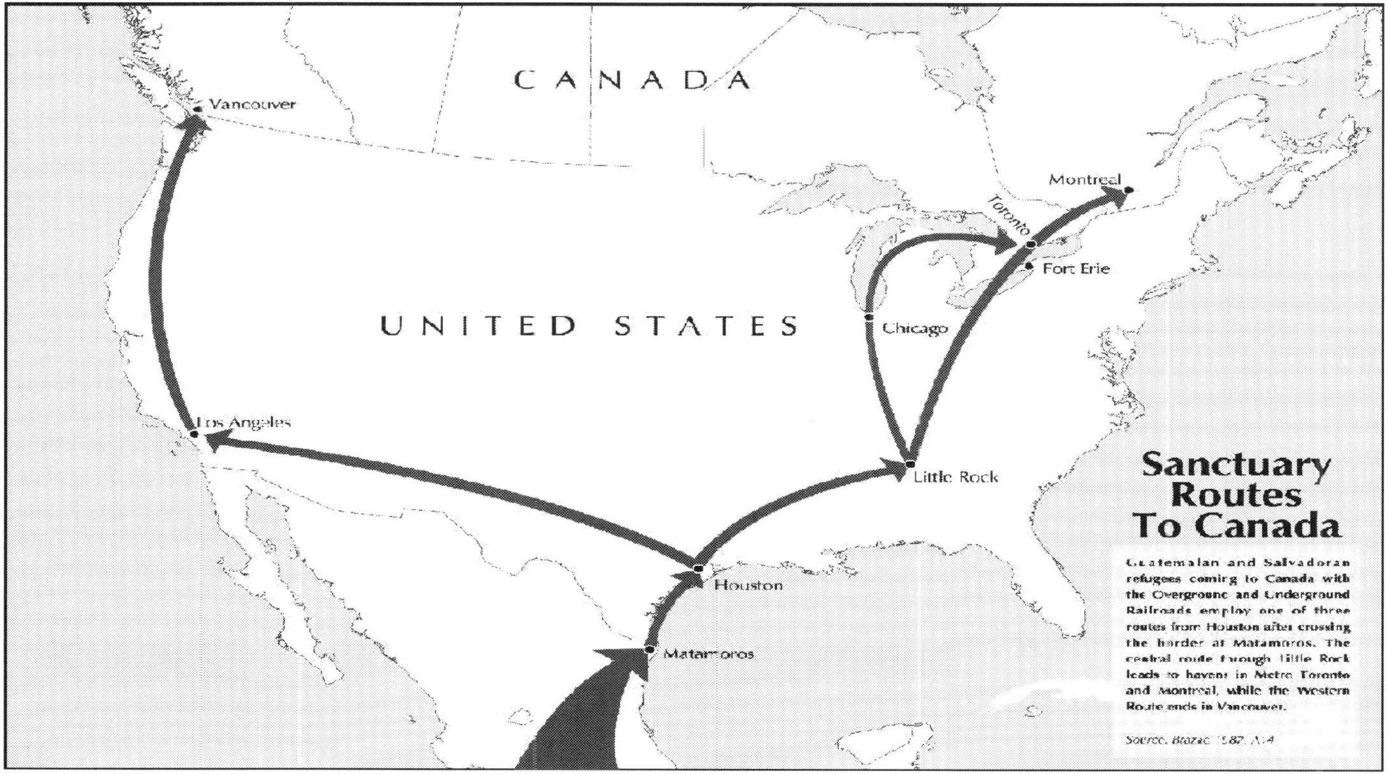

Figure 3.1 Sanctuary Routes to Canada

arrivals, Immigration Minister Benoit Bouchard threatened to force refugee applicants to remain outside the country while their claims were in process. For Guatemalans and Salvadorans, this policy change meant that if they were to apply at a consular office in the United States, deportation orders against them might be enforced before their claims were finalized in Canada.

In an alarmed response to American and Canadian policy announcements, increasing numbers bypassed both the Sanctuary Movement and the Overground Railway and opted for direct claims of asylum. Wilson (1987b) reported a doubling and tripling of refugee claimants in the early months of 1987 at Fort Erie, Ontario and Lacolle, Quebec border crossings, locations where once the number of asylum requests was so low that officials were not compelled to record statistics. In tiny Fort Erie, Canadian Immigration officials met as many as 100 refugees a day during this 'crisis.'

Swift government action followed, leading to 'crackdowns' on the perceived 'problem.' Tough interim measures announced on 20 February 1987 signaled a 'stone wall' approach to the refugees' plight (Brazao 1987). Then Prime Minister Brian Mulroney announced Bills C-55 (*Refugee Reform Act*) and C-84 (*Refugee Deterrents and Detention Bill*), indicating that all refugee claimants at the border were to be returned to the USA while waiting for their cases to be heard in Canada. Canadian officials turned away several hundred refugees at the border over the following weekend, effectively closing the doors to those who request asylum (Hess 1987). Imprisonment or detention in the USA compounded distress for many Guatemalans and Salvadorans, while others were left waiting for months in motels, convents, and solidarity houses along the border. Additionally, under this new legislation, to 'knowingly help or try to help a refugee claimant come to Canada without a valid visa, passport, or travel document' became an offence (Cleroux 1987). Quickly and decisively the door was closed and the refugee problem was contained.

Political Violence 1999-2005

Individual targeting of Guatemalan leaders and activists continued into the new millennium (Arellano and González Moraga 2000). Various refugee scenarios are evident as individuals, families, and whole communities reacted in myriad ways to the terror and violence that peaked in the early 1980s and continued in new forms, documented by Amnesty International (2003), Wilkinson (2003), WOLA (2003b), among others, through the 1990s and into 2005 with the targeting of Guatemalan leaders, activists, and journalists.

Additionally, Glaister (2004) and NACLA (2004), among others document the escalating homicide rate in 2004 and 2005 and point to the particular targeting of vulnerable women and men, particularly poor and indigenous peoples (Castillo Priego 2005; Tuckman 2004). Though far more men are recorded as homicide victims, Guatemalan activists argue that female murder victims are found at a rate of one per day (Lloyd 2004) with signs of rape, torture, and brutality reminiscent of the worst years of the internal armed conflict. For example, during a September 2004 visit to

Guatemala, Susana Villarán, in her capacity as the special observer for human rights with the Organization of American States (OAS), concluded that 'we now have a spiral of assassinations against women' (cited in Glaister 2004).[7]

Though not exclusively, the urban activist segment of the population tended and still tends to be accepted in Canada rather than the rural peasant population (see Chapter 4 for details of Canadian Citizenship and Immigration statistics). For example, at least five key witnesses and/or informants (and their families) in the Monseñor Gerardi assassination case sought Canadian asylum in 1999 and 2000. A number of people close to the case have been forced into Canadian exile. First, taxi driver Jorge Diego Méndez Perussina sought refuge in Canada on 25 February 1999 after providing eyewitness testimony. Méndez was quickly followed by Supreme Court Judge Henry Monroy. Death threats and lack of cooperation led to his 23 March 1999 departure to Canada after only two months on the Gerardi case. On 26 August 1999, the ODHAG and Canadian government assisted Jorge Manuel Aguilar Martínez, an ex-specialist of the military working in the *Estado Mayor Presidencial* (EMP), and his family to leave the country for Halifax after testifying on the case.[8]

Canada also received several high profile cases from Guatemala in the new millennium. In 2000, then Guatemalan President Alfonso Portillo, in an unprecedented move for someone in his position, chose to send his family to an undisclosed location in Canada due to death threats by members of the Los Pasaco kidnapping gang regarding the imminent execution of two gang members facing death by lethal injection. On the first day of summer, Guatemalan and Canadian news sources announced the secret departure of Portillo's mother, sister, brother-in-law, and two nephews days earlier (Arellano 2000a; CBC WebPost 2000). The climate of insecurity that blankets Guatemala appeared to penetrate the former First Family and their departure for Canada did little to suggest that the then President was confident in his ability to deal with destabilizing forces within the country. Critics charge that those *sin dinero* ('without money') cannot so easily ride out threats in a foreign country such as Canada (See Figure 3.2). As Lovell (2003) documents, Canada continues to act as a kind of safety valve for high profile cases such as news reporter Luis Barillas, recipient of the 2003 International Press Freedom Award, who remained in Toronto to seek political asylum after receiving a series of death threats.

7 José Eduardo Mora (2004) cites statistics provided by the Women's Protection Unit of the Guatemalan Attorney General's Office which indicate that, in a population of some 12 million, 489 women were murdered in 2004 as of December 23. Mora indicates that this count puts Guatemala at the 'forefront of the rest of Latin America with regard to the number of female murder victims,' ahead of Honduras with 171, El Salvador with 96, and Colombia with 297.

8 Two others related to the case found refuge in the United States and Costa Rica. Daily death threats (directed at both him and his family) compelled prosecutor Celvin Galindo to abandon his case and country for refuge in the United States on 7 October 1999. Later, attacks against Ronalth Ochaeta, director of ODHAG at the time, and his family led to their departure from Guatemala in 1999 as well (Palacios and Zelada 1999; Pop Barillas 1999).

Figure 3.2 Filóchofo Political Cartoon: Guatemalan President Portillo Sends Family to Canada[9]

Source: Filóchofo, *Siglo XXI*, 21 June 2000 http: //www.sigloxxi.com.

Whether returning after 15 years to cleanse one's conscience, as in the case of Julio César Pereira, or to demand justice for one's parents, as in the case of Wendy Méndez, the possibility to participate in a new phase of reconciliation is upon some Guatemalans in exile. Returns to Guatemala after years in exile can be seen to offer a suture in the transnational space of loss within the country. Individually, the suture may be strong and lasting, but the continued flight of Guatemalans to Canada suggests a reinforcement of Canada as a mainstay in the transnational refugee spaces of Guatemala. Chapters 5 and 6 highlight the multiple transnational social and personal spaces for Guatemalans in Canada and their families in Guatemala. As will be discussed, each individual and family grapples with the struggles of place making and identity negotiation differently. For some, the rupture of departure remains an open wound that never heals in exile, while for others transnational sutures enable the establishment of new lives in new locations.

The geographical spaces of transnationalism – including the spatialization of refugee movement and place making – is the subject to which we turn next. Using data from Citizenship and Immigration Canada (CIC), the Immigration

9 The main horizontal captions read: 'The President has announced that he will get his family out of the country on account of threats to their security … Good for you, Portillo … But what about the 12 million rest of us? Which country are you going to ship us off to? … [Figure with raised hand] I WANT TO GO TO CANADA! … Hey, you, what country would you prefer to go to?' The vertical caption requests that the municipal authorities responsible for water supply in Guatemala City get services resumed for a neighbourhood, Las Hojarascas, cut off for the past week.

and Refugee Board (IRB), foreign embassies, and other related sources, a dynamic population geography is articulated in order to situate the Guatemalan population in Canada in more detail.

Chapter 4

Government Policies and Refugee Dynamics: Geographies of Movement

It's a very hard life, savage and good at the same time.
(PEDRO)

Part of the challenge of understanding Guatemalan refugee transnationalism is the necessity to understand the political and policy context refugees and (im)migrants entered into when they arrived in Canada. Chapter 3 situated the historical context of political violence in Guatemala and refugee flight to Canada. In Chapter 4, the spaces of movement are charted using statistical data and interview sources to frame the dialectical relationship between Canadian refugee policy, multiculturalism, and Guatemalan population dynamics.[1] Chapter 4 develops a descriptive analysis of the effects on Guatemalan movement and the place making in light of Canadian refugee and immigration policy that appeared insensitive to the realities of genocide and systematic human rights violations in Central America during the 1980s. I argue that Canadian foreign policy and immigration/refugee policy functioned at various times both to facilitate and to impede refugee movement from Guatemala, ultimately cementing transnational ruptures rather than encouraging transnational flows.

In this chapter my intentions are two-fold. First, I discuss the necessity to draw links between policy and population dynamics. Analysis of the data provided by Citizenship and Immigration (CIC) and the Immigration and Refugee Board (IRB) allows the charting of population dynamics in light of government policy decision making. I also document the population characteristics of those who fled the spaces of terror in Guatemala and are creating living Canadian geographies. For some Guatemalans, new geographies entail links to Guatemala, while for others new lives entail place making projects without transnational ties. Gender, age, and place of residence are also significant.

At more length in subsequent chapters, I draw on people's own statements of experience in our interview conversations to reveal the often unacknowledged and silent experiences of the refugee decision making, transnational rupture, and the struggle at place making in Canada. In order that Guatemalan refugees and

1 Landolt et al. (1999) argue, in their study of Salvadoran transnationalism, that an analysis of transnationalism requires consideration of the dialectical relationship between grassroots and elite transnational practices. For Guatemalans in Canada, the relationship with Canadian government policy is central.

(im)migrants are understood as subjects rather than simply objects of repression and state policies, I try to balance statistical presentation with selected conversations.

No previous analysis exists of the limited range of Canadian data on the Guatemalan population. I see this chapter, therefore, as an opportunity to rectify that situation by offering as rich a portrait as possible, and to underscore the vastly different experiences from the more thoroughly documented American and Mexican migration and refugee scenarios (Loucky and Moors 2000).

From the Sources: Citizenship and Immigration Data

> It is impossible to think or write about refugee-related issues without some reference to statistics. (Crisp 1999, 1)

Data Sources and Methods

This discussion draws on two distinct data sources: statistical data and interview conversations. I obtained the statistical data from Citizenship and Immigration (CIC) in Ottawa and the Immigration and Refugee Board (IRB) in Toronto. I gathered together statistical information on Guatemalans and other Central American populations from a variety of sources such as Statistics Canada, CIC, the Enforcement Branch, foreign embassies, and so forth. At the same time, data were also obtained directly from the IRB Convention Refugee Determination Division (1989 to 2001) and the IRB Refugee Protection Division (1999 to 2004). According to the IRB Documentation Centre, specific country refugee data, at least of the sort I was looking for, are not available prior to 1989.[2] Tables and figures can only tell us so much so, in subsequent chapters, I draw on qualitative experiences of refugee transnationalism made possible through an examination of interview conversations with research participants as well where interview responses varied. Rather than extrapolate from particular experiences to a population at large, I prefer to use responses to offer personal reflections on broader processes. The present chapter gives priority to the descriptive analysis of the statistical data.

Relevant and available variables for the years 1980 to 2004 were identified in conjunction with the CIC Statistics Division. I obtained CIC data on Guatemalan permanent residents (age and gender provided) and refugee claimants that include: (1) numbers by port of entry and inland office; (2) numbers and locations of claims for political asylum (at the Canadian border and abroad); (3) immigrant class; (4) occupations upon entry; (5) numbers of minister's permit; (6) location of settlement by city and province; (7) number of deportation orders; (8) confirmation of departures; and (9) final destination of deportations.

In the quantitative survey that follows, it must be clear that data obtained from various sources cover different time periods and, therefore, it is impossible

2 For example, records from the 1980s are simply statistical counts of the various immigration classes (i.e., Convention Refugee, Family Class, Independent Immigrant, and so forth) with no accompanying descriptive information such as the claimants' locations.

to construct as clear a portrait as I had hoped. Nonetheless, given that no survey of Guatemalans (or all Central Americans, for that matter) has been generated in Canada and that the data are available for consultation, the information conveyed here provides some clarification. Limitations for cross-category comparison are evident in that data are not available in all categories for all years under consideration (1980 to 2004). Information on Guatemalan refugee claimants serves as an example of the difficulty of working with uneven data. Data are available on the number of Guatemalans by immigration class (including Convention Refugees, Designated Class, CR8 Dependants, those with Ministerial Permits, and such) for 1980 to 2004, but information on Permanent Residents by port of entry (POE) is available from 1985, while POE information for refugee claimants does not begin until 1990. Therefore, it is necessary to be a little imaginative in the interpretation of the available data.

CIC, IRB, and Canadian Embassies employ a variety of sub-categories under the broad terms of 'Immigrant' and 'Refugee.' Refugee claimants are those who enter the refugee determination system when they make a claim for asylum at a Canadian POE or in-land office. In selected years, Minister's Permits were issued to many Central Americans as a way to allow refugees to work while waiting for permanent residency. Permanent Residents are those who enter the country on a permanent basis through a host of government programs such as Family Class, Designated Classes, Convention Refugee, Assisted Relatives, and so forth (See APPENDIX ONE for a glossary of terms used). As will be noted below, the use of various programs changes over time given country conditions.

For the purposes of Figures and Tables in this chapter, I maintain the vocabulary of the Canadian government in order the highlight the variety of programs and avenues made available for movement to Canada. But for the purposes of discussion in later chapters, I continue to use only two terms: (im)migrant and refugee, though I stress that it is not entirely useful to distinguish between these two terms. In reality, the experiences of departure for the majority of Guatemalans in Canada are refugee-like, no matter that they were categorized as Permanent Residents (a category of 'Immigrant') upon arrival. This designation is directly due to government programming rather than an expression of voluntary departure.

Hollow Labels? Refugee/Economic Migrant/Immigrant/Designated Class

All those who arrive in Canada are conferred with some label supposedly defined by the circumstances of their arrival. Since analysis of CIC data entails an engagement with government categorizations, I have maintained their use in Figures and Tables in this chapter. But beyond identifying the program with which the individual entered Canada, are these categories a useful way to conceptualize population dynamics or are they simply hollow labels that betray the reality of the hard road travelled to Canada's safe haven? The categories are useful to identify government programs for the participants, but not the persons themselves. Analysis of the various avenues of departure and arrival is critical to understanding Guatemalan population dynamics, but it must be recognized that even those without the refugee label were (and are) considered to be in refugee-like circumstances. The labels tell us more about Canada's immigration programs than about the exact nature of departure from Guatemala. For example, according to the United Nations, a refugee is someone who applies for asylum in a country *outside* his or her country of origin whereas the Central American governments, via the *Cartagena Declaration on Refugees* (OAS 1984) argue for a broader definition to include 'persons who have fled their country because their lives, safety or freedom have been threatened by generalized violence,' among other threats.[3] Canada also established a number of special programs that conferred refugee status through special immigration status in a designated class on those accepted *within* Guatemala itself.

There is a call in the migration literature to include refugees and (im)migrants together in studies of population movement. 'Economic' or 'political' migrant characterization is, according to Bailey and Hane (1995, 171), 'an impoverished view of the range of mobility options that are available to, and practiced by, those who are uprooted.' Black (1993, 5) concurs and also stresses that past differentiation between economic and political migrants was 'inflexible, overly simplistic, and much too strict' for the realities of movement that include 'linkages and parallels between various types of forced migration' (Black 1991, 7).

Black (1993, 9) suggests that the primary inadequacy of some existing studies of refugees is their ahistorical approach that treats refugees as 'exceptional populations.' Singular causation also has been at the core of much conceptualization of economic migrants, immigrants, and political refugees (Cohen 1995). The processes of globalization within which contemporary refugee displacement and (im)migration is taking place calls for a more contextual approach within a place, and a time-specific analytical framework that illuminates the multiple causation and complex decision-making processes (Glick Schiller et al. 1995; Hamilton and Stoltz Chinchilla 1996). Holistic approaches reject the categorization of refugees as distinct from other kinds of migrants since, when historically contextualized, migration and refugee movements are often intimately connected by a host of socio-economic and political processes. There are connections between forced migration and other types of migration (i.e., economic as a result of political upheaval) that deserve consideration and exploration. Therefore, I chose to study those labelled as refugees and immigrants together, with an understanding that the experience of violence of the two populations varies, but as a result of the complexity of the conflict in Guatemala, those labelled immigrants and refugees are often one and the same.

3 The *Cartagena Declaration on Refugees* (OAS 1984) states that '[i]n view of the experience gained from the massive flows of refugees in the Central American area, it is necessary to consider enlarging the concept of a refugee … Hence the definition or concept of a refugee to be recommended for use in the region is one which, in addition to containing the elements of the 1951 Convention and the 1967 Protocol, includes among refugees persons who have fled their country because their lives, safety or freedom have been threatened by generalized violence, foreign aggression, internal conflicts, massive violation of human rights or other circumstances which have seriously disturbed public order.'

Charting the Movement: Policy and Population Dynamics

The largest wave of Guatemalan refugee and (im)migrant movement to Canada took place in the mid- to late-1980s and early 1990s. People on the move encountered a destination country dealing with a contested multiculturalism policy and rather extensive debate regarding immigration and refugee policy. This initial analysis begins with a brief review of the development of official multiculturalism, basic population characteristics of Guatemalans in Canada, and interconnected issues surrounding refugee and immigration policy change. These issues are followed by a descriptive analysis of CIC data and what I see as the dialectical relationship between policy and population dynamics that shape the spatialization of immigration and refugee movement and placement.

The key point in the following section is to identify the ways in which Canadian refugee policy plays out in a dynamic population geography. How, in the broadest sense, is the geography of movement mapped onto the Canadian landscape and, in turn, how does this mapping relate to the spaces of loss? Spaces of loss can be imagined as the voids left in Guatemalan communities, families, and organizations by the violent loss of over one million women and men through death, disappearance, and departure. Chapter 3 offered a brief 10-year overview of the many points at which policy and population dynamics interacted. In this chapter, particularly, we can note how, almost immediately, policy changes affect the number and spatialization of refugee claims.

Canadian Multiculturalism

Literature on the topic of Canadian multiculturalism is vast and fractured; detractors and opponents (Moodley 1983) and critiques of tolerance (Bibby 1990) confront proponents of pluralism and the anti-racist goals of multicultural policy in Canada (Kymlicka 1998; Mata 1994; Opoku-Dapaah 1994). As a country of First Nations peoples and immigrants, Canada has gone through many stages of adaptation, assimilation, and integration. Pre-1940s Canada was dominated by Anglo-conformity wherein immigrants and refugees were meant to renounce their 'ancestral cultures and traditions in favour of the behaviours and values of the Anglo-Saxon group' (Palmer 1975, 12). The notion of a biological merging of settled communities and new immigrants into a new Canadian type never achieved popularity in Canada. As the 1960s unfolded, demand grew for greater government recognition of ethnic groups and preservation of aspects of immigrant culture within the context of Canadian citizenship. The Royal Commission on Bilingualism and Biculturalism conducted hearings across the country on this issue which led to the 1969 passage of the *Official Languages Act* followed by Canada's first multicultural policy (Mata 1994). It became clear that Canada would have a policy of cultural pluralism *within* the framework of French and English bilingualism. In 1971, then Prime Minister Pierre Trudeau announced the new multicultural policy to the House of Commons (in Knowles 1992, 169) thus:

> The policy I am announcing today accepts the contention of the other cultural communities that they, too, are essential elements in Canada and deserve government assistance in order to contribute to regional and national life in ways that derive from their heritage and yet are distinctly Canadian.

Geographer Audrey Kobayashi (1993, 205) lays out three broadly defined stages to the development of multiculturalism: first, the demographic stage of concrete ethnic diversity without the existence of official policy; second, the symbolic stage, through which multiculturalism is officially acknowledged and promoted, but without commitments for real implementation; and third, the structural stage, at which 'legislative reform provides the basis for social change.' Canada has been, and continues to be, a multicultural country, but the multiplicity of ethnicities resulting from the changing nature of refugee and immigrant movement challenged the Canadian public's tolerance levels. No longer was Europe the main contributor of immigrants to Canada and an official policy of multiculturalism was not a guarantee against racial discrimination. Refugees and immigrants from the Middle East, Indo-china, South and Central America entered a society with, 'a clear and persistent history of racism and xenophobia' (Collins and Henry 1994, 526). In order to deal with the cultural and 'racial' diversity in Canadian society, the *Canadian Multiculturalism Act* was unanimously passed in 1988 in fulfilment of the structural stage of multiculturalism. The statement of policy presented in the *Act* established a new type of multiculturalism policy, which builds *inclusiveness* into Canadian society (in Mata 1994, 18):

> [T]o preserve and enhance the multicultural heritage of Canadians while working to achieve the equality of all Canadians in the economic, social, cultural, and political life of Canada.

With this pronouncement, there was a clear shift in policy from cultural pluralism as an ideal to the actual promotion of equality rights, anti-racist activities, and systematic removal of barriers to social, economic, and political participation for refugees and immigrants. The *Multiculturalism Act*'s approach to diversity is 'based on values and principles which allow immigrants and refugees to identify with Canadian society' (Mata 1994, 20). The goals of Canada's *Multiculturalism Policy* (1971) and the subsequent *Multiculturalism Act* (1988) strive to: (1) foster a society that recognizes, respects, and reflects a diversity of cultures such that people of all backgrounds feel a sense of belonging and attachment to Canada; (2) develop, among Canada's diverse people, active citizens with both the capacity and opportunity to participate in shaping the future of their communities and their country; and (3) build a society that ensures fair and equitable treatment and that respects the dignity and accommodates people of all origins (http://www.pch.gc.ca/multiculturalism/html/context.html#red).

A critical examination of the social context of refugee and immigrant experience in Canada, however, tends to reveal contradictions between a multicultural population and a multicultural policy, contradictions between what Carlos Fuentes (1985), in his Massey Lectures, termed the 'legal' country and the 'real' country. Fuentes brings attention to the gaping spaces that separate the 'legal' country of words, documents, agreements, and laws from the reality in the 'real' country of everyday life experience.

For example, Canada's *Multiculturalism Act*, a policy of pluralism and equality, was established in the same year the federal government was choosing to decrease refugees' access (particularly Central American refugees) to Canada with the passage of Bills C-55 (the *Refugee Reform Act*) and C-84 (the *Refugee Deterrents and Detention Bill*). Creese (1992, 123) suggests that the intention of the policy changes was to limit access to the refugee determination system and expand police powers, all in the name of deterrence of false refugee claims. Creese (1992, 124) further argues that this change in attitude was not the result of high numbers of false claims, but had more to do with the 'geopolitical realities of the generation of refugees and the non-European ancestry of most of them.' So whose multiculturalism is it after all?

Many observers in the edited collection, *Deconstructing a Nation: Immigration, Multiculturalism, and Racism in '90s Canada* (Satzewich 1992), recognize the reality of racism and intolerance as one of the main social issues Canada faces, while others suggest the problem is not intolerance, but too much tolerance offered to new Canadians and refugees. How have the experiences of Guatemalan (im)migrants and refugees in 'multicultural' Canada shaped their relations with their home country? Do Guatemalans in Canada use their relatively open space in Canada to reinscribe their transformed identity in the controlled spaces of Guatemala? Answering these questions may lead to a better understanding of the transnational networks that exist between Guatemala and Canada.

The policy of multiculturalism, in conjunction with refugee policy, does not overcome the unproblematic use of 'race' as a category naturally given rather than socially constructed. Rather than being used as an effective tool for anti-racism and equality, multiculturalism allows in some cases for the continuing racialization of (im)migrant and refugee groups (Smith and Feagin 1995). Rather than attaining 'inclusive' status, many refugee groups are segregated into the lower class sectors of employment and housing (Knowles 1992; Hawkins 1994). Radcliffe and Westwood (1996, 27) suggest that the 'racialization of the geographies of identities' occurs through the attribution of particular traits to racialized groups in the collective imaginations of citizens.

For example, perhaps Guatemalan Maya refugees and (im)migrants have a greater cultural connection with the First Nations people of Canada than the various ethnic groups to which they have been associated? Until recently, Maya peoples in Canada were not necessarily officially recognized as indigenous peoples; instead they are categorized together with Ladinos and other 'Central American refugees.' Until recently, it was not possible to officially recognize Guatemalan ethnic divisions among those in Canada that in many ways fuelled political violence and prompted their search for asylum. In the most recent 2001 Canadian census, 2,875 people self-identified as Mayas (1,440 women; 1,435 men).[4] Once we address the CIC data

4 Guatemala is the main country of origin of most Mayas though this figure may include some Mayas from Mexico and Belize (Statistics Canada 2004b).

analysis, the spatialization of refugee movement and settlement urges us to return to Radcliffe and Westwood's comment above.

Charting Population Characteristics

Survivors fortunate enough to leave the spaces of terror in Guatemala with their lives are creating transnational refugee geographies that encompass living Canadian geographies. Officially numbering 14,095 in the most recent Canadian census, their numbers are relatively small and so far their settlement has tended to be more permanent than temporary (Statistics Canada 2004a).[5] The figures that follow

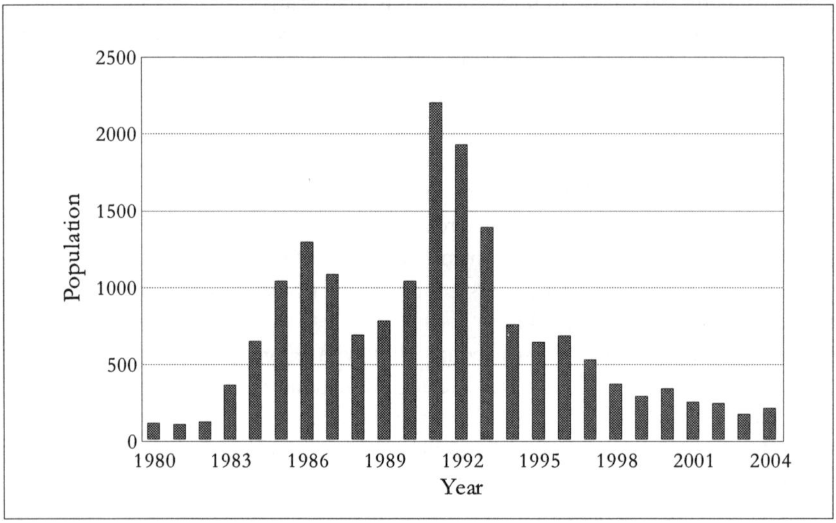

Figure 4.1 Entry of Guatemalan Permanent Residents, 1980 to 2004

document the presence of Guatemalans in Canada, that is, people whose country of origin is Guatemala. Limited data are available for those who self-identify as Maya beyond location in Canada (Statistics Canada 2004b). Figure 4.1 charts the year-by-year entry to Canada of 17,361 individuals between 1980 and 2004 (CIC 2004b). When these data, up to 2001, are compared with the census data, a review indicates that at least 2,613 permanent residents voluntary left Canada, were deported, or have

5 For example, in Simmons and Turner's (1997) study of Salvadorans and Guatemalans in Toronto, respondents choose to self-identify as immigrants rather than refugees or migrants.

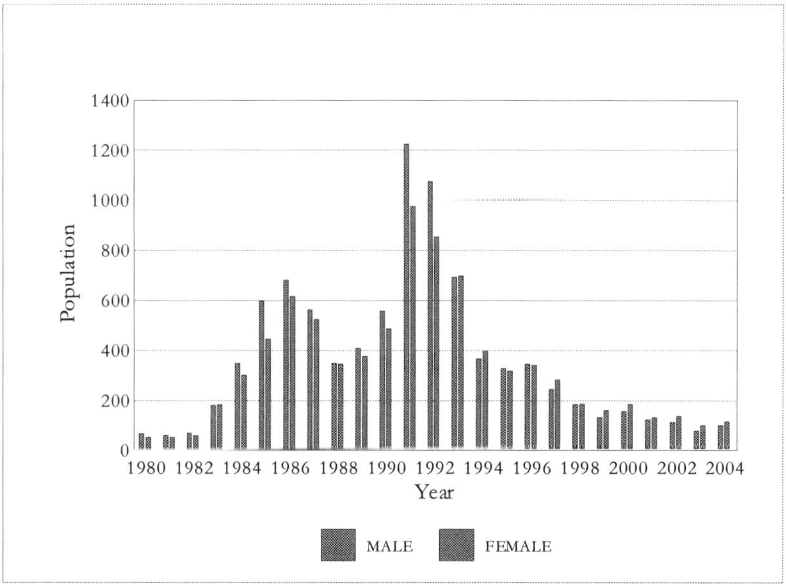

Figure 4.2 Gender of Guatemalan Permanent Residents, 1980 to 2004

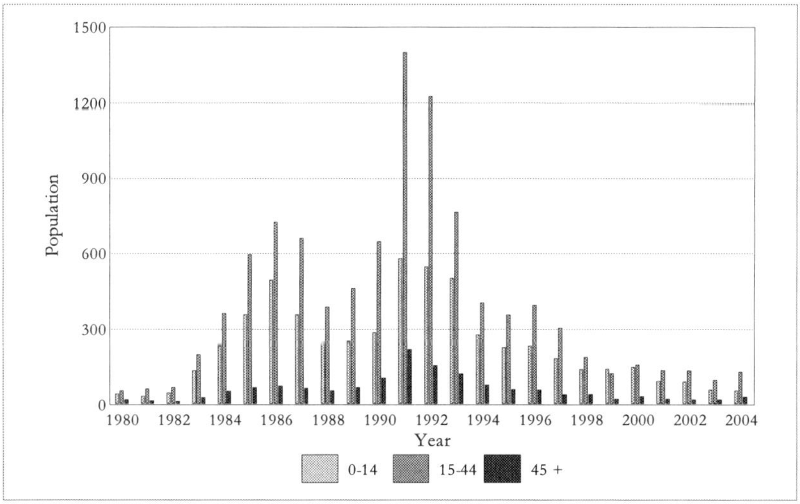

Figure 4.3 Age of Guatemalan Permanent Residents, 1980 to 2004

somehow been lost to bureaucratic record-keeping.[6] Therefore, we can estimate that 84 per cent of those who settled in Canada remain in the country.

Important characteristics of the population include age and gender distribution of the permanent resident population, as migration research consistently demonstrates a strong correlation between age and migration (Reyes 1997). Other important characteristics include immigration status, year of migration, and Canadian destination, which will be dealt with later in the chapter. Figure 4.2 charts the gender distribution while Figure 4.3 identifies the age distribution of the population upon entry to Canada.[7] Age and gender distributions are presented together in Table 4.1 and indicate that, overall, 48 per cent of permanent residents are female and 52 per cent are male. Even when we exclude the 0-14 age category, the proportion of females to males remains the same.

Table 4.1 Age and Gender Distribution, Guatemalan Permanent Residents, 1980 to 2004*

AGE	0-14	15-44	45+	TOTAL
MALE	2962	5440	631	9033
FEMALE	2826	4626	876	8328
TOTAL	**5788**	**10066**	**1507**	**17361**

*1999-2004: 0-14 category expands to include 0-17 and 15-44 category includes 18-44.

Figure 4.4 offers gender specific ratios to untangle the connections between the two dimensions. In the 0-14 year category, the proportion of boys is higher than girls particularly in the early years but evens out over time. In the 15-44 year category, at no point have more women arrived than men, though numbers are relatively close in some years. Clearly, more women occupy the 45+ category. A closer examination of the statistics reveals that among the 50-54 age category, the proportion of females (61 per cent) is higher than males (39 per cent) whereas the proportion of males to females in earlier adult age categories is 55 per cent to 45 per cent.

6 Immigration status of deported individuals is not available, therefore, I am not able to distinguish between voluntary and involuntary departure.

7 Age categories are divided into 0-14, 15-44, and 45+ for several reasons. First, we might assume that the majority of those in the 0-14 category are dependants of primary claimants, though Lovell's chapter, 'Q'anjob'al Canadian' (2000, 3-16) presents an example to counter this assumption. Second, the 15-44 range potentially captures even those young adults who travelled individually as well as those in their prime working years. Third, relatively few people over the age of 45 enter Canada as refugee claimants or permanent residents; therefore, this seemed an appropriate cut-off for a new age category.

The two adult categories are combined into a 15+ age category, which both statistically and visually confirms that males, in most years, are the slight majority of permanent resident entrants. This finding is inconsistent with broader world trends in the feminization of refugee movements (Martin 2001; Nolin and Goldring 2002). The UNHCR suggests that more than 75 per cent of displaced persons are women and their dependent children, while children alone make up approximately half of the world's displaced population (UNHCR 2001; UNHCR 2005, 5). Numbers are slightly lower in the Guatemalan case. For example, women and dependent children make up approximately 62 per cent of entrants and children account for 33 per cent of permanent resident entrants.

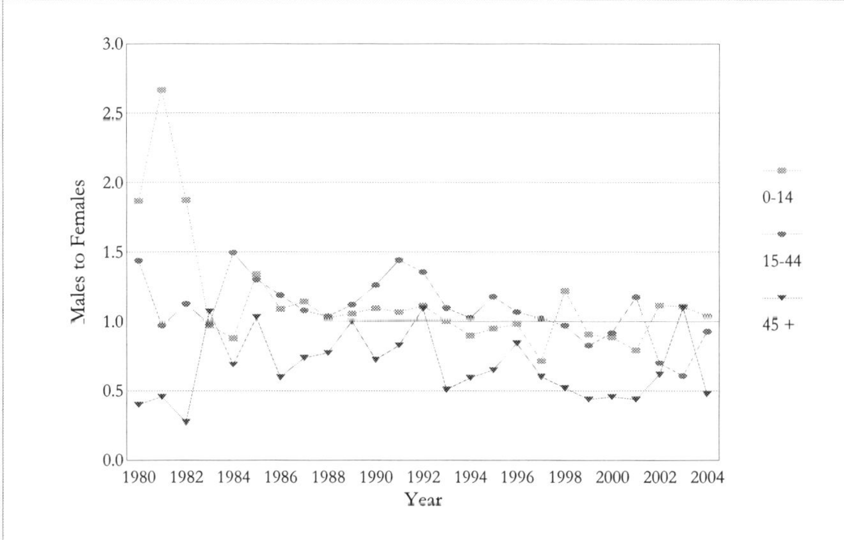

Figure 4.4 Age Specific Gender Ratios for Guatemalan Permanent Residents, 1980 to 2004

Guatemalans and Uneven Development in Immigration and Refugee Policy

In the 1980s, Guatemalan refugees and (im)migrants were entering Canada at a time of increased international migration and a world-wide explosion of refugee populations (Dirks 1995). Even though the Central American crisis generated more requests by Canadian solidarity and advocacy groups for generous programs than for any other refugee-producing situation during the 1980s, the Canadian government continued to keep acceptance numbers very low. Critical to this discussion are the conflicting agendas of the Ministers of External Affairs and Immigration, who normally operate in different spheres but by necessity were both drawn into action in the case of Guatemala. The Minister of External Affairs, with first-hand knowledge of the Guatemalan crisis and support of parliamentary sub-committee on external affairs, often argued for sympathetic programs to facilitate the entry of refugees to Canada. On the other hand, the Immigration Minister, responsible for the integrity of the refugee determination process, retained a defensive strategy and employed visa restrictions, emergency legislation, and deportations when deemed necessary. In the end, we see the 'uneven development' within immigration and refugee policy that guides policy direction.

Dirks (1995, 71-74) indicates that the Canadian government was less-than-enthusiastic about acting as host to Guatemalans seeking asylum and strategically imposed restrictions to their movement to Canada. The unfolding of Canadian pronouncements on refugee policy in light of the Guatemalan and Salvadoran crises push me to question Canada's humanitarian commitments to providing refuge to those in need. Looking at a contemporary example, we can ask why 7,000 Kosovar refugees were accepted and had their entry facilitated by the Canadian government (Sherrel and Hyndman 2004) while Guatemalan and Salvadoran refugees became 'illegal refugees' worthy of detention, deportation, and emergency legislation?

I argue that the changing geography of Guatemalan movement is intrinsically linked to: (1) Washington's policies of intervention as detailed by Cullather (1999), Doyle (2000), Menjívar and Rodríguez (2005), and Schlesinger, Nuccio, and Schirmer (1999), among others; and (2) American's subsequent denial of refugee status to those who fled the repressive forces in the region, as clarified by American Friends Service Committee (1988), Coutin (2000, 2004), Crittenden (1988), and geographers Mountz et al. (2002), among others, whose work focuses on the USA and Canadian Sanctuary Movements (Coutin 1993; Cunningham 1995, 2000; Leddy 1997, 2004) to be discussed later in this chapter.

In many ways, the story to follow is that of the implications of Washington's Central American wars for Guatemala and Canada. As Peter McFarlane (1989) and Jonathan Lemco (1986) ably document, the early 1980s was a period in which Canadian foreign policy was decidedly at odds with Canadian public opinion on Central America. Canadian officials were walking a fine line not only in terms of opposition to American intervention in the region, but also with regard to growing Canadian expressions of solidarity with the peoples of the region. Views diverged among Canadian officials themselves on the appropriate route forward.

Lemco (1986) clearly identifies the early trends associated with Central American refugee movement and changes in Canadian immigration policy. I want to update Lemco's statements and identify the geographical, and thus political and social, population dynamics in response to Canada's 'get tough' policy changes in the mid- to late-1980s that were, themselves, responses to Washington's 'get tough' policy directed at Central American refugees. The Canadian government's reaction was intended to deter potential refugee claimants from seeking entry into Canada (Lemco 1991, 160). Though it attracted criticism from many groups, there appeared to be widespread public concern regarding the social costs of accepting ever more developing world refugees. At critical moments in Canada's history, it seems, immigrants and refugees have borne the brunt of tougher immigration policy in order to appease the public's fear of 'bogus' claims, rapid increase in 'non-white' immigrant populations, and possibilities for the abuse of Canada's generosity.[8]

Before the initial period of Guatemalan refugee arrivals in Canada – the mid-1980s – Canadian policy-makers had paid scant attention to the Central American region. Writing in 1976, Ogelsby (1976, 100) confirms that ties between Canada and Central America were not close over the years. Lemco (1986, 120) indicates that it was only from the mid-1960s, under the leadership of former Prime Minister Pierre Trudeau, that Canada focused any serious attention to points south of Mexico. Canadian Catholic missionaries established contact in the 1950s, but it was 1962 before diplomatic ties with the five Central American republics and Panama were formally established (Ogelsby 1976, 100). Immigration to Canada from the whole of Latin America was minimal, which meant there were few personal ties and limited public knowledge of the region, its peoples, and its politics. In January 1979, three new designated classes of refugees were created including 'Latin American Political Prisoners and Oppressed Persons.' As late as 1982, however, Guatemala was still not included on the list of applicable countries, which included Argentina, Chile, and Uruguay (Kelley and Trebilcock 1998, 406).

Under the leadership of then External Affairs Minister Mark MacGuigan in the early 1980s, the Canadian government rarely voiced public political opinions in the region. MacGuigan led not only a 'quiet acquiescence' to American policy but, echoing American President Reagan's stand, attempted to repair relations with Guatemalan President General Efraín Ríos Montt (McFarlane 1989, 185). MacGuigan was eventually trounced out of his position and replaced by External Affairs Minister Alan MacEachen following resounding opposition to his 'pro-American' approach by academics, representatives of churches, unions, and all political parties in front of a special all-party external affairs sub-committee on Canada's relations with Central America (McFarlane 1989, 186). Under MacEachen, Canada's Central American policy shifted away from support of American policy to back-room opposition and sought influence through numerous aid projects undertaken by the Canadian International Development Agency (CIDA). For example, between 1982 and 1987, Canada gave more than $155 million to bilateral, multilateral, and NGO bodies (Lemco 1991, 6).

In the early- to mid-1980s, Canadian Immigration officials were clearly ill prepared when the first refugee claimants arrived at their foreign embassies and consulates. In 1981-2, Canada set aside only 1,000 places for all Latin Americans and projected estimates for 1985 only doubled to 2,000. After then Immigration Minister Lloyd Axworthy twice traveled to El Salvador in 1983 (January and June), 2,000 spaces were allocated for Central and South Americans that year. MacEachen also met with Canadian church representatives to prepare for his tour of Central America in October 1983 and received 1000 letters a week from more than 200 Central American solidarity groups (Lemco 1991). Through MacEachen, Canada

8 For an examination of the historical dimensions to Canadian immigration and refugee policy, see Kelley and Trebilcock (1998).

moved toward a clear break with Washington's policies of intervention. But dependence on American intelligence information and fear of American retaliation for bold pronouncements limited the scope of Canada's programs and activities (Lemco 1986).

After placing Guatemala on the B-1 list of non-deportable countries in 1981, Axworthy began to facilitate the entry of selected cases through the Mexico City embassy. McFarlane (1989, 201) notes that officials traveled from the Mexico City embassy into Guatemala every two or three weeks to interview prospective refugees and 'special immigration cases' and were willing to travel at a moment's notice to interview claimants in emergency situations.

But it was in 1984 that, for the first time, both External Affairs *and* the Immigration Department were seen by the Canadian public to deal with Guatemala and Guatemalan refugee issues simultaneously. The implications for Canada of the Guatemalan crisis became recognized and acknowledged through policy changes and grassroots responses and actions. Increasing numbers of asylum requests and support for refugee claimants from church, trade union, and solidarity groups, jettisoned the ability of Canadian officials to present the situation as an 'over there' concern and necessitated the acknowledgement of an immediate, urgent domestic dimension.

The limited measures suggested by Axworthy in 1983, though, were later compromised when, in 1984, the subsequent Immigration Minister, John Roberts, announced a visa requirement for Guatemalans in order to 'better regulate' refugee movement out of the country into Canada. So, where once refugees could board a plane and come directly to Canada, the visa restriction cut off this route and led refugees to pursue the much more difficult and potentially dangerous overland route through Mexico and the United States to Canadian embassies, consulates, and border posts.

Movement to the United States, though, was fraught with difficulty, with threat of deportation a constant concern (Hagan 1994); therefore, church, labour, and student organizations pressed for the Canadian government to accept Guatemalan and Salvadoran refugee claimants who could not find sanctuary elsewhere (Lemco 1991, 152). Through their efforts, among others, steps were slowly taken to come to grips with the situation. In 1984, Guatemalan refugees in Canada were included in the 'political prisoners and operational minorities class' and, therefore, special measures came into effect to reunite families and to allow those already in Canada to remain.

But eligibility for one of the spots in the refugee system at the time was made possible only if: (1) one had family members already in Canada; (2) one had a well-founded fear of persecution if sent back; and (3) if one was unsuited for rural resettlement in Central America due to above average educational attainment or career background (Lemco 1991, 152). *Campesinos*, the majority of Guatemala's population and the majority of the refugees, were routinely excluded as 'not fit for resettlement in Canada.' Therefore, the various programs such as the Designated Class, then, had some merit, but did not assist a great number of Guatemalans and, as North and CAPA (1990, 158) suggest, certainly did not reach the majority of Guatemalans in need.

Following the introduction of the Immigration Reform and Control Act (IRCA) in the United States, the crackdown on 'illegal' refugees in late 1986 and 1987, Guatemalans and Salvadoran refugee claimants looked north for asylum. Again, sympathetic to their dire circumstances, the Department of External Affairs recommended that the Canadian Government be generous in providing sanctuary to those claimants and to extend oral hearings to all of them. Unfortunately, this gesture of goodwill was short-lived and Canadian public perceptions went through a sea change within months from one of compassion to strong concern over the 'tide' of 'illegal refugees' who were 'flooding' the border. Government action followed and emergency policy measures were introduced.

Both *allusions* to policy change and the policy change itself triggered immediate population dynamics that altered the controlled geography of refugee movement to an 'out of control,' underground, panicked rush to and across the border. Solidarity organizations and refugee advocates facilitated their arrivals as best they could, but under Bills C-55 (*Refugee Reform Act*) and C-84 (*Refugee Deterrents and Detention Bill*) both the refugees and their advocates were dealt a harsh blow. Quickly, the 'tide' receded, the 'illegals' gave up their asylum claims, and Canadians were told that democracy had returned to Guatemala.

Susanne Jonas (1996a, 128) indicates that even against incredible odds, the stream of Guatemalan asylum seekers to the United States continued in the 1990s, such that from 1992 to 1994, the numbers of Guatemalan asylum applications were 'by far the highest for any country in the world.'[9] For the years 1980 through 2002, a total of 186,264 asylum applications from Guatemala to the United States were filed (Migration Policy Institute 2005).

But, as Evans and Kohrt (2004, 20) and McBride (1999) argue, 'bias permeates the US asylum system. Persons from Mexico, Central America, and the Caribbean are at particular risk of having genuine persecution cases denied as a result of this bias.' Consequently, few Guatemalan and Salvadoran applications have been successful. McBride (1999, 296) notes that from 1984 to 1990, only 1.8 per cent of 9,500 Guatemalan claims were successful and that rate remained constant across 43,915 Guatemalan additional requests submitted in 1992. Apart from the extremely low rate of acceptance of Mexican asylum cases, the Guatemalan acceptance rate is among the lowest of any country in the world. Jonas (1996a, 128) notes that the rate plunged in 1992 when only 63 of 44,000 [or 0.14 per cent] of Guatemalan asylum applications were granted.

Undeterred, Guatemalans continued the move northward in such great numbers that Deputy Attorney General Jamie Gorelick stated on 13 April 1995 that 'in 1994

9 Data compiled by the UNHCR (Population Data Unit) and made available by the Migration Policy Institute (MPI) indicate that indeed Guatemalan asylum claims, as a percentage of all asylum claims, for the years 1992 (42%), 1993 (24%), 1994 (24%), and 1995 (15%) were particularly high. Salvadoran claims comprised 51% and 59% of all asylum claims in 1995 and 1996, respectively.

the largest land-based mass immigration that we experienced was from Guatemala.' In mid-1994, Guatemalans constituted 30 per cent of all asylum cases pending in the United States (Jonas 1996a, 128). These official claims declined in the late 1990s and early 2000s – as undocumented migration levels increased – to 1,131 and 1,193 in 2001 and 2002, respectively (Migration Policy Institute 2005).

Seeing Through the Numbers

There are a number of ways to examine the available data in order to articulate the geographical implications of these policy decisions. First, I will examine CIC data to illustrate the official and contested spaces of refuge which include the solidarity spaces of both the Overground and Underground Railroads. Next, I examine the immigrant class and occupational categories of permanent residents in order to connect the ruptures of departure and spaces of loss in Guatemala with the spaces of refuge in Canada. Finally, I chart the timing and geography of deportation from Canada to identify changes over time.

Official and Contested Spaces of Refuge

To begin, let us examine the official spaces of refuge identified in a series of Tables created with data from Canadian embassies and consulates regarding applications for landing from abroad. Table 4.2 identifies the location of applications (cases and individuals) for landings by city of application for the years 1980 to 1999.[10] The 1,563 case (3,687 individuals) applications are sorted in descending order starting with the Mexico City embassy (671 cases, 1,642 individuals) which received 43 per cent of all applications, followed by the Canadian consulates in Dallas, Los Angeles, and Atlanta. Apart from a handful of cases made from consulates in Bogotá, Athens, Buenos Aires, Kingston, and Port au Prince, the majority of applications were/are made at embassies or consulates in American cities. Table 4.3 identifies that 53 per cent of all cases were made within the United States and that the average case consists of 2.4 individuals. Without an opportunity to regularize their legal status in Mexico or the United States and fearing deportation, many Guatemalans turned to Canada as an alternative.

So that the geographical implication of the IRCA policy decision is made clear, the applications for landing from abroad are differentiated by year of application in Table 4.4. Four key time categories include 1982 (before IRCA), 1987, 1992, and 1997 (immediately after IRCA and five and ten year intervals afterward). In 1982, one of the early years of refugee movement, Guatemalans made applications for landing only at the Mexico City embassy and the Dallas, Texas consulate. But, the fear of deportation from the United States led many Guatemalans (and other Central Americans) to seek refuge elsewhere in 1987.

10 Data not available from CIC beyond 1999.

Table 4.2 Guatemalan Applications for Landing Made from Abroad, by City of Application, 1980 to 1999

LOCATION OF LANDING APPLICATION	TOTAL CASES	TOTAL INDIVIDUALS
MEXICO CITY	671	1642
DALLAS	327	659
LOS ANGELES	189	533
ATLANTA	128	261
GUATEMALA	48	98
NEW YORK	40	91
SAN FRANCISCO	39	115
WASHINGTON	35	103
BOSTON	19	27
CHICAGO	18	50
SAN JOSE	16	29
DETROIT	9	18
BUFFALO	7	23
SEATTLE	6	10
MINNEAPOLIS	5	11
BOGOTÁ, COLOMBIA	2	7
ATHENS	1	3
BUENOS AIRES	1	1
KINGSTON, JAMAICA	1	1
PORT AU PRINCE	1	5
TOTAL	**1563**	**3687**

Table 4.3 Total and Percentage of Guatemalan Applications for Landing, USA vs. Elsewhere, 1980 to 1999

LOCATION OF LANDING APPLICATION	TOTAL CASES*	TOTAL INDIVIDUALS
USA	822 (53%)	1901 (52%)
OUTSIDE USA	741 (47%)	1786 (48%)
TOTAL	**1563 (100%)**	**3687 (100%)**

*Each Case = 2.4 Individuals.

A dispersed geography of claims is evident immediately after the IRCA implementation. No longer is Mexico City the primary source of claims, but Los Angeles and Dallas become key locations. Mexico is still prominent, as it is throughout the years, but Atlanta, New York, and San Francisco consulates become important sites due to the panic mentality that sent Central Americans to their closest consulate or through the Sanctuary Movement whose participants worked closely with the Atlanta and Dallas consulates (Crittenden 1988). After the immediate crisis periods of 1986 and 1987, the spatialization of applications recedes to a handful of locations in 1992 (with the primary source again the Mexico City embassy), and even further in 1997 to include only Mexico City and Guatemala City.

As mentioned in Chapter 3, in response to policy change, the orderly geography of requests for landing from abroad dissolved into the random, panicked, 'out of control' geography of a border rush to claim asylum directly. Unfortunately, it is not possible to chart the geography of refugee movement to the Canadian border in conjunction with the information above at this critical time, since the *location* of asylum request was not systematically recorded until 1990. But, we can examine the port of entry (POE) geography of refugee claims starting with 1990 data in Table 4.5 and POE geography of permanent residents with data beginning in 1985 in Table 4.6. The two Tables identify POE by province moving from east to west to north across the country.

In Table 4.5 we can note that between 1990 and 1999, 3,689 refugee claims were made at Canadian POEs and Inland Offices; Quebec (47.3 per cent), Ontario (35.3 per cent), and British Columbia (14.2 per cent) received the majority, while only minimal numbers arrived at POEs in Alberta, Manitoba, Nova Scotia, Saskatchewan, and Yukon. When refugee claims are examined by year, in Table 4.7, it is clear that the possibilities for making a refugee claim at a POE or Inland Office is much greater in Ontario and Quebec since there are so many entry points and inland offices. In the early 1990s, the majority of refugee claims are made in Ontario while Quebec takes top ranking between 1993 and 1997, at which point weight shifts back to Ontario POEs and Inland Offices.

Table 4.4 Guatemalan Applications (Individuals) for Landing Made from Abroad, by City of Application, (Before IRCA, Immediately After, 5 Years Later, 10 Years Later)

LOCATION	1982	LOCATION	1987	LOCATION	1992	LOCATION	1997
MEXICO CITY	101	LOS ANGELES	272	MEXICO CITY	91	MEXICO CITY	22
DALLAS	17	DALLAS	155	GUATEMALA	10	GUATEMALA	7
		MEXICO CITY	76	SAN JOSE, CR	9		
		ATLANTA	61	BOSTON	2		
		NEW YORK	45	BUFFALO	1		
		SAN FRANCISCO	33				
		BOSTON	9				
		CHICAGO	9				
		BOGOTA, COLOMBIA	7				
		MINNEAPOLIS	6				
		SEATTLE	6				
		DETROIT	4				
TOTAL	**118**	**TOTAL**	**683**	**TOTAL**	**113**	**TOTAL**	**29**

Table 4.5 Guatemalan Refugee Claims, Port of Entry, by Province, 1990 to 1999*

PROVINCE	TOTAL	% OF TOTAL
NOVA SCOTIA	5	0.10
NEW BRUNSWICK	28	0.80
QUEBEC	1613	43.70
ONTARIO	1301	35.30
MANITOBA	84	2.30
SASKATCHEWAN	2	0.05
ALBERTA	128	3.50
BRITISH COLUMBIA	525	14.20
YUKON	2	0.05
TOTAL	**3689**	**100**

* January to March.

Table 4.6 Guatemalan Permanent Residents, Port of Entry, by Province, 1985 to 2004

PROVINCE	TOTAL	% OF TOTAL
NEWFOUNDLAND	1	0.0
NOVA SCOTIA	19	0.1
NEW BRUNSWICK	42	0.3
PRINCE EDWARD ISLAND	2	0.0
QUEBEC	5017	31.3
ONTARIO	8466	52.8
MANITOBA	254	1.6
SASKATCHEWAN	14	0.1
ALBERTA	765	4.8
BRITISH COLUMBIA	1452	9.0
YUKON	1	0.0
NORTHWEST TERRITORIES	2	0.0
TOTAL	**16035**	**100**

The pattern for POE and Inland Office entry for permanent residents between 1985 and 2004 is roughly the same as for refugee claimants, though Ontario (52.8 per cent) is the primary receiving province with Quebec (31.3 per cent) close behind (Table 4.6). Border points and Inland Offices in British Columbia (BC) (9.0 per cent), Alberta (4.8 per cent), and Manitoba (1.6 per cent) receive significant numbers of Guatemalan permanent residents, while all other provinces and territories register between zero and 42 Guatemalan arrivals each. Examined over time, in Table 4.8, Ontario received the most permanent residents in all years except for 1991 when Quebec POEs were top of the list. A finer scale geography of refugee claims and permanent residents' entries is evident when data in Tables 4.9 and 4.10 are examined closely. Please see Appendix Two (Seeing More Numbers) for these two Tables that catalogue most of the POEs and Inland Offices where Guatemalan refugee claims and permanent residents arrived in Canada. First, Ontario, Quebec, and BC are key destinations for refugee claimants, with certain points within those provinces receiving the vast majority of claimants. For example, in Quebec, the Blackpool/Lacolle border crossing with New York, south of Montréal, received almost 70 per cent of all refugee claims made in Quebec. Sixty-three per cent of all claims in Ontario were made in the Fort Erie/Niagara Falls/St. Catharines/Hamilton region and a full 84 per cent of claims in BC were made at the Douglas POE and the Vancouver Administration office.

Only 0.7 per cent claims in Quebec were made at Dorval and Mirabel airports and a mere two per cent were made at the Toronto International Airport. It makes sense that few requests for asylum are registered at major airports due to the enforced visa requirement. The locations of refugee claims are more spatially distributed in Ontario, with 16 per cent of claims being made in the Windsor-London region, 15 per cent in the Toronto GTA, and approximately 10 more locations account for the rest.

An inverse geographical pattern is evident in POE data on permanent residents in Table 4.10. For permanent residents who, unlike refugee claimants, arrive in Canada with some sort of 'status,' airports are key POEs. For example, 25 per cent used Dorval and Mirabel airports to enter Quebec, 64 per cent arrived in Ontario at Pearson International Airport, and 44 per cent entered British Columbia at Vancouver's International Airport. Others arrived at Canadian POEs in a similar fashion to refugee claimants, but were granted permanent resident status through certain designated classes. The geography is varied in these cases but refugee boards and backlog offices granted permanent residence to significant numbers of people. For example, 33 per cent of Quebec permanent residents were granted status by the Montréal Refugee Board and 10 per cent from various Ontario refugee boards and backlogs.

The growing number of Guatemalans making refugee claims from the United States and at the border due to increased deportation activity is an under-acknowledged stimulus for the visa requirement. Table 4.11 documents the encouraging acceptance rates for Guatemalan and Salvadoran refugee claims until the mid-1990s after which acceptance rates fluctuate between 16 and 49 per cent for Guatemalans and 13 and 37 per cent for Salvadorans. Even with the yearly variations, these figures contrast with the extremely low acceptance rates in the USA, as discussed previously.

Table 4.7 Guatemalan Refugee Claims, Port of Entry and Inland Offices, by Province (with Number of Ports of Entry and Inland Offices) and Year, 1990 to 1999*

PROVINCE	ENTRY PORTS	1990	1991	1992	1993	1994	1995	1996	1997	1998	1999	TOTAL
NOVA SCOTIA	3	2	-	1	1	-	-	-	1	-	-	5
NEW BRUNSWICK	3	6	4	9	2	3	-	2	2	-	-	28
QUEBEC	15	108	197	233	217	224	256	162	148	62	6	1613
ONTARIO	41	142	214	256	169	135	137	84	80	65	19	1301
MANITOBA	2	1	9	6	5	12	12	11	14	13	1	84
SASKATCHEWAN	1	-	-	-	-	1	-	1	-	-	-	2
ALBERTA	6	16	18	59	10	6	4	8	2	3	2	128
BRITISH COLUMBIA	11	49	62	103	79	62	38	53	53	17	9	525
YUKON	1	-	1	-	-	1	-	-	-	-	-	2
TOTAL	**83**	**324**	**505**	**667**	**484**	**444**	**447**	**321**	**300**	**160**	**37**	**3689**

Table 4.8 Guatemalan Permanent Residents, Port of Entry, by Province (with Number of Entry Ports) and Year, 1985 to 2004

PROVINCE	ENTRY PORTS	1985-1989	1990-1994	1995-1999	2000-2004	TOTAL
NEWFOUNDLAND	1	-	-	1	-	1
NOVA SCOTIA	3	-	10	-	9	19
NEW BRUNSWICK	5	4	30	6	2	42
PRINCE EDWARD ISLAND	1	-	2	-	-	2
QUEBEC	20	1325	2550	732	410	5017
ONTARIO	52	2764	3827	1308	567	8466
MANITOBA	4	106	97	35	16	254
SASKATCHEWAN	3	5	6	2	1	14
ALBERTA	10	235	323	158	49	765
BRITISH COLUMBIA	16	463	482	316	186	1452
YUKON	1	-	1	-	-	1
NORTHWEST TERRITORIES	1	-	2	-	-	2
TOTAL	**117**	**4907**	**7330**	**2558**	**1240**	**16035**

In response to the implementation of the IRCA, two patterns of movement are evident. First, as noted above, we see the multiplication of the controlled geography of embassy and consulate requests over time. Where once the requests for landing came only from the Mexico City embassy and the Dallas consulate, by 1987, Guatemalans are making requests for landing in Canada at consulates throughout the United States. Second, all of the Tables above suggest that refugees redefined the spaces of refuge from 'asylum control' in the Canadian embassies and consulates to 'asylum demand' at the country's border. Once the officially recognized routes such as the Overground Railroad (United Church of Canada 2004, 18) that collaborated with the Atlanta and Dallas consulates could no longer fulfil the needs of an increasingly desperate population, the clandestine Underground Railroad emerged to whisk all Guatemalans and Salvadorans to the Canadian border as never seen before (Cunningham 1995). Hundreds also arrived on their own, with no assistance from solidarity groups, in a panic move wherein zones of exclusion at the border were redefined into the 'known, the made, the constructed' (N. Smith 1993, 90). These limited and limiting responses illuminate a lack of connection with the escalating problems in the Central American region or, at the very least, as North and CAPA (1990) suggest, a lack of innovative action.

Table 4.11 Guatemalan and Salvadoran Refugee Claims, Acceptance Rate, 1989 to 2004

YEAR	GUATEMALANS	SALVADORANS
1989	89%	83%
1990	76%	78%
1991	72%	76%
1992	64%	32%
1993	56%	23%
1994	NO DATA	NO DATA
1995	57%	37%
1996	49%	22%
1997	23%	13%
1998	20%	14%
1999	20%	18%
2000	17%	16%
2001	22%	16%
2002	16%	27%
2003	32%	32%
2004	24%	21%

Source: IRB, Immigration and Refugee Board (1999; 2005a).

Requests for asylum at Canada's POEs were a hitherto extremely limited phenomenon; therefore, 'new spaces of interaction' (N. Smith 1993, 90), we might say, were created in which Guatemalans and Salvadorans transgressed the official boundaries of acceptable behaviour and established new ones. Maritime arrivals were previously experienced in Canada, but this crisis stands as the first time in which the Canada-USA border became a contested zone of refuge. By acting swiftly and moving to the borders, refugees dissolved the spatial boundaries that confined asylum procedures to embassies and consulates and inscribed their presence at the border where they could not be turned away. In order for refugees to take Canada up on the offer of 'sanctuary' and 'asylum,' therefore, established procedures needed to be forsaken for heretofore-unknown strategies.

Then Prime Minister Brian Mulroney and Immigration Minister Benoit Bouchard had to be seen to rein in this 'out of control' frontier mentality and wild geography through the implementation of new border regulations. Through the *Refugee Reform Act* and the *Refugee Deterrents and Detention Bill*, the government shed the values that Canadians hold close in times of tranquillity to dam the flow through emergency legislation and the criminalization of assistance. While the Canadian government was able to maintain asylum requests to controlled embassy and consulate spaces, Guatemalan refugees were identified as 'political refugees,' 'true refugees,' and so forth. Once these same people were compelled to challenge the embassy spaces and confront authorities at the border, thereby expanding the scale of asylum requests and taking the government at its word, the bounds of identity shift and refugees were labelled as 'would-be refugees,' 'illegal aliens,' 'bogus,' and so forth. As Neil Smith (1993, 101) argues, 'it is geographical scale that defines the boundaries and bounds the identities around which control is exerted and contested.' Once the government reconfigured their identities from legal to illegal, true to false, genuine to bogus, policy was changed to deal with their transgressions.

Ruptures of Departure and Categories of Arrival

Immigrant class and occupational categories of permanent residents are examined in order to connect the ruptures of departure and spaces of loss in Guatemala with the spaces of refuge in Canada. The first rupture of refugee transnationalism emerged as the spaces of terror began to incorporate spaces of loss through death, disappearance, and departure of leaders, teachers, indigenous peoples, and activists. The loss of leaders, intellectuals, and educated people through assassinations and disappearances was compounded by the departure of survivors and those likely to be targeted due to their activities to countries such as Mexico, Canada, and the USA.

The findings in Table 4.12 represent the occupational categories of Guatemalan permanent residents in Canada upon arrival in the 1980s, 1990s, and the 2000-2004 years. The results indicate the necessary departure of people from a wide range of occupational categories that represent a significant drain from progressive Guatemalan sectors and future generations. For example, high frequency categories include New Workers, Students, Dependent Children, Home Workers, and Occupations Unique to Primary Industry. A full 26 per cent of the permanent residents are categorized as New Workers and 25 per cent are Students (which is a separate category from Under Aged Dependants or secondary school students). Dependent children make up 16 per cent of all permanent residents and seven per cent are Homeworkers. Also noteworthy are the many people in the health occupations (doctors, nurses, health promoters, and so forth) and those in the category 'Social Sciences, Education, Government Services, and Religion,' which includes university professors, college instructors, and government workers.

University and college students comprise 25 per cent of all permanent residents since 1980 and unknown numbers of refugee claimants. When we examine the documentation of 433 deaths and disappearances of university students and faculty members, as noted in Table 4.1, in conjunction with the 4,267 students accepted into Canada and listed in Table 4.12, a clearer picture emerges of state-directed violence against progressive Guatemalan intellectuals and how Canada acted as a kind of safety valve.

Exile outside Guatemala for survivors and family members of victims tied to union activity often began in Mexico City before leading people to Canada. It is clear from my interviews with women and men in THOMASBURG – many of whom were student activists in Guatemala – that Mexico City was the first stop for the majority of USAC student activists who fled Guatemala before acceptance as permanent residents by foreign embassies. Once Mexico City became untenable as a long-term solution, Guatemalans presented their cases to the UNHCR office to be granted Convention Refugee status. With this designation in hand, the Canadian Embassy then facilitated transfer of individuals and families to Canada as Permanent Residents rather than as 'refugees.' This labelling explains the high number of people listed in the various 'Immigrant' categories rather than in the 'Convention Refugee' category in the CIC records. In reality, the majority of 'Immigrants' are in fact *bona fide* refugees, but through the UN and special programs at the Mexico City embassy and consulates in the USA, people were given permanent status rather than adding them to the lengthy refugee determination process. Others made direct petitions to the Canadian Embassy in Mexico City and Guatemala City for asylum.

Immigrants arrive through various 'immigrant classes' and we can note that the most significant immigrant classes, in descending order, are Convention Refugee (4,624 or 27 per cent), Designated Classes (4,569 or 26 per cent), Family Class (4,357 or 25 per cent), and Other Independent and Skilled Workers (2,257 or 13 per cent). All other immigrant classes account for only nine per cent of the permanent residents. Appendix Two contains full details on the raw numbers and percentage scores of each immigrant class (Table 4.13).

Of course, the significance of each category changes over time. For example, 70 per cent of individuals in 1980 arrived as Family Class immigrants, while only 1.7 per cent arrived as Convention Refugees. By 1983 and 1984, though, the proportion of Convention Refugees increased to 46.6 per cent and 68.7 per cent respectively, and continued to fluctuate between approximately 17 per cent and 46 per cent in the following years. Designated Classes were introduced in 1984 to facilitate the entry

Table 4.12 Occupations, Guatemalan Permanent Residents, 1980 to 2004

OCCUPATIONAL CATEGORY	1980s	1990s	2000-2004	TOTAL
NEW WORKER	687	3416	367	4470
STUDENT	1495	2403	369	4267
DEPENDENT CHILD	1215	1510	n/a	2725
HOMEWORKER	589	557	117	1263
OCCUPATIONS UNIQUE TO PRIMARY INDUSTRY	695	361	18	1074
OCCUPATIONS UNIQUE TO PROCESSING, MANUFACTURING & UTILITIES	400	430	10	840
SOCIAL SCIENCES, EDUCATION, GOV'T SERVICES & RELIGION	334	291	30	655
SALES & SERVICE OCCUPATIONS	310	168	40	518
NATURAL & APPLIED SCIENCES	166	193	20	379
ART, CULTURE, RECREATION & SPORT	109	86	3	198
HEALTH OCCUPATIONS	112	76	8	196
RETIRED	59	96	17	172
BUSINESS, FINANCE & ADMINISTRATIVE OCCUPATIONS	43	74	39	156
TRADES, TRANSPORT & EQUIPMENT OPERATORS	47	58	17	122
MANAGEMENT	6	64	16	86
OTHERS	16	19	169	204
TOTAL	**6283**	**98**	**1240**	**17151**

of persecuted and displaced peoples who might not necessary qualify as Convention Refugees. This category gained real significance in the early 1990s when it accounted for 52.1 per cent and 57.5 per cent of all cases in 1991 and 1992. The Family Class again becomes a key category in the late 1990s as more Guatemalans who arrived earlier are able to personally sponsor relatives; rates fluctuate between 28.5 per cent in 1996 and 47.1 per cent of total arrivals in 1994.[11]

Deportations and Departures from Canada

Another set of CIC data includes statistics on deportation orders, confirmed departures, and final destinations of confirmed departures for the years 1980 to 1998.[12] The 252 deportation orders and 837 confirmed departures reached significant numbers during the 1990s. Though 837 is a relatively low figure for a 20-year period, I argue that it is the *geography* of the final destination that is the critical dimension to Canada's involvement with Guatemalans and which receives little attention due to the difficulty in obtaining the information.

In 1981, then Immigration Minister Lloyd Axworthy added Guatemala and El Salvador to the B-1 list of non-deportable countries. Consequently, no deportation orders or confirmed departures are noted in 1981. Along with the 1984 introduction of the visa requirement, North and CAPA (1990, 159) note the establishment of a moratorium on deportations to Guatemala and El Salvador. In the intervening years, the IRB registered 16 deportation orders and 70 confirmed departures. Again, no deportation orders or confirmed departures are noted for 1984 and numbers remain small until the 1990s.

The final destinations of confirmed departures from Canada are of grave concern. Table 4.15 lists the 13 countries to which Guatemalans have been deported between 1980 and 1998 with the USA and Guatemala by far the most common destinations. A startling picture emerges when we examine both total departures and per cent returned to the USA and Guatemala.

During the early 1980s, when political violence peaked, Canada deported failed claimants or others deemed undesirable directly to Guatemala. For example, in

11 Between 1980 and 2004, 6,937 Guatemalans gained entry with Minister's Permits that are usually issued to those with a compelling need to come to or remain in Canada for a limited amount of time and who might not qualify as Convention Refugees. Those with Minister's Permits are entitled to work while waiting for permanent residency in Canada. Appendix Two: Seeing More Numbers contains Table 4.14 that lists the number of Minister's Permits issued to Guatemalans between 1980 and 2004. Numbers rose significantly between 1987 and 1989 when many Guatemalans arrived at Canada's POEs and Inland Offices. Until 1995, the return to Guatemala of those with Minister's Permits was not recorded and, therefore, it is not possible to identify how many voluntarily returned and how many applied through other channels to remain in Canada.

12 The IRB regularly publishes figures on removal orders even though until recently the CIC Enforcement Division, not the IRB, actually enforced the orders (Kelley and Trebilcock 1998, 435). Since its creation in December 2003, the Canada Border Services Agency (CBSA) is now responsible for removals.

1982, 1985, and 1987, 100 per cent of departures ended in Guatemala. In 1983 and 1986, 78 per cent and 82 per cent respectively were sent to Guatemala. The decade ended with the final destination of departures divided equally between Guatemala and the USA. Those who landed in the USA were subject to deportation directly back to Guatemala, but Canadian tracking figures are not available to confirm the fate of these souls. See Appendix Three for the testimony of a deported Guatemalan man for whom deportation to Guatemala meant a return directly into the hands of the military.

Table 4.15 Final Destination of Confirmed Departures, 1980 to 1998

DEPARTURE DESTINATIONS	TOTAL
USA	429
GUATEMALA	361
MEXICO	25
EL SALVADOR	5
NICARAGUA	5
PERU	4
COSTA RICA	3
UNKNOWN	3
ARGENTINA, BELIZE, GUADELOUE, EUROPE, JAMAICA (1 PER)	5
TOTAL	**840**

Contrary to humanitarian traditions, the Canadian government removed the special program that sheltered Guatemalans and Salvadorans from deportation in response to increased numbers of Central Americans coming to Canada from within the USA. Interestingly, though, this policy shift did not lead to widespread deportations as experienced in the USA. Three confirmed departures are documented in 1987, none in 1988, and four in 1989. Though rare, many in the Canadian public were not prepared to support the deportation of a single Central American to situations of risk. For example, Bryden (1987) notes the outcry from solidarity groups over the deportation to the USA of a Guatemalan threatened by death squads. Through the early- to mid-1990s, the USA became the favoured site of deportation/departure, while 20 to 40 per cent were sent back to Guatemala. By 1996, however, numbers almost are equally split between the two countries.

After the immediate furore over Bills C-55 and C-84, limited follow-up research charts the long-term impact of policy changes into the 1990s. Documentation on deportations allows a window onto government action. While Bill C-84 enabled the detention of refugees who arrived without proper documentation until their identities could be established (North and CAPA 1990, 160), Bill C-55 enabled the removal of any Central American refugee who arrived via a 'safe third country' (meaning from the USA) back to that safe country.[13] A high percentage of removals to the USA is noted after the implementation of the measure.

Guatemalan and Canadian Living Geographies

For those who managed to gain refugee status, permanent residence, and citizenship it is important to chart out the living geographies that situate their place making and settlement in Canada. Their places of residence are charted by province – organized east to west to north – for the census years of 1986, 1991, 1996, and 2001 in Table 4.16, with Ontario (5,820 or 43 per cent) and Quebec (4,460 or 33 per cent) receiving the majority of permanent residents.

Clearly, though, Guatemalans are inhabiting new spaces in most provinces of the country, though in fewer numbers and under more physically isolated circumstances in provinces such as Manitoba (245 or 1.8 per cent), Saskatchewan (90 or 0.7 per cent), New Brunswick (35 or 0.3 per cent), Nova Scotia (30 or 0.2 per cent), and most intensely in the Northwest Territories (ten or 0.1 per cent). The provinces of British Columbia (1,725 or thirteen per cent) and Alberta (1,235 or nine per cent) and are the middle-range destinations for Guatemalans in Canada. These figures are consistent with other refugee and immigrant populations in Canada. Interestingly, the prairie provinces of Alberta and Manitoba have a fair number of Guatemalans, a presence I attribute to heavy lobbying of local church and solidarity groups for group sponsorship. Obviously, we do not know the extent of those without documentation or who overstayed their visas and chose to go underground.

A finer scale to the geographical spaces of refuge is available in Figure 4.5A, Figure 4.5B and Table 4.17 when the cities of settlement are charted for those same years. Table 4.17 indicates that, according to the last census, the highest number of Guatemalans live in Montréal (4,015), quickly followed by Toronto (3,525), Vancouver (1,360), and Ottawa-Hull (685). Contrary to Lemco's (1986, 134) statement that 'most Central American refugees are settled in rural Canada,' urban settlement currently predominates according to more recent data on Guatemalans: compare, for instance, the limited Guatemalan Canadian living geographies (13,680 Guatemalans) mapped in Figure 4.5A and Figure 4.5B with the more speculative American Guatemalan geographies (1.5 million documented and undocumented Guatemalans) graphically represented in Figure 4.6 (Rodríguez 2000).

13 Fifteen years later, in late 2004, the Canadian and American governments signed the Safe Third Country Agreement which requires refugees to make their claims in the first 'safe' country through which they pass. Therefore, refugee advocates such as the Canadian Council for Refugees (CCR 2004) argue that most Latin American refugees are effectively restricted from making a refugee claim in Canada.

I became intrigued with the geographical impact on southwestern Ontario close to several major POEs. Consequently, I identified five towns and small cities in this region of Ontario with Guatemalan populations ranging from a handful to 300 for interviews and conversation to be discussed in Part Three.

Table 4.16 Guatemalan Population in Canada, by Province, 1986 to 2001

PROVINCE	**CENSUS YEAR**			
	1986	**1991**	**1996**	**2001**
NEWFOUNDLAND	-	-	-	-
PRINCE EDWARD ISLAND		-	-	25
NOVA SCOTIA	-	85	20	30
NEW BRUNSWICK	-	10	10	35
QUEBEC	1885	3115	4305	4460
ONTARIO	1790	3620	5820	5820
MANITOBA	55	195	280	245
SASKATCHEWAN	-	50	110	90
ALBERTA	265	840	1130	1235
BRITISH COLUMBIA	335	1015	1575	1725
YUKON TERRITORY	-	-	-	10
NORTHWEST TERRITORIES	-	-	10	5
CANADA	**4325**	**8920**	**13270**	**13680***

*13,680 IMMIGRANTS & 415 NON-PERMANENT RESIDENTS = 14,095

Source: The Nations Series– Immigrants in Canada, Statistics Canada (1986 to 1996); Statistics Canada 97F0009XCB01003 (2001 Census), accessed February 2, 2004.

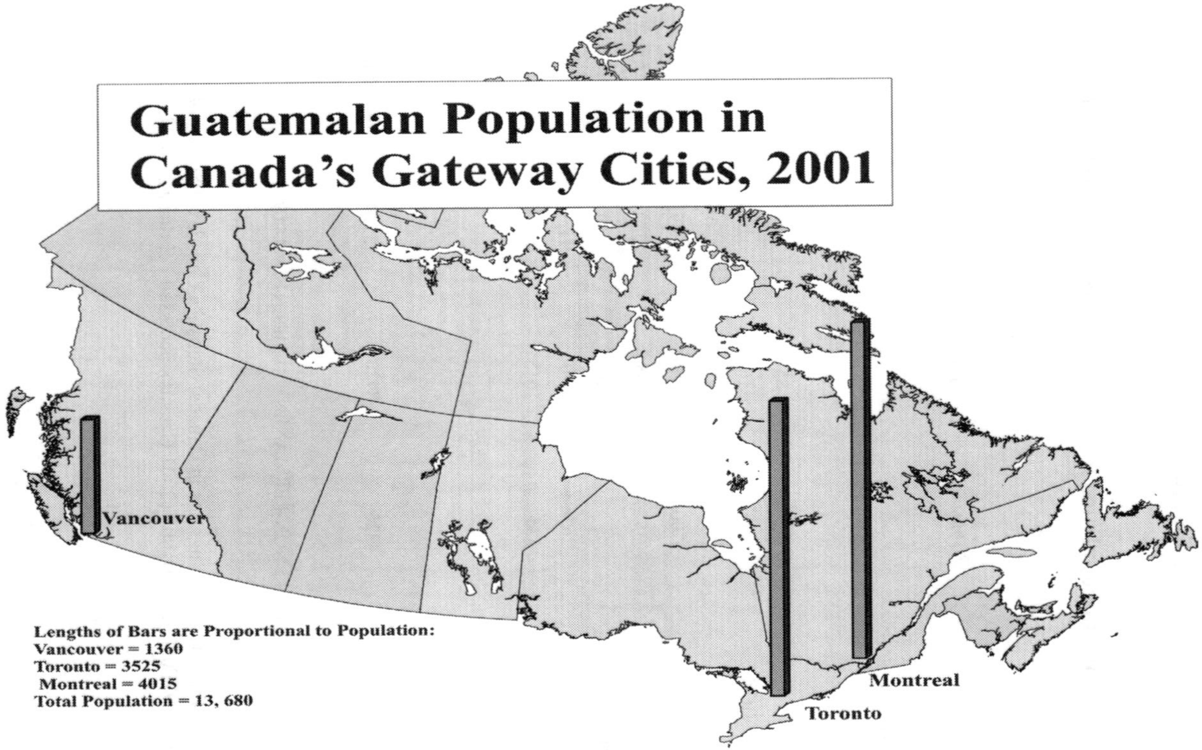

Figure 4.5A Guatemalan Population in Canada's Gateway Cities, 2001

Source: Statistics Canada, 2001 Census, Topic-based Tabulations (Immigration and Citizenship), CMAs and CAs.

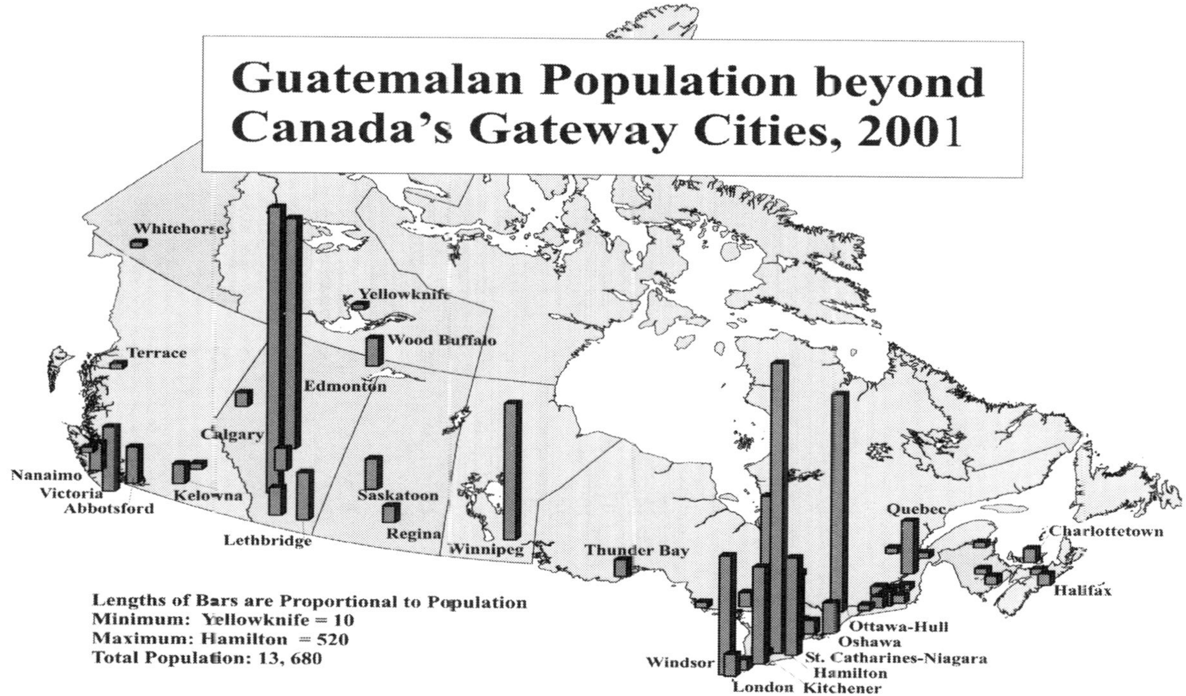

Figure 4.5B Guatemalan Population beyond Canada's Gateway Cities, 2001

Source: Statistics Canada, 2001 Census, Topic-based Tabulations (Immigration and Citizenship), CMAs and CAs.

Table 4.17 Guatemalan Population in Canada, by City, 1986 to 2001

CITY	CENSUS YEAR			
	1986	**1991**	**1996**	**2001**
NOVA SCOTIA				
Halifax	0	60	15	20
NEW BRUNSWICK				
Saint John	0	0	10	15
QUEBEC				
Montréal	1700	2885	3825	4015
Sherbrooke	10	25	135	15
Québec	20	25	70	95
Trois-Rivières	0	0	15	0
Chicoutimi - Jonquière	5	0	10	10
ONTARIO				
Toronto	1470	2185	3485	3525
Ottawa - Hull	200	445	1045	685
London	70	185	400	175
Hamilton	20	270	370	520
Kitchener	20	180	315	280
St. Catharines - Niagara	0	50	280	175
Windsor	10	190	135	215
Oshawa	25	60	80	115
Sudbury	30	25	40	25
Thunder Bay	10	20	20	30
MANITOBA				
Winnipeg	45	185	270	245
SASKATCHEWAN				
Saskatoon	0	15	95	55
Regina	0	35	15	30
ALBERTA				
Calgary	135	415	505	515
Edmonton	90	220	265	415
BRITISH COLUMBIA				
Vancouver	250	765	1360	1360
Victoria	5	65	80	115
CANADA	**4325**	**8920**	**13270**	**13680***

* 13,680 Permanent Residents + 415 non-Permanent Residents = 14,095.

Source: The Nations Series – Immigrants in Canada, Statistics Canada (1986 to 1996); Statistics Canada 97F0009XCB01003 (2001 Census), accessed on February 2, 2004.

Summing Up

Consistent with Stephen Castles' (2002) work on transnational migration, Leo Chavez (1994; 1997, 62; 1998), a leading scholar on Mexican and Central American migration to the United States, argues that transnational migrants threaten a singular vision of the nation because they allegedly bring 'multiculturalism' and not assimilation. Appadurai (1996, 11) also stresses that globalization and mass migration are not the stories of cultural homogenization or Americanization. Rather, there is room to explore specific geographies and specific cultural groups so that the nature of locality as a lived experience in a globalized, deterritorialized world can be addressed (Appadurai 1996, 52). In this chapter, the geographies of movement have been charted in order to establish a foundation on which to narrate gendered experiences of refugee transnationalism. The challenges to Canadian policy is a subject to which we return in the final chapter, but one that encourages a critical reading of the specified, contextualized, and historicized refugee journeys that are presented here and articulated in Part III.

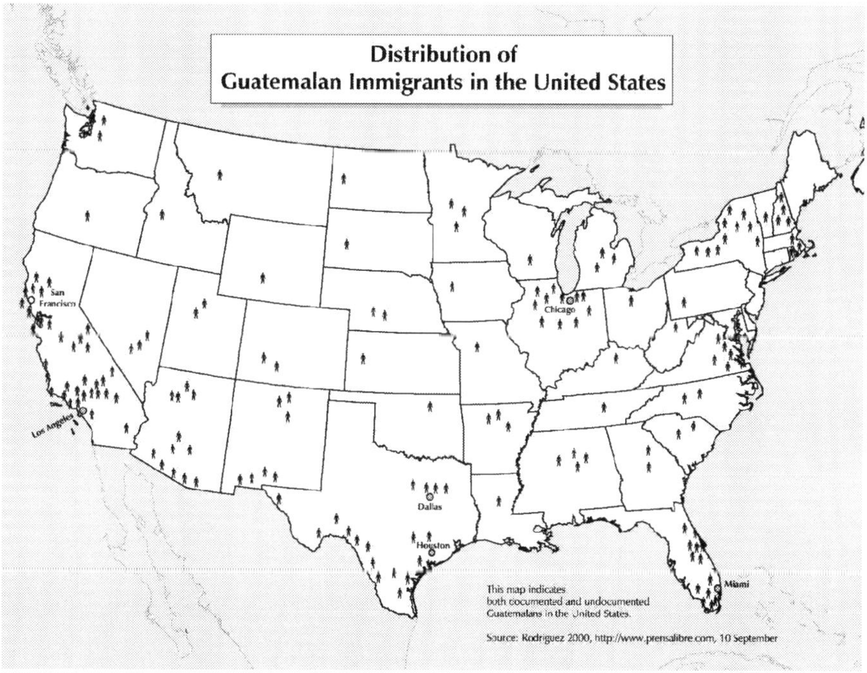

Figure 4.6 Distribution of Guatemalan Immigrants in the United States

PART III
Spatializing Gendered Transnational Identities

Chapter 5

Transnational Ethnographies: Gendered Narratives of Rupture and Suture

We are what we do, especially what we do to change what we are: our identities reside in action and struggles.
Eduardo Galeano (1992, 139)

On 8 December 1976, MIGUEL woke at 5:30 am, as usual, to run to the local shop for the morning's paper. In its pages he read the words that confirmed what he already suspected, that the Secret Anticommunist Army had included his name on a list of people targeted for execution. MIGUEL, an electrician and head of a major trade union in Guatemala City, survived two kidnapping attempts before seeking asylum in Canada.

In 1988, guerrillas left ROBERTO for dead with a machete cut to his head and buried his father alive in a rural community in Baja Verapaz. ROBERTO waited two years to uncover the truth of his father's murder and marry his love, CARMEN, so that they could flee Guatemala together.

On 31 October 1993, ELENA and her children joined RICARDO in SUMMERLAND; two years after RICARDO had fled death threats related to his union activity in Guatemala City. RICARDO's flight was swift. Trying to come to terms with his decision, ELENA acknowledged to her mother, 'Well, I believe that here there isn't much to choose.' She immigrated to Canada to join her husband and to keep the family together.

In 1992, in a bid to escape a life of misery working on a banana plantation, ANA paid $2,500 to a 'coyote' for a dangerous journey to El Norte before making up a story of union participation, intimidation, and rape in a bid to escape to Canada.

Introduction

Who are these survivors I have called MIGUEL, CARMEN, ROBERTO, ELENA, and ANA? Their disparate stories come from some of the 14,000+ Guatemalans living in Canada as refugees, landed immigrants, and new citizens. A great many are directly targeted victims of Guatemala's 36-year internal armed conflict; others are former government and military personnel who obtained landed immigrant status for the security of their families; still others are victims of Guatemala's grinding poverty and spiraling insecurity.

Central American migration to the north of the continent is growing in size and complexity. However, as Casillas (1995, 7) points out, 'what we know about this phenomenon is still woefully inadequate.' Ten years later, this statement still holds true. Casillas suggests that many migration questions await answers in part 'due to the difficulty of conducting research in countries of origin,' which encourages research on countries of transit or destination at the expense of holistic, transnational research. My desire to conduct research in Canada and Guatemala grows out of a responsibility to address the simultaneity of experiences rather than symptoms and outcomes inadequately discussed in isolation.

I am interested in how political violence and new refugee spaces in Canada work together to create particular kinds of social space constituted by rupture, connection, yearning to return, denial of past, new opportunities, lies, and concocted life stories, identity re-negotiation, and recognition. The spatializing of transnational identities must be situated within a recognition of the simultaneity of complex articulations that include: (1) political violence and a fundamentally racist nationalist ideology; (2) government policies and refugee dynamics; and (3) receptivity, addressed in Parts One and Two. Concomitant articulations of identity transformation and multi-scaled social spaces are addressed here through refugee and (im)migrant narrations.

This chapter and the one that follows are organized around a core of individuals whose stories are drawn from our interview conversations. Pieces of what they have to say are woven together through poignant and intense memories of the participants as well as those who know them best, family members in Guatemala. Our meetings took place over the course of 10 months in 1999 in several locations in southwestern Ontario. I then spent two months in Guatemala operating in short travel bursts from a base in the old colonial capital of Antigua to meet with family members who resided in various parts of the country. In the frantic days and quiet evenings spent with each family – meeting parents, aunts, uncles, cousins, brothers, sisters, grandparents, and neighbours who also had relatives abroad – I came to understand the need to step back from my academic preoccupation with connections, circuits, and continuities and simply listen to, and focus on, the ruptures, tears, and silences conveyed in their words.

Of course, refugees and other displaced people who lived through the ruptures of civil war, internal armed conflict, and political violence somehow bring together an existence in new locations. In questioning how to approach survival and new spaces of belonging, I turn to Watts (1991, 12) who refers to Stuart Hall (1989) to suggest that he understands identities as 'points of suture, points of attachment, points of temporary identification … [one] only discovers who one is because of the identities which one has to take on in order to act.' In-depth interview conversations, then, open us to myriad ruptures and sutures, or points of attachment, of refugee transnationalism. Mobility has been the centrepiece of much research on transnationalism, but given the circumstances of refugee lives and my geographical bent, I am particularly interested in the 'points of attachment' or the transnational sutures that refugees operationalize locally in the reworking and constitution of new identities. Immobility often becomes the centerpiece of refugee transnationalism. As Nyberg Sørenson (1998, 246) suggests, 'it is necessary to listen to how migrants themselves interpret their situatedness.'

If one is to carry on after surviving terror and flight, there are necessary compromises and temporary measures employed to function in new circumstances. Of course, shades of identities are not completely interchangeable but there is flexibility and site-specificity as to how we see ourselves and perform or present that understanding to others. Watts (1992a, 123) points to the lack of consideration of how people define themselves, 'how identities are cobbled together to act in new spaces.' Therefore, for a geography of Guatemalan refugee transnationalism to embrace the richness and complexity of the contemporary Guatemalan diaspora, an engagement with what Behar (1996) calls the 'individual realities' of refugee and (im)migrant lives must be central to it. Transnational culture and new social relations are played out through individual lives, in particular places and at particular times.

In this chapter, I make room for the voices of some of the thousands of survivors in Canada through three 'ethnographies of the particular' (Abu-Lughod 1991, 149) or transnational ethnographies. I create personalized accounts that address the personal and social impacts of so many atrocities of Guatemala's 'hidden war' (Manz 1988), the emotionally draining experiences of rebuilding lives in exile, grappling with transnationalized identities, and re-establishing and forging new social relations within and across borders. I edited interview conversations, highlighting certain aspects of their testimony and concealing others.

After holding back for so many years and having so few opportunities to speak about their experiences and private sufferings, their words often flowed without restraint. My questions often sparked a nerve regarding the immense personal cost associated with exile in Canada for all people involved. Reflecting on our conversations, I think that it is quite impossible to imagine what it was like for the participants to work through the memories and then to speak of the moment when past and present realities are joined, when here and there, the road behind and the road ahead, are linked, if briefly, in a moment of deep reflection; when all the abstract discussion of 'transnational social spaces' and 'living across borders' is pin-pointed to a specific moment or experience.

The words of the participants about their departure from Guatemala reveal a lot about the moment in which we spoke in Canada. As Marguerite Feitlowitz (1998, 16) found with survivors of Argentina's rule of terror, depending on circumstances, 'memory may be clear or dim, fluid or clotted.' Physical distance and the passage of time allow a certain kind of analysis and reflection that is missing when sharing immediate, close circumstances. Immediacy, though, is prominent in discussions of the creation of new relations, alliances, and identities.

Interspersed between the transnational ethnographies are voices of many other Guatemalans who share their experiences of refugee flight, transnational connections and ruptures, and identity re-negotiation. Interview conversations reveal the diversity of people and the commonalities of experience. Female and male participants in my study include members of the university student movement, union members and leaders, wives and girlfriends of those directly targeted by security forces, former male and female members of the *Partido Guatemalteco de Trabajo* (Guatemala Workers Party, PGT) and the *Fuerzas Armadas Rebeldes* (Rebel Armed Forces, FAR) guerrilla organizations, an agricultural co-operative member, a former military intelligence agent, and a former member of the *Estado Mayor Presidencial* (Presidential General Staff), among others.

The Guatemalan women and men I interviewed in Canada had a mean age of 36 and 40 respectively, with education levels ranging from elementary to advanced university. Forty-two per cent were female. In Guatemala, the men worked as union leaders, general labourers, university students, and entrepreneurs; women worked as office staff, in factories, as social workers, dentists, and university students. Eighty-four per cent came from larger cities or the capital while only 16 per cent came from smaller, rural communities. Ninety per cent indicate that they did not have knowledge of English before their departure from Guatemala and 16 per cent still do not speak English more than five years after arrival in Canada. Twelve of 19 are married, three are single, two are widowed (one widow and one widower), one male is divorced and one woman is living through a bitter divorce and child custody battle. In Canada, women work as hotel and night shift office cleaners, in an accounts payable office, in part-time daycare, and as homemakers. Men's occupations range from labourers in a greenhouse, poultry farm, and an airplane parts factory, kitchen staff, a landscaper / caretaker, and a union leader. Jobs often are unstable, seasonal, and part-time. Legal status includes refugee claimants, convention refugees, landed immigrants, and Canadian citizens. Arrival in Canada ranged from more than twenty years ago to the first day in the country, while over 60 per cent of participants arrived between 1989 and 1994. All participants live in southwestern Ontario, the majority in single-family dwellings, but some single participants share apartment space with one or two others.

The transnational narratives included here reveal the ways in which events, memory, and places transform identities. They describe how, seemingly overnight, radical thinkers become marginalized inhabitants of suburban Canada, enemies become friends, and the strong and confident become weak, nervous, and anxious. The interview conversations reveal the diversity of people, the commonalities of experience, and the profoundly transformative role that political violence and exile play in the lives of women and men in Canada and their families who remain in Guatemala. Within the narratives we hear the meaning attached to the reconfiguring of shattered identities as people negotiate the process of 'reweaving the torn' (Taylor 1998), mending one's sense of self, and reinventing one's place in the world.

Not only have the displaced been transformed by their exile, but so too have their family and friends who stayed behind. Exploration of the social, cultural, and economic relations with those who remain in Guatemala reveals the cultural meanings and significance attached to the transnational ruptures and points of attachment within and across both countries. Transnational fieldwork, then, affords us a window into relations that constitute transnational social spaces.

Personal traumas on family left behind are one of the most profoundly painful aspects to emerge from the transnational interviews. For those who 'felt in their own flesh' (ELSI) the brutality of the political violence, but were unable to leave Guatemala for myriad reasons (such as the need to look after aging parents, limited financial resources, lack of a travel visa) the separation of loved ones is extremely difficult and is described as 'a violent loss' (ELSI) and 'like a death in the family' (JOHN).

One might ask, are all the stories one? There can be no over-arching experience of transnational rupture due to the complexity of circumstance, socio-cultural and political baggage carried by each individual, the variety of new social spaces encountered and created, and the multiplicity of possibilities for identity redefinition and suspension. All of these factors play a role in the forces of interplay between local circumstances and interconnectedness of social spaces spanning here and there. John Berger (1998, 13) paraphrases Antonio Gramsci, who argued that it is not enough to know a set of relations existing at a given moment. One also needs to know the 'story of formation … because every individual is not only a synthesis of existing relations, but also the history of those relations.' Transnational ethnographies illuminate some of the social relations embedded in historical and contemporary complexities.

After composing several transnational ethnographies, I discuss the spatialization of transnational identities, in which I argue for a differentiated sense of refugee transnationalism that focuses on the many ruptures and sutures of identity and acknowledges the power of the internal differentiation *within* the Guatemalan exile – (im)migrant population.

Transnational Ethnographies

PEDRO[1]

With bravado and apparent confidence, PEDRO looked directly into my eyes as we shook hands for the first time in December 1998. SISTER BETH introduced us in the kitchen of CASA LIBERTAD, a refugee transition house in BEVERLY, on the morning that PEDRO crossed the SULLIVAN-BEVERLY Bridge in his bid for political asylum. SISTER BETH's assurance that I was not with Immigration helped to set PEDRO at ease and she explained that our conversation would not interfere

1 I fluctuated between using real names and pseudonyms depending on the request of the participant. If a pseudonym was requested then all associated names are concealed as well. Pseudonyms are used for all place names in Ontario, Canada and Guatemala (except Guatemala City, where the population base is large enough to offer anonymity if needed). PEDRO's brothers in Guatemala chose LA HAVANA as a pseudonym for their *aldea* [village]. BRUCE and JOHN apparently were cheeky when choosing their own pseudonyms: 'BRUCE WILLIS' and 'JOHN SMITH' but were serious with their request that I not return the cassette tape or transcript to them by mail in case either landed in the wrong hands. Also, pseudonyms are capitalized as are words which were emphasized during our interview conversations.

with his refugee application. We agreed to meet again the next day and continued to meet regularly over a six-month period.

Twenty-nine years old, with military-style shaved black hair and an intense gaze, PEDRO explained how, having deserted the army and successfully dodged their grip for a few years, he began to fear for his life after receiving a number of threats once he resettled in LA HAVANA. He left Guatemala on 5 October 1998. With no contacts or plan in mind, PEDRO made the dangerous journey through Mexico and the United States on his own, and came to Canada directly:

> I had to leave very fast. Yes. First, I slept on the riverbank in a secret place. I knew very well where to go because I fished in those rivers all the time and I knew of hidden places. So I hid myself for the night and then I went to my house and they said they knew I was coming because they went to look for me … some spies, I suppose. Three times they were there and talked to my mom and dad. So I told them, "I won't send cards, you never hear from me, don't worry about it." My mom was crying and my dad…. I walked in the mountains, asking for rides, and in this way I arrived at the border of Mexico without money. Without money and without food. I crossed at Roma, Texas. [It lies] close to Monterrey. I worked on a ranch for two or three days and they gave me food. I walked for a long time, like five or seven days in the mountains. I didn't know anyone. Nobody. I wasn't brave, how do you say? Without knowing, without knowing anything. I crossed with the name of God, asking, and in this way, I went. But I suffered a lot. No food, sleeping on the mountain under the rain.

As with many young men in the military, PEDRO did not enlist but was pulled from the street and forced to endure brutal training exercises. 'See this?' he asks in Spanish while pointing to two large bumps and a scar on the top of his head. PEDRO explains:

> Here I have two blows to the head but the bigger one is from the military. It's from when I was in the military. They put like this … with my hands behind my head and dropped me to the floor on my head so that I would learn everything. Ummm, my life is full of suffering. I've suffered a lot.

Leaving was not easy for PEDRO even though he was escaping violent conditions in which he might be called upon to fight his own countrymen and women:

> When I came on the road I knew that I could not return to Guatemala, never again. When it is my country and I feel proud to have been born there, even though it is a bad country. Right? Like you feel proud to be Canadian, proud to be a Canadian. And even if Canada were a bad country, or communist … but you always feel proud of where your parents are from, where your blood is from, where you were born. Right? So when I left Guatemala, I left with tears. I came crying when I crossed to Mexico. Like that, I was on this side and I looked at Guatemala and I knew that I can't anymore. I can't go back.

Each time we met, PEDRO would reveal and conceal as necessary. It was more than a month from our first meeting when he disclosed that he was not being entirely truthful. But what was he to do? Who was I? Couldn't I be with Immigration? The police? How could he know I was who I said I was? Some level of trust developed, though, as we pieced together our relationship and he began to hear of me through other Guatemalans in the area. But, instead of throwing away my fieldnotes and starting from scratch with PEDRO, I chose to see his revelations as a problematic for qualitative research: why do some people find it necessary to be less than truthful interviewees? How can researchers know what the participants say is 'true?' How many interviews do we conduct before they are labeled as 'reliable?' What role does violence and vulnerability play in the answers participants offer in our conversations?

These questions go beyond the scope of this chapter, but I include them here to flag the partiality of all that follows. The ethnographies of the particular and all interview conversations are vividly partial, temporary, and shifting. Transnational interviewing, too, adds complexity and contradiction to the mix. Of all the transnational interview conversations, those with PEDRO and his family in Guatemala best demonstrate the incomplete, imperfect, and limited character of engaged qualitative research. This statement is not meant to downplay or discredit our findings; rather, I mean to extol the virtues of an engagement with complexity that acknowledges contradiction and different ways of seeing.

During our last meeting in Canada, PEDRO assured me that somehow he would contact his family to let them know of my planned arrival in LA HAVANA. He requested that I take along some letters and gifts for his family and gathered them together with great affection. A purse and dress for his mother, shoes for his father ('Tell him I've only worn them once.'), hand-written letters addressed to his brothers, sisters, and parents, and photographs with his new girlfriend in HOPE. He was the only participant to use me as a personal courier, even though he was the most recent arrival to Canada.

Several weeks later, a long and isolated gravel road surrounded by sugar cane brought us to LA HAVANA. PEDRO's brother, BRUCE, was waiting for us as we stepped off the bus in front of the community phone and family house.[2] 'Oh my God!,' he shouted in English, 'you made it.' Starving for English-language conversation, BRUCE explained that he recently returned to Guatemala from the Midwest United States in a (failing) attempt to legalize his status. Lonely for his wife and young son, BRUCE was keen to serve as intermediary and speak to us of the family's migration experiences. He invited us to the garden behind the house and introduced us to his sister, TERI, mother, JOSEFINA, father, MANUEL, and many nieces and nephews. JOSEFINA went off quietly to read the letter from PEDRO while BRUCE and TERI made conversation.

TERI expressed how nice it was to hear of PEDRO since she had not seen him in 'so long … seven years. The kids really don't know him except from photos,' she

2 Finola Shankar (1999), my research assistant and travel companion, participated in all family meetings and interview conversations with me while in Guatemala. Her qualitative research experience on organic coffee production in Guatemala proved valuable during our interview conversations.

explained. 'Seven years?' I thought to myself. TERI talked of his 'vice of drinking' and BRUCE added that he had a real lack of responsibility and never sent money to the family. Everyone said they were greatly relieved to hear of his efforts at legalizing his status in Canada and that he seems to be settling down.

So, what of his statements during our interviews, in which he confirms that he left Guatemala in October 1998? Seven years since his family have seen him? What went on in the intervening years? This contradiction raised a dilemma for Finola and me. Do we ask directly about the conflicting accounts? Who do we believe and why? If we believed the family how could we believe everything else PEDRO shared with me?

Our confusion must have been apparent to the family. We chose to carry on, however, in the hope that more information would clarify matters. We spent two days with the family and met three additional brothers, in-laws, and neighbours. Each person warrants her or his own biography, as they shared freely aspects of their life stories. But it was a more formal interview conversation with BRUCE and brother JOHN that proved most revealing. JOHN received PEDRO's call about our visit to LA HAVANA and was prepared for our arrival. When I asked JOHN where PEDRO said he was going when he left Guatemala, he replied:

> I think that, perhaps, I think of that he had in mind that one day he'd go to Canada. Yes, I imagine, right? I think of him … he said that I am going to help in this point that I am giving. I THINK … then, in this way, *pues*, thanks to God he went.
>
> What day did PEDRO leave? Was it this year?
>
> He left on October 5th. October 5th, perhaps.
>
> In which year?
>
> Last year. Uhum. October 5th. October 5th.

BRUCE did not support or contradict his brother's statements – which concurred with PEDRO's comments. Instead, he spoke of his migration experiences that seemed to urge his brother to reveal more of the 'truth' than PEDRO's concocted story. BRUCE fled Guatemala as a 14-year-old after the disappearance of their older brother who worked with the military:

> I have already lived the experience of the other side of the story, right, because I went to the United States when … *pues*, a little after, weeks after the assassination of my brother…. With fear and looking for something better, right, and thanks to God, I was able to study in the United States … and I cried and asked God to help me and thinking always, thinking "Will I return to see my family again?" "Will I have peace in my life" and things like that passing through one's mind, right?

JOHN opened up, though, when we asked how PEDRO's flight from Guatemala affected the family and him in particular:

> I speak of what, as a brother, one feels when a brother distances himself from the family because we lived together for a long time right? Everything, at least I have passed a lot of time with my brother right? And we miss him, we miss him a lot and it was very hard for us from the first time when my brother GUILLERMO, on the 17th of March I believe of '86 when he died, right? So from there we lived some quite bitter years, right, firstly for his disappearance, because he was disappeared [and] he was found like at two months.... I don't remember a lot. And well, *pues*, in the end we can feel more than anything this, this pain, right because like the years go passing by, one goes filling the days, one goes on forgetting them, right? [half laughs]. But the truth is that, the truth is that we don't know, right, what the hate is that these people who did this crime with my brother have. With our family right because they started with PEDRO threatening him and everything ... they sent his first anonymous [letter], *pues*, you don't pay attention to it. I said to him truly I don't believe that there will be a problem. But shortly after receiving the second, the second threat, yes, he had to leave, *pues*. For us it was quite hard. And more than anything with me, *pues,* because my brother [BRUCE] has been there [USA] for more time, right? And know that he left, *pues*, I have felt, I have felt quite alone as well. There was a little fear as well, right, because also it could be that they persecute us, these threats right?

So in the end, JOHN was the 'good brother' and told us what PEDRO wanted him to convey: that he left Guatemala in October 1998 with thoughts of coming directly to Canada. Family members did not openly question his answer but went about telling their own version of the family's migration experiences. Later in the afternoon, BRUCE explained how he assisted PEDRO as a teenager in the United States while both lived an undocumented, 'illegal' existence in El Norte:

> He was young, got tangled up with the wrong crowd, drugs, alcohol … he hit rock bottom and came to me in the Midwest for help. I gave him a few bucks and told him to get his act together. That's when he went to SULLIVAN and decided to try Canada.

JOHN, too, wanted us to know the 'true' circumstances of PEDRO's departure and therefore after dispensing with PEDRO's story line carried on with his own version of events. It was up to us, as researchers, to identify the strategy of brotherly loyalty within the family narratives. It became clear that the inventions we live by are sometimes necessary compromises made in extreme situations. Our interview conversations and research framework had to be flexible enough to identify the many strategic choices of participants.

The lack of support from family, contacts, and money available to individual refugee claimants such as PEDRO reinforces disconnection from family and friends:

> Arriving at the border they asked me if I had friends, family, money … from where I came … and I had nothing, nothing … no family, no friends, no money, no house, no nothing so they gave me directions to CASA LIBERTAD … a house there in BEVERLY that helps refugees. But for me it is hard here in Canada because people here think one comes to tell lies, that one comes to say, "Ahhh … more money ... that the money is worth more."

> One time I called. I called home when I arrived … no more than a quick hello to them because for me it's very expensive to call. And I don't have enough money. [Can you write to them?] Agh, yes but … perhaps no, no I think because there when they see letters sent from Canada or the United States there are many thieves who steal them. Perhaps there is going to be money or something in them so I don't send any. It's difficult. "*Correos seguros*" [courier services] are more expensive so right now I'm not able until I start to work then. For now, no.

Transnational interviewing allowed the suspended space of unknowing to emerge from our discussions with family in Guatemala. Rather than the maintenance of 'transnational circuits' or 'networks,' those affected by political violence must deal with the rupture of social relations when circumstances disrupt communication and face-to-face contact. JOHN expresses that the suspended spaces of refugee transnationalism operate at the family level, particularly when communication is limited and the journey north is dangerous:

> So this was very hard for us because we didn't know where he was, where he was going, or what he was doing, who he was with, if he was eating, or if he wasn't eating. But knowing that he is … is already there and he told us he was well … we felt quite happy, right? Because we know that there, nothing will happen to him, right? …. It was very hard. It was very hard. I think that it was almost like losing a brother because one doesn't know how many people leaving Guatemala lost their life just because they wear Nikes. Or they steal money. A little while ago my brother-in-law went [to the USA]. They stole his money, they stole his money and they hit him, so one doesn't know. It was very hard for us…. True, we want to see him but the reasons that we have already said do not permit it, right?

New identities develop in order to survive without community or familial support in Canada, as PEDRO explains:

> You're a new baby in Canada [PEDRO laughs] … My life never existed before here. It is like it never happened. Yes, because here I feel Canada … I don't speak the language, I don't know how to speak. I didn't know how to read. I didn't know where to go … I didn't have a home. I still don't have a mom and dad here. Right? A new life, a new baby. That of Guatemala is past but it's always on my mind … When I have my own children I am not going to be able to tell them something good [about Guatemala] because nothing good ever existed.

****

MIGUEL CIFUENTES

MIGUEL CIFUENTES, a prominent Guatemalan union leader and President of the National Confederation of Workers in the 1970s, became perhaps the first Guatemalan accepted as a political refugee in Canada. Our interview conversation begins in the living room of his home and later moves to a sofa in the kitchen. The tape recorder, most appropriately, was set down on Volume II of the REMHI

(1999) report, Los mecanismos del horror [The Mechanisms of Horror], kept visible by MIGUEL in the family's living space. Our interview begins with discussion of the first of many ruptures – of being specifically targeted by the military forces, two attempted abductions in Guatemala City, internal exile within his own country – being ripped away from family, friends, activism, and occupation.

MIGUEL requested that our discussion of his forced departure be situated within the political culture of state terror and urban violence directed at the popular movement and his growing politicization throughout the 1960s and 1970s. The rupture to family relations is central to the trauma of MIGUEL's internal exile and forced departure, as he explains:

> The popular movement was completely destroyed. The leadership and a lot of people was forced to leave the country … those who make it. And a year later, that repression became a massive repression in the countryside with the policy of earth … scorched earth policy that you know very well about that. So anyway … this is what FORCED me to leave the country. That situation, right? Because I was living already in exile in my own country. I couldn't visit my family because I knew that if they get me at my place, not only they want to harm me, but they're going to harm my family. So I couldn't visit my family, I couldn't stay with my family anymore … I was sleeping in some friends' houses and cheap motels and I always have a set of clothing with me … so it was very difficult.

MIGUEL maintained his deep commitment to struggles of the popular movement even when faced with intensified insecurity and ongoing surveillance:

> We knew that the death squads were running from the National Palace … We understood for each of us there were, I don't know, maybe about 10 members of the security forces watching us all the time … this is why at that time the repression was very selective …

MIGUEL describes here two critical moments at which he knew without doubt the impossibility of his situation, the realization that the death squads added his name to the list of targets and the kidnap attempts in broad daylight. MIGUEL coped by drawing on a close circle of trusted colleagues, discipline, and laughter:

> This is why I was forced to leave finally to Costa Rica [and later Canada] … My name was published on December the 8th, 1978 and I left, I made the most difficult decision that I ever, ever made in my life … it was to leave the country and I left and I remember it was April the 14th, 1979. It means that I spent a couple more months, it was like, I don't know, it was like the most HORRIBLE nightmare … the uncertainty, right?

> In 1978, the repression really became very, very … very strong and the Anti-Communist Secret Army became very active … and it was scary because the death squads, the Anti-Communist Secret Army published some list of people that are going to be executed, right? But, suddenly the death squad starts to kill people that not necessarily were on the list. So that put you on the spot and say, "Wait, who is next?" Right? So on December the 8th of 1978 when I arrived to the National Confederation of Workers, the secretaries were crying and I said to them, "Why are you crying?" and they said, "Well, you didn't hear the

> radio?" And I said … I was playing a game, right, and now I don't know if I regret it … [laughs a little] but I hear at 6:00 – I was awake everyday at 5:30 in the morning and went to buy the newspaper, read the newspaper – and my name was published on one of the lists of the Anti-Communist Secret Army and I read it again … I hear it on the radio. So and when I arrived and the secretaries were crying and I said, "Well, what is wrong with you?" They said, "Well you know what happened?" and I said, "Well, no." "Your name was published in the … in one of the lists of the government Secret Army." And I said, "Well let me see." And I read it, right, I knew it but I was playing a game. So I said, "Well I am very upset about this." And they said, "Well why?" But I mean [I said] angry, right? And they said, "Well why?" "Because I am not number one on the list!" [big laugh]. It was … now I say it was a stupid joke but in those moments of tragedy … I think [in] Guatemala, you have to LAUGH, you know what I mean? It's like laughing is kind of therapeutic. I firmly believe that. In Guatemala people say … well, you can be with a lot of sorrow in your life, but you HAVE to cope with reality, you know? Not to escape reality but to cope with reality we learn to laugh because we learn to cry, you know?
>
> This is why I say that I am very lucky to be alive and also I survived two attempts to be kidnapped, you know, the last one was April the 9th [1979] when I … unfortunately I had to go to the city hall to pick up my ID, my *cedula*, that was in there, and I was walking … at that time really, really I experienced what was TERROR and … I just saw … in Guatemala the *policía judicial* was using the Toyota Jeeps and Toyota Land Rovers and I saw a jeep, a white jeep … and I wasn't using my glasses that day, I was using some contact lenses [he laughs a little] … so my eyes were red …a lady said to me, "Are you OK or are you crying or are you on drugs?" [he laughs] And I said, "My contact lenses." And she was laughing. So anyway that day I saw this jeep and I say, "Oh, my gosh" [fear conveyed in his voice] you know, and I believed I shouldn't go out, you know, the decision was that I was leaving Guatemala, it was made the decision, I had to leave the country, that I shouldn't be in the street, right? But I … somebody … at that time you HAD to go personally to pick up your ID. So anyway, on my way, when I saw the *judiciales* jump and with their guns and pointing, right? So I tried to run and I couldn't, you know? I felt my legs this heavy and I lost my vision, I almost peed my pants, you know? … honestly … suddenly I just … it piqued what my grandmother was telling me all the time, right?

Earlier, MIGUEL told me his grandmother said:

> "MIGUEL, don't let them take you alive because we don't like to live with the uncertainty and the question in our minds and our brains and our head." "What happened to MIGUEL? Is he still alive? Is he dead? Did they torture him?" And all those questions, right?
>
> So I run and it was unbelievable … Seventh Avenue in front of the city centre, civic centre …in front of the National Bank, Banco de Guatemala, the … Supreme Court of Justice … and the city hall … so finally I go and I was very close to being struck by a big truck but it was the best at that moment. But when I achieved to cross the street another car come, a Ford, a very old Ford, without license plates and red and the top was white … so another group of guys jump with the guns. So at that moment it was a lot of people over there because it was almost lunchtime and so the ladies start to say, "Don't kill him! Assassins!!" So people were … And I was screaming, right? "I AM MIGUEL CIFUENTES!!" Because I was well-KNOWN to be the president of the CNT and the president of the workers of the

> Central America Tobacco Company. And I managed to go to city hall and.... I went in hiding until the day of my departure. And that was kind of tragic, right?

MIGUEL describes his forced departure as a rupture on many levels including citizenship, identity as a union leader, family relations, and participant in the fight for social justice in Guatemala:

> I firmly believe and still I think that to belong to a union and to be a union leader is a constitutional right. But the reality is that in Guatemala that was considered a crime. And I think that the high punishment that I have been paying, is that I have been ... when I made the most difficult decision to leave the country ... is that they take the right to live in your country. My right to be a Guatemalan citizen, to live in my own country was taken away ... was taken away the right to be with my community, my family, my community ... my community and friends and I was kind of teared [torn] away from the fight for peace and social justice in Guatemala. That is very painful. It was very painful and it's still very painful.

Strained and stressed family dynamics emerge as a profoundly painful rupture for MIGUEL. In response to my question regarding the family impact of his departure:

> Well ... I think that it was a relief in some ways ... because I was AWAY and I was ALIVE and I was still alive.... I firmly believe that they embraced what I was doing ... that what I was doing was the right thing to do. So I think that it was a relief but also caused a lot of pain in the dynamic in my family ... and now it's like 20 years later ... and it's a generation that I really don't know in my family, you know?

The social disintegration of 'communities of association' in addition to the dismemberment of physical 'communities,' such as towns and villages, of course, functioned on fear, suspicion, and silence – entrenching political divisions within the country and reproducing them in exile. In response to my questions, 'Is there a feeling that there is a "Guatemalan community" in your city or is that too strong of a word? Are there too many conflicting realities of what people have lived through?' MIGUEL responds:

> Ya, I think that, listen, I cannot deny and I always speak with my heart. I wish all those who left the country for political reasons, you know, that we can have a real community, you know. And I think that with the time we forgot the real meaning of solidarity among human beings and I think that was what prevailed in the last years since we came to Canada ... was the political divisions, right? Politics divide the community here. This is why I cannot say that we have a community.
>
> This is an example that how painful also exile can be right when ... instead of coming together, you know, and be there for each other, you know, the personal agendas, the political agendas also come ... and that maybe it's a shame to say but that is the reality.
>
> I sometimes I ask to myself, "How this is that even in a social movement that has been looking for changes in our countries," let's put it very clear, "in the revolutionary

> movement there ALWAYS has been divisions." And I say, "Well, is it that those negative forces always exist? That made the life of the people even more difficult? You know what I mean?" And that has been the other part of how painful the exile can be, in my case, that is some of the other reality, you know, that I feel that in somehow I was kind of betrayed by some people that I considered were my closest friends, you know.

In addition to the many ruptures of departure, arrival, and betrayal in exile, MIGUEL also articulates a painful suturing of fractured identity through a tentative return to Guatemala:

> Well, I went in 1994 first with a group of people from Canada and I have … kind of friends, two members of the Union of the Steel Workers who were my companions, right? At least to be witness if something was wrong. But, ya, it was the first time … it was kind of … very moving experience … it was like a dream, you know, I was pinching my cheeks to see if it was a dream or not [he laughs]. But it was a strange sensation, I don't know, it was kind of psychosis of terror coming back … the flashbacks, you know. But I was feeling like I was floating, that I was walking in the air … and at certain points I was quite nervous, you know, walking in the street…. In 1994 the situation was still very bad…. I couldn't go to my family, right, I was staying in a hotel, you know. And when, when I had the opportunity to see my family, when I saw my aunt … I just jumped from the car, I don't know, but I think my friends from the Steel Workers thought that I was crazy, you know [smiling]. Can you IMAGINE after 15 years to see somebody from your family!? And I couldn't say anything. I just hold her and I think that our hearts and the whole was telling everything, you know, ya it was like a dream, it's like a dream, it's like being born again.

So, perhaps opportunities do not exist for effective solidarity among Guatemalans in Canada, but MIGUEL sees the possibility of contributing to the process of social reconstruction in Canada through a transnational suture of skills and experience transfer:

> When I left the country, I couldn't come to Canada and just say, "Well Guatemala no longer exists for me, right and say well I'm comfortable and I don't care anymore." I think that we can be instrumental, you know, to the rebuilding of communities, for example, and the rebuilding, why not, of the trade union movement…. So and I think that can be helpful but the main question is, "Are there going to exist the conditions for Guatemalans to go back and try to do something?"

When asked if he thinks of his time in Canada as a time in exile or a process of becoming a Canadian or a mix, MIGUEL responds:

> You know … [long pause] Somehow we can attach also to this country. And I think that it's a country that the culture and the people that embrace us, you know, that help us to become accustomed to a certain extent to this culture. It's a difficult process, these 20 years in Canada … [but] I was fortunate to meet and build a beautiful network of friends…. And NOW working for a union, you know, I represent what I can say, the working poor, you know. And it's kind of … it's another strong root in this country. But certainly what I can say is I wish I can have two hearts, no? One dedicated to Guatemala [laughs hard] and one

dedicated to Canada. But certainly, loyalty to this country too and I think somehow we have been contributing to this country, too, one or another way.

****

CARMEN and ROBERTO

CARMEN and ROBERTO, a young, newly married couple full of hope and commitment to issues of social justice, fled Guatemala for Canada at the first opportunity in 1989. As an engaged university student and social worker, CARMEN was firmly committed to exposing brutal working conditions in rural Guatemala and injustices experienced by union members in the sugar industry:

> Yes, yes, I, I have many difficulties there [Escuintla] with the owners of, landowners, ya. Many times they told, not only me, the owners, the people who I was working with, they told us if we continue doing some kind, that kind of organizing, they said, "You're going to disappear" ⌊nervous laugh⌋. Yes, ya, they were very clear on that.

Dedicated to her research and activism in rural communities, CARMEN withstood intimidation and threats by the security agents of landowners and those who work for the army while working on her Master's thesis at Guatemala's national university, the Universidad de San Carlos (USAC):

> I … maybe I … have something in my blood! [we both laugh] That's what my husband says because like when I was writing about unions he told me that [she laughs], "Don't do that!" And when we have our presentations, we invite many peoples and some of our friends told us, "Oh my gosh! You're CRAZY!" [she laughs]. But sometimes, like, you have to do that … like it's something that you don't feel like you have to be quiet … somebody has to tell, to tell EVERYTHING … what is going on, what happened in … because someday, our hope someday that something change.

But it would not be CARMEN's problematic activities that spurred the couple's flight from Guatemala. During our conversation, CARMEN moved from forcefully describing her own encounters with the darker forces of society to almost whispering the case of her husband, ROBERTO. In response to my question, 'Now you had said that the difficulties that your husband's family had were with the guerrillas and again you hear less of that than problems with the army and the military and the police … was that particular to the area that they were living in?' CARMEN answers:

> Yes, Yes. That was like, you know, in many places in Guatemala when the army … go to do like mass … mass killing … my father-in-law and two people were in that village, they owned a truck and sometimes the army just go there and they ask them to, to, to give them the truck … and it wasn't like they ask you, "Could you please…?" They, they told them, "You have to give us the truck" and they used the truck to go to other villages and kill people … to transport soldiers … you know, from one place to another and because the guerrilla was working in that area, area … they decide that those three people were doing something for the army … and they decide to kill. It's kind of between … you

> can't do anything for the guerrillas because the army and you can't do anything for the army because the guerrilla … and they were between, between them and then they kill, they killed, like that night when they came into the village they took the church and they put all the people inside the church and they took those three people and one of them … they killed one in the centre of the village in front of all … in front of everyone and they told them, "This is one way to teach you don't to help the army" and then they took the other, the other two and the other one, after they push my husband and let my husband … because they thought that he was dead [CARMEN gets very quiet] … yes, and … after they, they leave the other ones maybe two kilometres after and my father-in-law, they didn't find him after two years … later …. That was in SAN VICENTE, close to SANTA CATARINA.

Not only was ROBERTO left for dead after receiving a machete cut to his head, but his trauma was exacerbated during the two years in which the location of his father's body was unknown:

> Then they, like the whole family, were like … with too much pressure or stress because some people, sometimes they call them and they said, "OK, I think your father is with the guerrillas … they took him to some place and la la la" and during two years they were looking everywhere, you know? But after, like, after that time the army find one member of the guerrilla who participate in that … in that time … and he told them that they killed like ... they didn't kill him. They just put him in some bag and they … put it in a hole and just put some [motions like covering with dirt] …

'On no,' I whispered while CARMEN's eyes filled with tears. She continued:

> [It] was terrible … like my husband was, was terrible sick, you know? Like he was depressed and all the time he was thinking someday he find some people who, who know, that he knows he participated. He said, "I'm gonna kill them, I'm gonna kill them." But thanks to God, we moved to here, like for us it was hard but he's OK now. He still remembers many things like … sometimes … he didn't have any picture of his father because the house was burned…

While I visit with CARMEN's family in VISTA HERMOSA, Guatemala, her sister, ELSI, reflects on the family's perception of the reasons for their departure:

> Carmen didn't have problems like this we say … but the question of ROBERTO, yes is a little serious, a little hard … there they have to live, right, because they killed his father, one of his sisters, him … to him they left for dead so, truly for him the situation was very strong and the guerrilla went in to SAN VICENTE, Baja Verapaz, SANTA CATARINA and all this where he lived it was very strong, right? … It was a little easier for them to look for a place farther to improve their life in the case of ROBERTO, right. It was no longer tranquil like before they married. Practically, immediately they went [to Canada] because they knew that they were not going to be able to be here tranquilly, right? Because it was a little that, he couldn't be settled in one place because he felt the fear right that at any moment and he could be recognized and to say that we believe you were the one. Him more because I believe that the father appeared [dead] *pues* [she pauses] … I believe that they had already married when the body of the father … [was found] buried, right,

> so. They told them where he was and all, right? They had to verify how to be and all but I think that this was the reason that they, he took the decision to go, right? The same emotional instability that he had, the impassable, the non-confidence, we say, until they left here ... More than anything, it was emotional instability. He had a lot of fear.

Throughout our three days with CARMEN's family, ELSI and ENCARNACIÓN, CARMEN's mother, offer fragments of the family's experience of political violence, CARMEN and ROBERTO's departure, and the transnational ruptures that affect the entire family. Inevitably, the comments shared in quiet moments around the dinner table or through conversations following the 'interview conversation' illuminate far more than the words captured on the cassette tape. During a calm moment in her fabric shop, ENCARNACIÓN shares how ROBERTO lived the violence *en su misma carne*, in his own flesh – 'imagine living here after that!,' she implored.

When CARMEN and ROBERTO attempted to return to Guatemala in 1994, ENCARNACIÓN remembers that ROBERTO never left the VISTA HERMOSA house, nor returned to his family home in SAN VICENTE for fear that he would be the target of *vengazas*, death by community members as revenge for past family transgressions. His father was more involved in the local political violence than had been revealed to me in Canada and, therefore, if detected in SANTA CATARINA, ROBERTO might be the focus of retaliation and revenge.

But ENCARNACIÓN appeared shocked to find out that ELSI also shared with us the family secret of how she lived the political violence in *her* own flesh. During our visit the previous evening we asked ELSI how CARMEN's flight from Guatemala affected the family, if it was more difficult for them to deal with the rupture because she fled the country due to ROBERTO's troubles. ELSI's reflections moved from the cousin who refuses to baptize her daughter until CARMEN returns to stand as her godmother to her own missed opportunities to flee; from the details of ROBERTO's troubles in Santa Catarina to the role of the Canadian Embassy in determining the shape of transnational connections through the visa application process. After speaking at length, ELSI then connects CARMEN's experience with her own:

> In the beginning, *pues*, like all beginnings it is a little harder, right? And for, for me personally, it was quite violent that CARMEN went. She is my littlest sister. I, they say, I gave her piggyback rides and I fed and cradled her. So for us, like I say, it was a little violent, no? In saying, "Well but why?" But there is also understanding because, *pues*, if it were for his security, right, because if I had sent him ... if I had maybe the sufficient strength to join him and to say, *pues*, there are problems here, *pues*, let's go and save life, right? Better that he would be alive.

From this rather cryptic response, we later learn from ENCARNACIÓN that ELSI's *compañero* was macheted to death, chopped up, and returned to her in a bag known as a costal when she was one month pregnant. ELSI lived the political violence in her own flesh and eight months later gave birth to a son. Eighteen years later, she wishes she had the strength to flee the country with her love and live the rupture of exile like CARMEN:

> Better she didn't go but once she was married they [parents] couldn't say no.

CARMEN explains how, eight days after their marriage, she and ROBERTO caught a flight bound for New Jersey with a plan to come to Canada as refugee claimants:

> We [went] to Guatemala [City] ... Guatemala to USA and in USA we took a bus and then we ask for refugee at Montréal. Ya. And then the nightmare began [she laughs].

The nightmare of exile began from the first moments at the border and it continues in multiple scenarios for her young family. Trauma, fear, difficulty, depression, anger, and complete sadness consume CARMEN and ROBERTO even 10 years after their arrival:

> And like the trauma like when we came here we were not too healthy ... not too easy for us because my husband has some trouble that all that had happened. I ... it was difficult to come here because I left all my friends and family, EVERYTHING. I was SOOOO depressed, so angry. For us we are living because we HAVE to live [sad laugh] you know? You are alone in this country, only with your kids, you think all about if the kids are growing up without cousins and all the rest of the family and ... because that's because you feel like something is not ... something is empty, you know?

CARMEN talks about the multiple barriers she faces as a refugee woman, though she often reflects how her difficulties are shared by ROBERTO. Difficulty with the English language and underemployment are critical elements to their unhappiness and instability in Canada. Employed as a social worker and an electrician in Guatemala, CARMEN and ROBERTO's occupational situation in Canada creates constant stress and frustration, as CARMEN relates:

> Yes, after the baby was born, BRIAN born in February, and then I start to work as a cleaner in a building. I remember the first ... the first time that I start to work ... I cry a lot. I was washing the washrooms and I was crying and crying because I was saying, "Oh my God, this is our future."

From respected professional to janitor in a few short months, CARMEN expected the humiliation to be short-lived and that her experience would prove valuable in her new country. But almost 10 years later, their struggles continue as ROBERTO obtains part-time work in nearby factories and farms, when he can, and CARMEN attempts to move from volunteer to part-time work:

> Ya, if you are living under, under stress all the time ... because it's difficult for us ... living as immigrants it's difficult for us to find a good job … first it was only 2 ½ hours but I said, I told my husband, "OK, I'm gonna take this job because I need Canadian experience." But it's like a daycare, drop-in program for mother's groups. And then ... they pay me the same ... $6.85 and it's pretty difficult for me. I have almost 6 months there … Being volunteer, just volunteer…. Ya! And I talked to the supervisor there and I told her, "See this is my situation. I don't want to be under this, this stress more time ... like

> I'm losing time ... I have to do something else. And I don't want to be rude I just want to do something GOOD."

Between laughs, an exasperated CARMEN goes on to articulate the many barriers she and other refugee women face in obtaining satisfactory employment -- low salaries, few hours, difficulties with childcare, and lack of opportunities to learn English in the workplace – leading to intensified social isolation:

> I said, "OK, how much are you going to pay me?" and she says, "$6.85" "For how long?" "2 ½ hours." "Oh, excuse me!" [she laughs] ... like what, crazy! Like I don't know ... I don't know, how can I take that? I told her "My husband has to find a job and we have to take care of ROSA ... and she said, "OK, you can drop ROSA in some daycare" and I said, "Uh, first day cares are expensive" ... I told her, "OK, look for 2 ½ hours I get $16 for the morning, you know. Then I have to pay $6 for bus. Then and I have to pay daycare like anyway if they give me a subsidy in the daycare ... I have to pay $30 a month. $30 a month, plus the bus ... it's not too much money ... $6.85, it's like NOTHING! I know that they pay $8.50 for the students." "Ya, ya. I know that they pay that." But for me, $6.85.

> Then because I told her [social worker] that I want to improve my English [but] I was sitting in my desk watching people or doing nothing and sometimes they just put me to cut paper or do some crafts [laughs] … And I say, "Oh my gosh!" I was so upset and I called her and said, "Look, I asked you for a place so I can practice my English" and she said, "Oh, that is the BEST place where I can send you" ... and I said, "Look, if I have to lose time I'm going to sit at home doing that and maybe I'm gonna learn more watching TV..."

As a suture to their fractured existence, CARMEN and ROBERTO place great importance on bringing together Guatemalans in the region. Others recognize their leadership efforts and are tentatively receptive:

> Yes, we try to align the relationship between all the Guatemalans who live here. It's difficult ... like you know work with people is ... its good/bad. But at the same time, it's like a good experience ... also if you are not in your country ... it is difficult because you have to see if they have time if they work ... but it's nice, it's really nice. Ya, like last year for example we went to ... we organized a party just for Guatemalans. It was like a lunch and a dance for the Guatemalan people. It was GREAT and we were really happy because that was the first time and this year we want to have another lunch and it's like ... good for us here.

Forging new social relations with fellow Guatemalans proves difficult, though, due to a host of practical reasons that limit opportunities for group activity to once or twice per year:

> The other thing is the transportation, you know. Some people don't have cars [and] here Sundays we don't have a bus and you have, you can't have a chance to go ANYWHERE. Lifestyle for us is changed a lot because as I told you before Saturdays for us is family reunion. And here we are alone ... we don't have family ... our family is my husband, my

> children and me ... that's it. And it's very difficult to find some person, family who can stay close to you like that because of maybe they have a different religion or because they work too much or because the level of education is different or many, many things here that you have.

Deep connections and solidarity are largely absent for CARMEN and ROBERTO, as they, like other participants, keep much of their life stories hidden from other Guatemalans and avoid asking too many questions. Half- truths and concocted histories allow local social relations to develop – however shallow – as a refuge from profound loneliness and isolation. Even if new friends might have been enemies, or at least adversaries, in Guatemala, the avoidance of probing too deeply into reasons for departure from Guatemala allows a union representative to befriend a man with military connections. Social relations among Guatemalans in southwestern Ontario, therefore, are fragile.

More central to CARMEN and ROBERTO's identities though are the ways in which they remain close as a family unit in Canada and how those relationships with family in Guatemala are renewed as often as possible through twice-monthly telephone conversations and rare family visits from Guatemala. The Canadian Embassy twice granted CARMEN's mother a visitor's visa but has repeatedly denied ELSI the opportunity to see her sister in Canada. For ROBERTO, family connection is maintained more through memory than concrete relations, as communication to his family's remote community is rare:

> No, she [ROBERTO's mother] doesn't want to visit here and she's very sad like she's, she ask ROBERTO why he still stays here and she ask him to go back there because she doesn't like that we spend all our life far away from home. But for us now, like I tell you, for us now with our kids, with our family ... now THIS is our family, we still have family there and we miss a lot our family but we have to do this because we don't want that they, the future, they suffer the same.

Even through all the difficulties of a transnational life of exile, CARMEN remains guardedly optimistic of a future return to a new Guatemala, a Guatemala of opportunity:

> For our kids … if there are any opportunities to come back to Guatemala and live there, there with MY kids. YES I do. Maybe when I get older! [she laughs]

Though grateful for Canadian citizenship and the 'luxury of freedom,' CARMEN's social spaces and personal identity are bound to Guatemala:

> After one year, after one year, we get out Canadian citizenship, Guatemala signed for double citizenship and we have both … Yes, now I am belong to here and there [both laugh]. But your mind is there [she laughs].

Very telling is CARMEN's rapid response to my question, 'How do you see yourself? Like, if somebody said to you in Guatemala, 'Oh, you live in Canada now, you're Canadian.' Would you say yes?':

> No, no. No, I'm Guatemalan [she laughs]. Ya, here ... like we are proud to be in Canada. We are proud to have help from Canada. We are thankful for that. But ... we can't lose ourselves ... we can't change that, we can't change that.

CARMEN then reaches for a copy of her thesis on unions in Guatemala, flips to the front page, and points to her dedication:

> And we dedicate the book to all the workers. And we found a nice poem … this one, it's beautiful … oh we thought it was PERFECT. Ya ya. Oh I LOVE this poem and this is like … this is … it's like you are SEEING me, you know! Because this is the way I feel. I told you before that they can take you away … but you have all the things in your mind and they can't change anything. Like if you feel like you have to do something for the people, you have to do it. And I don't know, I think that God knows why I am here.

****

Gendered Articulations of Rupture and Renewal

As mentioned earlier, I came to understand the spatialization of transnational refugee identities by thinking through the geographical, social, and personal spaces of transnationalism. The historical context and statistical survey of CIC and IRB data of Part II identify a rougher scale of analysis, while the interview transcripts and fieldnotes allow for a finer scale of analysis of the personal and social spaces. The personal expressions of transnationalism tend to focus on voices, echoes, and the reach of memory and on what we can call the 'personal spaces' of exile using the language of difficulty, yearning, isolation, longing, and floating to relate to questions of personal identity and citizenship. The discussion that emerged on the social spaces focused on the struggle of place making in Canada and transnational social relations that connect the 'here and there.' In these conversations, responses dealt with barriers and obstacles to integration, lack of 'community,' ruptures and sutures of social relations, and financial obligations.

Political violence, as action and process, is gendered. This fact, of course, has consequences for who comes to Canada, for what particular reasons, and the potential for return. As noted previously, Guatemalan women and men appear in almost equal numbers in Canada yet women's voices are all too often absent from studies of migration and refugee flight. Therefore, I set out to present a selection of gendered narratives that emerged during our interview conversations. Samuel Dunn's (2000) research with Guatemalan men in Toronto and transformations of their identities and gender relations stands as a critically important counterpart to this exploration of the way that both women and men talk about their experiences. As Wellmeier (1994, 78) suggests in her study of Guatemalan Mayas in Florida, to understand the 'texture of life in exile' researchers must explore the categories that are meaningful to Guatemalan women and men. Though many topics overlapped, women who I spoke with put more emphasis on the myriad barriers to integration (such as limited childcare opportunities, underemployment, and lack of English-language skills), strong sense of social isolation, and limitation of primary relations to their immediate family in Canada and family in Guatemala. Men, on the other hand, tended to stress the limitations of 'ethnic solidarity' and employment contacts, opportunities of learning new skills, and deep ruptures from Guatemala and fear of return.

Sarah Mahler (1998, 83) points to an expanding literature documenting 'how male and female migrants differ with regard to their desires to return home permanently,' which suggests that men wish to return home to recoup higher status while women try to settle family in the new country. In this case study, the reverse is what most applies. Most male refugees indicated an inability to return permanently due to threat of political violence and the possibility that 'they' would be waiting for them. Women, on the other hand, expounded at length on the choice and/or necessity to remain in Canada for the children's sake … safe, secure, *tranquilo*. Most women, though, articulated a desire to return home if possible once children received their education in Canada.

Rupture and Renewal

Social theorist Craig Calhoun (1995, 51) writes:

> If we start from the view that human beings can and indeed very commonly do inhabit multiple and internally differentiated social worlds … then we are led less to consensus as the orientation of communication.

Though identity is a problematic category of analysis, I agree with Richard Wilson (1995a, 260) who suggests that 'identity, more than any other issue, has generated dialogue between foreign and indigenous social commentators' in Guatemala and therefore requires attention. Juanita Sundberg (1999, 120; 2004), too, observes that 'identity is a shifty "social fact" and is not easily pinned down for analysis. Rather it appears to be formed and maintained through interactions with others.' Instead of attempting to specify a new 'Guatemalan-Canadian' identity, then, I shall highlight some of the tensions and inconsistencies that participants live with, create, and fight against in their attempts to live through the transnational rupture.

There can be no definitive benchmark from which to analyze identity transformation. It is an ongoing process rather than a static 'thing' or product. Instead, the participants and I seemed to use a range of events that critically influence identity transformation. For some, the moment of realization that state forces targeted them is a key moment of disengagement from the inclusive 'we' to an 'us and them' dynamic. Others identified the moment of departure, the step across the national border, as the illuminating moment. For others still, it was not until they found themselves requesting political asylum at the border that 'reality' hit and both self- and externally recognized identities changed. Of course, for all, the process of negotiating a sense of self and belonging continues in Canada but each person notes a critical juncture, a dislocation, which marked a point at which a certainty of identity came into question.

Guarnizo and Smith (1998, 20) delineate two strands of contemporary identity research. First, postmodern cultural studies present a free-floating, individual identity developed through self-formation. On the other hand, empirical studies of bi-national migrants situate identity as 'embedded in socially structured and politically mediated processes of group formation and collective action.' I agree with Guarnizo and Smith's assessment that rather than allowing the two visions of identity to drift on their own, that they be brought together to account for the external forces of competing situations, local conditions, media imagery, and immigration discourses which all affect the negotiation of identity. As Calhoun (1995) argues, identity is relational and contingent on changing social spaces. Guarnizo and Smith (1998, 21) contend that 'personal identity formation in transnational social space can best be understood as a dialectic of embedding and disembedding, [as] contextual but not radically discontinuous.'

In many ways, Guatemalan refugees and (im)migrants affected by political violence metaphorically oscillate between the reality of the social spaces of their existence (material circumstances and concrete social relationships) and reconfigurations of personal identity in a space that we might call personal or psychic space. The most personal, dream-like 'space' (Appadurai 1991) allows internal re-workings, re-inventions, re-creations of a sense of self, all the while the 'external self' (that identity recognized by others) moves along a continuum of known or recognized identities. It is in this personal or psychic space that individuals come to grips with the most damaging, deeply felt aspects of political violence and the ensuing ruptures that throw into question all sense of identity and belonging as one moves into and out of dislocation, within and between national territories and personal senses of citizenship and belonging.

There appears to be a discernible development of what Doreen Massey (1994) identifies as a progressive sense of place that recognizes identity in relation to other places, other layers, other aspects of identities. A progressive sense of identity understands the relationship between place and identity to be what Don Mitchell (2000, 272) refers to as a 'web of interconnections' with other places and other identities. Mitchell (2000, 276) persuasively argues that new identities have always been 'forged out of violent processes by which a truly global market or network was constructed.' In exploring identity transformation, then, we are not beginning with some sort of true essence that is radically altered by displacement but rather an understanding that, as Taussig (1993) puts it, identity is a constant interplay and process of construction and decomposition.

We all deal with our own hybridity, whether we acknowledge it or not. Rupture and deliberate renewal characterize hybridity of the displaced, while a more unconscious renewal accompanies stable, more secure life stages. Identity is more than merely externally determined change, Calhoun (1995, 222) argues, but individuals challenged by internal tensions and inconsistencies, 'can seek to transform [themselves].' The relationship between place and identity transformation can be thrown into conflict, butting heads and causing sparks, such as when CARLOS discusses his hatred of the English language and denial of the reconstruction process offered by refuge in Canada.[3] Even though CARLOS acknowledges that Guatemala is a 'country of damage,' he thinks that language and age work against him in Canada. 'Canada is wrong for me,' he says, 'it is not the experience of the flesh … I feel out of my reality. I hate the English language, I hate using this language.' In many ways, CARLOS feels his relatively comfortable life in Canada is a betrayal of FAR's fight against 'imperialist gringo' intervention in Guatemala. A limbo existence, then, of neither here nor there is proving too much for CARLOS, as daily he contemplates a return to uncertainty in Guatemala. Safety and security have come at the expense of 'truly living' on the path to the 'new Guatemala' envisioned in his FAR days. The various levels or layers of identity can rebut, grate, slide, mesh, or overtake each other in the process of recomposition.

On the other hand, the relationships between place and identity transformation can also mesh and allow for place to imbricate one's sense of personal identity in new and exciting ways. Despite her arrival to Canada as a refugee, JUANA deliberately shed the label 'refugee' and rather sees her identity is a blending or merging of positive attributes:

> I don't know, I don't like that word … when you said, 'refugee,' the first thing, probably not to you, but the first thing that comes to mind is like the people from AFRICA, you know, they are like suffering and they're dying and they're running away or something like that. So, that's why it's like uh … a SAD word, you know, for a person that … that's really in BIG trouble and physically and mentally.
>
> [My identity] it's a mix. DEFINITELY no doubt about it. Ya, because right here I have Canadian friends. I go to school with Canadians and I'm not too like them. You know, I'm different. But when I'm there [Guatemala], I see that I'm not the same person. Like

---

3 CARLOS, a FAR operant and political science instructor at USAC, traveled extensively in Europe, Honduras, and Mexico as a FAR operant in the 1960s but returned to Guatemala in 1971 only to be kidnapped on 20 October 1971 and re-appear on 2 December 1971. As a university-backed FAR supporter, CARLOS then traveled to El Salvador, Spain, and France until his much-feared second return in 1974 when he began to feel like a refugee within his own country. He recounts how on Sixth Avenue in downtown Guatemala City he felt everyone looking at him, touching him, but managed to carry on and start teaching as a political science professor at USAC. He reflects on a quiet life in the early 1980s when he never looked for friends and always felt eyes on him. But after a kidnap attempt at his home in 1987, when he managed to wrestle the gun away from one of his assailants, he and his family escaped to the north of Mexico where they started a small business. 'Mexico was ready to explode,' he remembers of the early 1990s, and so he successfully petitioned the UNHCR in Mexico City for acceptance as a Convention Refugee. Third country resettlement options of France, Australia, and Canada were offered to CARLOS, his wife, and two children. The family arrived as landed immigrants to Canada where CARLOS's sister-in-law arrived one year earlier.

you know, I've changed a little bit. It's because I've got the Canadian culture a little bit in me. So, I'm a mix [she laughs]. DEFINITELY no doubt … If I'm here, I will say I'm from Guatemala. If I'm in Guatemala, I will say I'm from Canada! [she laughs] … I guess I'm trying to get the best out of both worlds. So, I'm half and half [laughs again] … It's like you take people, the person, out of the country but you cannot take the country out of the person.

Ethnicity and Identity

Much of the work on identity in the Guatemalan context focuses on indigenous identity transformation and, as Grandin (2000, 222) states, ways in which the 'state's counterinsurgency was experienced in racial terms.' Though, until recently, Canadian census categories do not allow for an ethnic breakdown of Guatemalans in Canada (indigenous or Ladino) but, given the findings in Chapter Four and recent census data, we can safely reckon that the majority are Ladinos. Among my long-term participants, only two of 19 in Canada identified themselves as indigenous. In terms of questions of ethnicity, most Ladino participants in Guatemala and Canada found it particularly difficult to articulate their sense of ethnic identity. ANA's response is typical of most responses I encountered:

IIIII [drawn out] don't know ... but my family from my mother's side, I think they are, you know, my grandma she's, her father is from I don't know ... you know, the Spain people ... *mestizos*, like maybe, how you can say that … I think maybe *mestizos* ... or Ladinos. I don't know.

[Question: So neither word you really use very much, no?]

I know the Indian people, you can tell the Indian people SOOO well, you know. You see the face or the way they talk and you know they are Indians. But when somebody, like me, I don't think I'm Indian [little laugh]. I don't know, I say I'm not, but you never know [laughs].

JUANA expresses the same tentativeness of ethnic identity:

Ya most of the people, we are mixed. Okay there is, for me, there is only two groups: the Mayans and the *mestizos*, mixed ones, so I will say we're mixed, we're not pure Mayan. And pure Mayans are the ones all dressed up in their costumes, they have their rituals, so I would say mixed. But more, I don't know, I don't know… I think most of the people [in Canada] are…. We're *mestizos* because we're not 100% Mayan and not 100% White, we're *mestizos*.

PEDRO's brothers BRUCE and JOHN retain competing expressions of ethnic identity:

BRUCE: Spanish. And now in terms of culture we are *campesinos* [rural peasants]. We are poor *campesinos* because the land does not respond.

> JOHN: We're like, Ladinos. Better we say Ladinos. We have blood of the natives but we don't want to admit that we are Indians but that we are only Spaniards.

ELSI in VISTA HERMOSA articulates the primacy of national identity over ethnic identity that is more commonly heard among Guatemalans in Canada:

> Ladinos [but] we are *Guatemaltecos* [Guatemalans] … yes, first and before everything, right? From the beginning … all are of the same nationality with the same rights, with the same identity even though different groups … but all belong to the same nation … we are equal … We can say that even though we are a Ladino group, we all came from or rather, *pues*, we can't say that we are of pure blood.

For example, through the establishment of a 'Guatemalan folkloric group,' Ladino refugees and (im)migrants in GLENWOOD, HOPE, and SUMMERLAND are refashioning indigenous songs, dances, and clothing as 'traditionally Guatemalan' for consumption by Canadians and ethnocultural funding bodies. Additionally, the progressive Ladino participants are identifying with a proud indigenous past and distancing themselves from the repressive elements of their home country and those connected with the government and military forces now in Canada. Everyone tells me that CARMEN is the driving force behind the 'Guatemalan folkloric group.' She laughs when I point out the 'ethnicity twist' that sees Ladinos wearing the traditional clothes of Mayas and performing indigenous dances for multicultural presentations in the region. 'Yes, it's a little strange, isn't it?! But, I have always felt close to the indigenous people of Guatemala.' When we discuss this situation with CARMEN's sister, ELSI, in Guatemala, she agrees that traditions are '*bien importante'* for the whole family, and CARMEN in particular

Citizenship and Identity

Those interested in the examination of identities have been led, Calhoun (1995, 218) argues, by our theories often to 'underestimate the struggle involved in forging identities.' Calhoun goes on to assert the need to recognize 'tensions inherent in the fact that we all have multiple, incomplete, and/or fragmented identities … and the possibilities for our salient constructions of identities to change in the context of powerfully meaningful, emotionally significant events….' It therefore makes sense to understand the struggle over self-identification for participants as somehow a merging of a once taken-for-granted sense of 'Guatemalan' identity with a new, place-based, acquired identity as 'Canadian,' 'refugee,' 'immigrant,' and so forth. Such an orientation suggests that we must recognize an identity continuum where people fluctuate given place and positionality, between 'Guatemalanness' and 'Canadianness' (whatever those two terms mean to each individual), between inclusion and exclusion, remaining and returning, rupture and suture. It also is a powerful statement of self-realization to resist those acquired classifications (or external recognitions) to answer, 'Guatemalan,' to my question of self-identification.

This identifier – 'Guatemalan' – is itself, however, not without contestations, and in reality the question of who can be Guatemalan underpins much of the irrationality that drives state violence.

It is not so much that a core identity is ruptured, as it is always shifting anyway, but that displacement stresses decomposition over construction. There is no template of identity transformation and therefore each person follows his or her own schedule. For example, when we talk about identity and citizenship there seems to be a continuum between Guatemalanness and Canadianness that shifts over time and depends on who is asking the question. For example, ANA, GLORIA, ALBA LUZ, CARMEN, LILLIAN, JUAN, and FRANCISCO, all see themselves differently – at different points on the continuum – though all have dual citizenship or landed immigrant status.

ANA states: 'I feel Guatemalan. But I'm a Canadian now. But my traditions are from Guatemala.' GLORIA, on the other hand, prefers not to talk about her life before Canada. Unfortunately, silence and denial of her Guatemalan past encourages GLORIA to state firmly that she is 'Canadian. Not Guatemalan Canadian. Not Guatemalan. Canadian.'[4] Identity and identification are rarely, if ever, straightforward concepts and processes. ALBA LUZ, for instance, imagines her apartment in HOPE 'real Guatemala' while 'Canada is outside,' beyond the living room window. She explains:

> One feels like part of the culture or one feels like one ... not specifically a Canadian, but one feels more part of Canada … that you are in the country and you follow routines of the country and do the things that they do here. Or you still feel 100% Guatemalan [we all laugh] … I would feel better in English and in everything. I would feel better but ... beans are always on my mind [she laughs] … on the tortillas ... on the beans … on the bananas. Ya, Cati, I feel that I am here without being really here.

ALBA LUZ's mind is Guatemalan while her body is Canadian – cleaning hotel rooms, carrying out the routines of daily life, struggling through the Canadian legal system. LILLIAN, though, reflects on how life in exile encourages her to 'feel more Guatemalan now,' rather than Canadian and reaffirm her Guatemalanness to those she encounters in Canada. 'A more global viewpoint' is the benefit of four years in Canada but a sense of Canadianness remains illusive for LILLIAN.

Thirty-three year old FRANCISCO's 'long, frightening, and exhausting' 1992 journey to Canada led to feelings of being 'rejected and defensive' since his 'university education was not valued' and farm work and office cleaning were the only employment options available. After six years in THOMASBURG, though, FRANCISCO now 'feels Canadian' as he 'did not like the first Guatemalans' he met in Canada nor encounter 'spaces of friendship' in a 'Guatemalan community.' For FRANCISCO there is a duality between his communal, 'selfless' identity as a

4 GLORIA chose not to participate in this study beyond our initial meeting because dwelling on her Guatemalan past, she states, is unhealthy and counterproductive to her personal transformation in Canada.

Guatemalan and individual, 'selfish' Canadian identity particularly exacerbated because his small family did not know of his need to flee.

JUAN's identity shifts depending on his positionality, geographical location, and those with whom he interacts:

> Part of me is Guatemalan … well, a lot of me [he laughs] I was BORN there! But as far as how I feel? There was a time maybe that I, that I … this is what I want to be, you know. But I think that I have changed in the last 10 years, maybe five…. I'm not promoting Canada when I'm there! [in Guatemala] [he laughs] If I'm in Guatemala, I'm Guatemalan…. We as immigrants have the option of becoming part of the country or just becoming … not being part of the country but just being there. And it seems to me, like United States, you go you work and you send money. Canada you come you assimilate to the society and become part of Canada and THEN if you get a chance you send money. So it is … the difference is that I'm here in Canada and going to get an apartment, pay my rent, and have … to adapt to this society I have to have certain things which in the United States, I don't need that. [In the United States] I can live with 20 other people in a one-bedroom apartment and save my money and send it back…. I mean I'm going to come to the country and make it my home. I'm going to invest in the country. At the same time, I won't forget my family. I'm not saying that I'm going to forget entirely about them but I'm going to let them know that now I'm part Canadian. And that I have dreams.

Summing Up

Through the three transnational ethnographies and the multiple voices threaded into this chapter, I have considered how Guatemalan women and men in Canada define themselves after forced migration and, as Watts (1992a, 123) puts it, how 'identities are cobbled together to act in new spaces.' Political violence often is infused in refugee identities, affecting a differentiated sense of refugee transnationalism. The spatializing of refugee transnationalism is influenced by the ruptures and sutures of identity, the Guatemalan and Canadian national contexts of displacement and refuge, and the power of internal differentiation among Guatemalans. Transnationalized identities are complex and are best addressed through the individual realities articulated by Guatemalan refugees and (im)migrants in Canada and by their families in Guatemala, as they are forged through primary social relations and active contacts in both Canada and Guatemala. To the social spaces of refugee transnationalism we now turn our attention.

Chapter 6

Social Spaces and Immobility of Refugee Transnationalism

Both REMHI (1998) and CEH (1999a) confirm a deliberate strategy on the part of the Guatemalan military to destroy 'communities of association' such as unions and student organizations, and to dismember physical communities, such as towns and villages. Political violence was aimed at destroying any notion of community, either as a physical entity, the very fabric out of which Mayas construct their relations with each other, or as 'communities' of association. A close reading of the transnational ethnographies and the voices of other participants reveals the ways in which political violence, refugee exodus, and immigration policies engender a shift in primary social relations from face-to-face experiences of proximity that are associated with 'communities' to those that stretch across borders. 'Weak ties,' (Carrasco et al. 1999; Rose et al. 1998) on the other hand, play a prominent role in the face-to-face experiences confronted in new refugee spaces in Canada.

In this chapter, I set out to elucidate the contours of new social spaces forged by Guatemalan refugees and (im)migrants in southwestern Ontario, spaces characterized by the maintenance and establishment of primary social relations within and across multiple scales. In order to explore these new social spaces, an analysis is necessary of the ruptures of departure, 'suspended spaces' of unknowing, contradictory spaces of exile, and categories of arrival.

Some parallels exist between Guatemalan transnationalism in the Canadian and American contexts, particularly regarding the role of state violence in initiating forced migration and refugee flight as identified by Popkin (1999), Prensa Libre (2000), Stoltz Chinchilla and Hamilton (1999), and Hamilton and Stoltz Chinchilla (2001). On the other hand, particularities of the Guatemalan Canadian population urge a new reading of Guatemalan transnationalism. Single generation refugee flight, as individuals or family units, encompasses much of contemporary Guatemalan migration to Canada rather than multi-generational labour migration that grew out of the original refugee experience to the USA as documented by Burns (1993), Fink (2003), Foxen (2002), Hagan (1994), Hamilton and Stoltz Chinchilla (2001), Loucky and Moors (2000), Moran-Taylor (2004), and Rodman (2002), or the collective experiences of Mexican refuge revealed in the work of Montejo (1999a, 1999b), Nolin Hanlon (1999), and Nolin Hanlon and Lovell (1997; 2000). Rather than employing a 'transnational communities' approach, advocated by Portes (1996a) and Portes et al. (1999a, 1999b) among others, though, the experiences of Guatemalans in Canada require an exploration of the politics and possibilities of multi-scaled social spaces as the primary means of coping in exile.

Transnationalism is a complex process that involves, as Guarnizo and Smith (1998, 29) argue, macro- and micro-dynamics. The macro-dynamics of the Guatemala-Canada connection are dealt with in Chapter 4 through an examination of the influence of immigration policy. In this chapter, I propose to explore the micro-dynamics of transnationalism by examining the destruction, alteration, and creation of social fields of relations within the social spaces of refuge and migration.

But what is transnational social space? According to Nyberg Sørenson (1998, 244) it is a 'metaphor for the lived experiences' of migrants, in her case, Dominican migrants. Transnational social space bears the potential for bringing experiences from different times and different locations into 'one single field of analysis.' As Bondi (1993, 99) argues, 'geographical metaphors, though, must be informed by conceptions of space that recognize place, position, location, and so on as created, as produced.' Transnational social spaces, therefore, are the spaces of social relations created and produced by refugees and (im)migrants that join together particular places in two or more countries. 'Transnational social space,' then, is more than a metaphor for lived experience, as it is comprised of 'primary social relations' forged and maintained across multiple scales and 'weak ties' present in the lived experiences in exile or migration.

Drawing on interview conversations and my fieldnotes, I am interested in how Guatemalan women and men work to transform and create social relations, given the ruptures of 'community' and 'concrete social relations' (Calhoun 1992) induced by political violence. We occupy, create, influence and interact with any number of social spaces in a given day, week, year, or lifetime. In this chapter, I focus on a few distinct 'social spaces' that emerge as particularly relevant for the people with whom I spoke. They include border, suspended, and paradoxical spaces. Of course, the social spaces might have been defined differently if I had spoken with the 'gate keepers' (border officials, Embassy staff, military commissioners, and so forth) rather than Guatemalans themselves. But my goal is to begin to understand the ways in which political violence becomes deeply imbedded in and ruptures 'community' relations, and the ways that people continue to rely upon primary social relations stretching across borders when face-to-face 'community' connections are untenable.

Transnationalism and Social Space

Transnationalism explores the dynamic interactions between home and adopted countries, and reveals the social, economic, political, and cultural fields that span borders and boundaries. Transmigrants, the term of choice of Glick Schiller et al. (1992a) are described as social actors who, while clearly influenced and constrained by political and economic hegemonies of both countries, are actively involved in developing and maintaining multiple, layered, fluid identities and relations – familial, cultural, economic, religious, organizational, and political – that span the borders of several societies (Basch et al. 1994). A transnational conceptual framework seeks 'to examine relations between displacement and ethnic identity' (Basch et al. 1994, 106) and must be situated economically and politically within the changing global capitalist system and arenas of political conflict, best attempted in a historically and politically informed ethnographic context.

Peggy Levitt (2001b, 197), also, argues that individual migrants cannot be understood in isolation from transnational social fields.

> The transnational social fields that migration engenders encompasses all aspects of social life. Though they may arise at first in response to the economic relations between migrants and non-migrants, social, religious, and political connections also emerge which constitute and are constituted by these arenas. The more diverse and thick a transnational social field is, the greater the number of ways it offers migrants to remain active in their homelands.

Therefore, transnational refugee displacement and (im)migrant movement must be understood as situated within the forces of globalization and what Castles and Miller (1993) denote as our 'age of migration.'

One definition of globalization refers to the processes through which the world has become ever more closely and intensely interconnected (Kearney 1995). Many researchers of the myriad phenomena of globalization indicate that the paradox of this age of interconnectedness is the revival of nationalist sentiments, heightened nation-building processes, and the establishment of new statehoods (Hobsbawm 1990). Clearly, the land of this earth is generally divided into national territories, those multi-coloured shadings on the world map, each of which attempts to represent a culture 'placed' within that national territory. In this world of national spaces, where space has been conceived as partitioned and discontinuous, we have tended to naturalize this connection in such a way that the 'people and place are permanently territorialized and rooted' (Malkki 1990).

Social, economic, and political activities that take place within nations are becoming 'stretched' across the globe such that activities, events, and decisions in one part of the world can have immediate significance for individuals and communities in geographically distant parts of the world (Featherstone 1995). Along with this spatial interconnection, Pierson (1996, 170) identifies a 'deepening' and intensification of interaction across borders and a penetration of global processes into local communities. Some would identify this as a shift from the centre to the periphery (Appadurai 1990, 1996; Balibar and Wallerstein 1991), though more current theoretical discussion of globalization implies a decay of this distinction (Kearney 1995; Power 2003; Wellmeier 1995). New forms of capital accumulation and quickening mobility of ideas, communications, and goods, are seen to be tearing apart any sense of tightly bounded spaces (Rouse 1995b).

Refugees, (im)migrants, exiles, and other transnationals are living lives that 'challenge bounded categories in a world that is still built on nation-states and "race" placing' (Basch et al. 1994, 268). Precisely because these spatial-cultural habits have seemed so natural and permanent, Lavie and Swedenburg (1996, 3) argue that 'recent changes in the cultural organization of space [have] caused rather severe surprise and shock among those accustomed to thinking according to such dualities.' Globalization and the reconstruction of meanings of places are happening within a world that is already unevenly developed, both socially and geographically. Consequently, the mass movement of world populations has enormous local implications.

From Community to Transnational Social Relations

In contrast to most of the literature on Guatemalan (im)migrants and refugees in Mexican and American contexts, which focuses on the collective orientation of return negotiations and transnational community connections, respectively, this project employs a transnational refugee approach that focuses on the individual as an active agent in multi-scaled social relations. Generally, as Black and Koser (1999) note, there has been little research on the relationship between refugees and their countries of origin, though recent work on diasporas addresses how collective communities in exile maintain links with home countries.

I situate my examination within the transnational literature on communities, social fields, and identities (see Chapter 2) rather than within the literature of network analysis. Only recently has network analysis recognized that the 'material and physical conditions in the receiving context foster or hinder immigrant networks' (Menjívar 1997a, 2) and the dynamics of kinship-based social relationships. A transnational framework instead urges researchers to deal with the material and physical conditions of both sending and receiving contexts in our conceptualizations of cultural, social, and personal transformation.

The kinds of social life people create in a transnational context have received growing attention in recent years, with studies of diasporas, borders, and other de-territorialized settings in which people practice culture. Many researchers interested in transnational practices and processes talk about 'new social spaces' that are said to be created by migration processes whereby (im)migrants cultivate social networks that span political and geographic borders.[1] As Sarah Mahler (1998) indicates, though, there is little agreement on the nature of these social spaces. Do we mean transnational community organization and association (Popkin 1999; Chinchilla, Hamilton, and Loucky 1993), 'communities' (Loucky 1996; Portes 1996a), labour networks (Kohpahl 1995), circuits (Rouse 1991), or social fields (Mahler 1998)?

As noted in Chapter 3, the growing literature on the Guatemalan population beyond the national borders is restricted to Mexican and American locations where often Guatemalans function collectively in places of new settlement. Attention is directed to community-to-community links, chain labour migration, remittance sending behaviour, and emerging social and economic impacts of home community associations in exile (IOM 2004; Popkin 2003). The 'community' focus of much recent research is consistent with the ways in which Guatemalan migration to Mexico

1 For recent work in the Americas context, see Portes, Guarnizo, and Landolt (1999a, 1999b), Bailey (2001), Bailey et al. (2002), Hiebert and Ley (2003), among others. Crush and McDonald (2000) bring attention to southern African transmigration.

and the United States operates and the ways in which (im)migrants understand their experience.

Different realities are evident, however, in the Canadian context. Single generation refugee flight, as individuals or family units, encompasses much of contemporary Guatemalan migration to Canada rather than multi-generational labour migration that grew out of the original refugee experience to the United States. Though Vancouver, Toronto, and Montréal serve as primary destinations for Guatemalans, as with most refugee and (im)migrant populations in Canada, thousands live scattered across the country in small- and mid-sized towns and cities. In response to the varying reasons for departure from Guatemala and the resulting dynamic population geography evident in Canada, it is imperative to shift attention from a bounded sense of community (as face-to-face association) to transnational social relations.

Hannerz (1996, 92) reminds us that communities used to be thought of as (and for some still are) 'small, tangible, face-to-face entities unproblematically situated in space.' Forced and voluntary migration urges researchers to imagine communities as something else, as social spaces composed of relationships spanning borders. 'What is personal, primary, small-scale,' Hannerz (1996, 98) argues, 'is not necessarily narrowly confined in space, and what spans continents need to be large-scale in any other way.' Wellman (1996) suggests, though, that if the unit of analysis in research becomes 'active contacts' – co-workers and physically close neighbours, rather than primary relations – then many 'ties' are local. Menjívar (1997a, 1997b; 2000) reminds us, furthermore, that network analysts often examine immigrant 'ties' to explain how local relations are not necessarily the most important, as physical proximity does not mean strong social support or primary social relationships. Wellman's 'active contacts' can be composed entirely of thin associations rather than deep relationships maintained across multiple scales. To thin relations and weak ties I will return near the end of this chapter.

New social spaces do not necessarily refer to geographically defined spaces contained by thin political borders, but spaces defined by social relations that, through their particularities, are geographically located. Gupta and Ferguson's (1997b) influence is also evident in my endeavours through their focus on the social and political processes of place making. I did not focus on a discrete 'Guatemalan community' in Canada nor identify transnational Guatemalan communities as evident in Canada. Rather, I stress the social fields of relations forged by women and men in one region of Canada that extend to people in close-by towns and to their families in Guatemala. Hannerz (1996, 95) suggests that Calhoun's (1992) focus on 'concrete social relationships' and delineation of four categories of social relationships – primary, secondary, tertiary, and quaternary, that move from physical co-presence to surveillance-type interactions – are instructive to this conceptualization. Calhoun's notion of 'concrete social relationships,' can be extended beyond their original intention to apply to primary relations that do not require physical co-presence but social action across borders.

When the above concepts are grounded in social reality, it becomes clear that refugees and (im)migrants are entirely 'bound' by the political, social, and national contexts of both (if not more) countries even if they are able to cross borders with ease. Guarnizo and Smith (1998, 13) also urge a social grounding of transnational studies. They write:

> Specific kinds of migrants [and refugees] and specific local and national contexts abroad shapes not only the likelihood of generating, maintaining or forsaking transnational ties, but also the very nature of the ties that migrants can forge with their place of origin.

In our interview conversations, we focused on the extraordinary events of political violence, flight, exile, and return that serve as benchmarks in the lives of many Guatemalans in southwestern Ontario. By examining these events, the discourse of rupture, connections, isolation, and continually feeling 'out-of-place' is given priority and the impact on families physically separated is dealt with. Rather than a concern for discussions of the everyday activities that shape adaptation and adjustment to 'Canadian life,' we focused on the challenges of maintaining and forging primary social relations in a transnational context as well as the presence of 'weaker ties' that constitute everyday social relations in Canada. While some migrants and other transnationals are able to communicate with family through video, fax, phone, email, and transportation, others, such as the Guatemalans I spoke with, often are caught up in local space by the lingering fear of reconnection, relative poverty, and what Mitchell (2000, 278) identifies as 'increasingly unjust reconfigurations of space, radical geographies of cleavage, and social unevenness.'

Politics of Multi-Scaled Social Space

Henri Lefebvre (1991, 110) writes:

> Every social space is the outcome of a process with many aspects and many contributing currents, signifying and non-signifying, perceived and directly experienced, practical and theoretical. In short, every social space has a history.

How do we understand the contributing currents – the contradictions and antagonisms – that constitute social space? Geographical scale, Neil Smith (1992) argues, is the central concept to a spatialized social theory. Straightforward sequential narratives are unhelpful, then, when working through the spatializing of transnational relations. Instead, N. Smith (1992, 60) invokes John Berger to stress the necessity of wrestling with the 'simultaneity and extensions of events and possibilities' that influence transnational existence. Levitt and Glick Schiller (2004) also see that, in such a way, multiple contexts and times – simultaneous, overlapping, and contingent – are brought into a single field of analysis of transnational social spaces and identities. Pile and Keith's (1997, 27) urging to examine key sites in the 'political landscape of lived space' is, therefore, applicable to my concern with the spatialities of refugee transnationalism as participants are embedded in and create social relations of obligation, allegiance, opportunity, and so forth.

Refugee narratives from Canada and Guatemala inform the discussion of multi-scaled social space. Rose's (1997) notions of paradoxical space in addition to Laurie's (1997) contradictory space offer the conceptual tools with which to deal with the spatializing of transnational relations affected by political violence. Laurie's (1997, 239) contradictory space is incorporated to move beyond a focus on the dualism of here and there to 'third space', or places 'beyond the grounds of dissimilarity' that allow for an examination of ruptures and connections. Laurie (1997, 239) explains that Rose's (1993) paradoxical space highlights the 'importance of contingent relationships in allowing "simultaneous occupation" to occur.' First we begin with the dismantling of community and straightforward connections before examining the ways in which new transnational relations stitch together ruptured lives and new social relations. The barriers and opportunities of the paradoxical spaces of refuge in Canada are examined to see how freedom without power and freedom as power function together to shape transnational social relations.

Dismembering and Disintegrating 'Communities' and Connections

Critical to an understanding of the shattering of 'community' in Guatemala is a 'radical undermining of certainty' (Rose 1997, 202) through the manipulation of space by state forces, of the sense of belonging, and constructive engagement with fellow citizens and the state. Paradoxical and contradictory spaces are created as terror operationalizes, Aron (1989) notes, to turn worlds 'upside down, where things become their opposites.' Neighbours and friends become the killers of your father or mother, the military talks of being your protector, and sacred places become massacre sites. The particular cruelty of the Guatemalan military is demonstrated by their ability to perpetuate terror by drawing in the whole of society as accomplices in the manipulation of space and social relations. Through the military installation of civil patrols across the country terror was perpetuated in some way by every family in every village, the result of which has been psychologically shattering (Manz 2004; Warren 1993; Zur 1994). Civil patrols were, in the words of the CEH (1999b, Item 50), 'used by the State to cause social disintegration.'

Paradoxes emerged in the interview conversations, similar to Feitlowitz's (1998, 151) findings in Argentina, when people initially deny knowledge of violence but in the next breathe share their experiences or thoughts on particular events. Terror that accompanies political violence thrives on the many lies, denials, silences, and half-truths that survivors and willing participants learn to perpetuate for their own survival and that of dependents. When we asked families in Guatemala about the past and present local situations, the usual first response from almost everyone was, '*tranquilo*,' as if the violence passed them by, as if they did not witness what they saw or acknowledge the direct impact of violence. Further questioning usually encouraged responses that shifted from denial of insecurity to descriptions of some violent act they witnessed.

For example, while in LA HAVANA with PEDRO's brothers, BRUCE and JOHN, and sister-in-law, SUZIE, we asked about the *aldea's* experience during the violence.

Everyone's first response was that all was tranquil and quiet. But over the course of the day, BRUCE and JOHN point to the spot on the patio, 'right there,' and recounted how SUZIE's father was shot by 'bad men' about seven or eight years ago, just across from where we were sitting. She later confided to us that her brother, who lived next door, stopped her from going out. It was good, she said, because 'who knows what they would have done to me.' Shortly after, while SUZIE rode the local bus with her uncle, she witnessed his murder at the hands of masked men who hauled him off the bus and shot him on the side of the road. 'Over there,' JOHN directs our eyes to the nearby tree where another man was hung for all to see. And the cane fields that line the one road joining the *aldea* to the closest town are associated with sexual violence, murder, and dumping of bodies:

> They took the teacher off her motorbike and put her in the cane field, left her on foot, and hit her. Another teacher here, [name], they also took her off her motorbike and put her in the cane field and everything. The *señora*, [name], that they also killed there – drowning.

Now in HOPE, Ontario, JUAN's initial reaction is to deny knowledge of political violence.

> I'm not … politics were nothing … wasn't something that we discussed in my family. I don't think we were on either side … we didn't know what was happening. Myself, I don't know what was happening until I came here.

A few moments later, however, he describes its personal impact:

> … and you can't help to see all the things that happened at the time. I was 15, 16 … you're at a party and you can see … because you were a target in a way. And that's one of the reasons I guess sometimes guys move. … Ya, you might be called upon to fight your own people.

CARMEN's sister ELSI in VISTA HERMOSA, Guatemala first suggests no family difficulty and moments later mentions, in rather coded terms, her *compañero's* brutal murder before the birth of their now 18 year-old child:

> But before we talk about the question of problems, this of the internal mess that there was, more or less some 30 years previously, perhaps. Or rather it was long but we didn't live it here in the urban area. But the people who were very compromised possibly had more information … that is to say many people, because I know of many people from here, from VISTA HERMOSA who had many problems … but with this family, *pues*, I want to tell you that there was nothing. Right?

> So sometimes you lose heart a little but because, *pues*, it doesn't matter that one says "I am not afraid of anything, I am not afraid, I don't have [a reason] to be afraid, right? Because I have not done anything, I am not doing anything, bad, right?" So but already having passed through this alive I tell you that when the blows are like this, so close to the family and all, *pues*, you have reason to feel the fear because I felt it in my own flesh, no?

Denial of family participation in opposition activity is evident with the families of student activists who often came from middle-class and professional families. LILLIAN and CONCHA relate how their parents in Guatemala often denied knowledge of their problematic activities and forced departure from Guatemala – perhaps as a survival strategy or perhaps out of regret. LILLIAN was raised in the capital and brought her talents as a dentist to the PGT after she returned 'shocked' from a month-long rural excursion. LILLIAN wanted to finish her dentistry program at the same time she worked with the PGT so as not to hurt her family. But her involvement with the guerrilla organization required drastically changed behaviour, to operate out of safe houses in the capital, and to maintain multiple identities. Using false names and constantly lying to her family led to 'silent suffering' and the need to flee to Mexico without telling her family. LILLIAN suggests that 'families feel *vergüenza* [shame] and fear about their children's clandestine activities.' 'Oh, she's on a scholarship to Spain' became her family's concocted story when asked of LILLIAN's whereabouts.

While visiting ISAIAH's mother (LILLIAN's mother-in-law) and extended family in GUADALUPE, San Marcos, we asked if ISAIAH left Guatemala for Mexico in 1982 because of the violence. ISAIAH's mother, MIRANDA, said, 'No, he had a *beca* [scholarship] to attend UNAM in Mexico City,' to study civil engineering before moving to Canada four years ago, 'where he had a *beca* to go as well.' Even all these years later the lies that families live by continue to strain social relations and bolster ruptures over connections.

Within Guatemala, new face-to-face communities are thrown together out of the shattered pieces of longer-term 'local communities' (Wilson 1995a). Others are transformed by the coming together of new ties of association developed during the refugee experience in Mexico (Stepputat 1994a, 1994b) or through the newer wave of evangelism (Garrard Burnett 1998). Linda Green (1999, 9), among others, charges that the devastation of communities – people and places – was massive and 'went far beyond physical destruction and murder.' Green (1999, 7) documents the ways in which political violence is imbedded in the daily lives of survivors in Guatemala, but she stresses the need not only to examine alienation and violence but also the possibilities for creativity and collective dignity. Green explores how violence marked the lives of Guatemalan widows on a daily basis and examines the creative ways in which some of the widows construct 'alternative forms of community' in the midst of their suffering and survival.

Terror and political violence cannot be downplayed, therefore, as the repercussions continue to be felt by Guatemalans both within and outside its national borders. It is a 'country of damage,' CARLOS says of Guatemala. It is a 'country of *masoquistas* always needing an oppressor,' charges LILLIAN. CONCHA relates the country's violent tendencies to the words of poet, Otto René Castillo, who describes Guatemala as 'a good mother with bad children.' Political violence functions on fear, suspicion, and silence that work to entrench political divisions within the country and reproduce them in exile. Those in Canadian exile have the dual challenge of maintaining social relations to Guatemala with little possibility of communication and forging new social relations through 'weak ties' in Canada (Carrasco et al. 1999; Rose et al. 1998). That challenge seems to be the crux of transnational refugee social space, the forging and re-forging of social relations and identities within and across borders rather than the development of new 'communities of association.'

Creating New Spaces of Primary Social Relations and Weak Ties

Transnational social relations that create and produce social spaces operate at, and across, multiple scales and become key to our analysis. I identify, therefore, not so much a 'politics of locality' as a 'politics of multi-scaled social space,' in the parlance of Soja (1998). We all live in multi-level scales, not just nations, and so we must examine the various scales at which de- and re-territorializations take place. An entire range of social relations is 'stretched out' over space, between Guatemala and Canada (and often Mexico and the United States), between families here and there, between asylum seekers and those from whom they fled (usually the police or military forces), and so forth. Forced migration and refugee movement, according to Hannerz (1996, 98) work to 'extend the reach of direct relationships' through transnational social space, a concept that must be seen as a workable rather than a contradictory one.

Hannerz's (1996) examination of global 'transnational connections' leads him to ask: Is the global always shallow and the local necessarily deep? Can there be depth to transnational social fields and shallowness to local, face-to-face connections? Such questions for me lie at the heart of transnational studies. Many transnational studies examine how transnationalization is enacted in everyday life, in decision-making, in local events and activities, and ways of seeing, enacted through 'community' (Mountz and Wright 1996). But Guatemalans in southwestern Ontario refer not to 'community' but to practices and processes at the scales of the home and individual – scales at which feminist and critical geographers such as Longhurst (2004), McDowell (1999), and Valentine (2001) are situating their work.

In support of his call for a politics of scale, N. Smith (1992, 76) refers to Harvey's (1973) statement that 'while the rich express their freedom in their ability to overcome space, the poor are imprisoned by it.' In the Guatemalan context, it is clear that the social fabric was torn apart both for peasants and urban social activists, but that ethnicity and class, particularly, differentiated the timing and type of atrocities (as noted in Chapter Three), as well as the geography of displacement. The majority of the refugee population – poor, rural indigenous peoples – relied on their own feet to find a place of refuge. Peasants, mostly indigenous peoples, sought refuge in the mountains of Guatemala (Falla 1994), refugee camps (Montejo 1999a, 1999b; Nolin Hanlon 1999; Nolin Hanlon and Lovell 1997; 2000), rural settlements in southern Mexico (North and Simmons 1999), or worked their way through the dangerous passage landscapes to an 'illegal' existence in the United States (Loucky and Moors 2000). Considerably fewer managed to escape to Canada due to restrictions in the Canadian immigration selection process and lack of resources to finance an escape route on their own.

Of course, some of the participants, such as PEDRO and ANA, did find their ways to Canada by their own means. ANA, a 36 year-old woman in WINTERBURN, describes her harrowing journey from Guatemala and the final stretch to the Canadian border at BEVERLY, Ontario:

> I got to Guatemala [City] to meet my aunt, she's going to bring me to the *coyote* … [with] 20 young people. We came to the border, to Tapachula, by Galgos [bus line], by bus and from there we have to cross in the border. We took a Mexican visa, we have like a tourist visa … By bus until *Distrito Federal* … we took airplane there to Tijuana … then we have to walk. Ya miles, miles, ya everybody together ... and there in mountains ... ya was FREEZING. A *camión*, a truck, like to cross to Los Angeles ... the *camión* was big like MARCO's truck … but inside the people squishing like animals ... like *culebras* [snakes] [she laughs] when we arrive to San Diego. Immigration do that [knocks table twice] to the *camión.* "Are you OK?" You have to say, "Don't answer if they ask 'Are you OK?'" "*¿Está bien, la gente allí*?" "*Nada*." You don't have to answer. And Immigration was knocking [knocks table five times lightly] "ARE YOU OK?" "Everybody ... somebody!" "*¿Todos están bien allí*?" "*¿Cómo vamos*?" He was making that question and nobody answered and the driver say, "Oh, I don't bring nobody." "OK, go ahead." And then they call the people to pick you up and pay the money.

ANA and her cousins then continued on to Canada after working in exploitative conditions in California for two years:

> … we came by plane … to SULLIVAN and we took a taxi and then we say, "Can you bring us to Canadian Immigration, please?" and he say, "Where are you going?" he was asking, I know he was Spanish … "Are we going to Canada? Ya, please bring to Canadian Immigration, no America," I say. "I don't want to go to Guatemala," I say, "Please." And I was SCARED because I don't know what this guy, all the way from the airport to the border was so LONG. I didn't know, it was night, you know. It was freezing and night. We were suffering. We suffered a lot.

Urban social activist survivors, on the other hand, often made their ways to Costa Rica or Mexico City as a place of first refuge (Bottinelli et al. 1990), though others managed to obtain asylum in Canada and Australia through the UNHCR in Mexico City or direct petitions to Embassy officials. As discussed in Chapter 4, the Canadian government facilitated the immigration of particular types of refugees and (im)migrants. Canadian immigration and refugee programs targeted urban-based, 'employable,' mainly middle-class, Ladino, political refugees at the expense of rural-based, mainly indigenous, *campesinos* who comprise the majority of refugees in Guatemala (see Chapter 4). Examining the outcomes of political violence and Canadian government strategies allows us to understand who is here, who is still in Guatemala, who they left behind, the places they create for themselves here, and the spaces, places, and lives that are altered by their departure.

The Canadian government facilitated the resettlement of many former student and labour activists to THOMASBURG, Ontario. MATEO, an indigenous leader from Guatemala City, relates how the Embassy facilitated his family's flight to

THOMASBURG in 1998, 24 hours after his meeting with the Canadian Ambassador. CARLOS, a 55 year-old longtime FAR operative, along with his family, chose Canada as a third country re-settlement option from Mexico City in 1993 and was directed to THOMASBURG. Former student activist, CONCHA, too, received Canadian government protection in 1993 after a decade-long exile in Mexico City following her activist husband's disappearance.

Of the six participants from THOMASBURG, all report their anger over the willingness of the Canadian government to facilitate settlement to Canada of those with government, military, police, and paramilitary ties. From LILLIAN's perspective, officials of the Guatemalan government request favours of their operatives and says, 'Do this and we'll get you to Canada.' But, she continues, 'their behaviour gives them away. They talk and cry when they get drinking. Then they go to the evangelical churches and confess to the people.' In Green's (1999, 64) study of devastated Maya communities, a priest recounts how 'many ex-soldiers would get drunk before going to confession, where they intermittently sobbed as they related to him in brutal detail what they had done and seen while in the army.' ALBA LUZ, CARLOS, ISAIAH, CONCHA, and others relate similar experiences in the Canadian context, where former soldiers and police are drawn to evangelical churches and openly confess their sins in front of a receptive congregation. All four indicate that the violator's sins emerge in the public spaces of church where they are likely to be embraced for 'having the courage' to start anew.

As an example, during our meeting in her WINTERBURN home, ANA describes the circumstances of her husband's family's departure:

> [MARCO's father was] … a witness from some shooting [ANA points her hand like a gun] … shooting people ... from government and he was working for the government. Ya, and he saw something like they ... burying the people alive ... and they were looking for him … that's why he have to leave the country right away and he applied for the whole family because in Guatemala if somebody owes something ... they don't care if you die ... no, they have to kill all the dependents, so, ya, that's why they are here.

Financial resources also enabled some Guatemalans to fly directly to Canada to request asylum or to obtain legal entry into the country. But, even for those who fled economic circumstances related to the politically volatile situation, there is no straightforward characterization of social relations. Personal contacts in the Canadian Embassy enabled ALBA LUZ, her then-husband, and young child to leave Guatemala:

> So Catherine, my story was like this. I went to the embassy of Canada … to a friend in the embassy of Canada and I told her my story that it was very difficult in Guatemala. I had a baby girl who was very sick … I didn't earn very much money, like I was telling you. So, well, my friend did me the favour and I went the embassy of Canada and happily, *pues*, they gave me Canadian residency.

For those particularly targeted by state or paramilitary forces, as well as former state agents, fear of communication with family and return can cement the rupture and lead to suspended communication and knowledge of changing country conditions. The rupture is almost complete for 54 year-old JOSÉ who started as a soldier and later became a military specialist.

> My mission was very, very delicate because I had to look after the security of the President's activities, the operations. When he went on business or whatever, we went too. I hope I am able to serve you enough, but really, I don't like to talk about this. It's very … very sensitive … I knew all the skulls … all the underground they had for torture, killing the people and everything. I know all of this. For this, I am not able to go there … I don't want to return there, it's possible that I'll never go. I was so damaged that I'm sure I don't want to return there. For what? Why return? You want me to return there?

The only connections JOSÉ maintains are 'with my family, nothing more. I separated from all of that.' JOSÉ lived an undocumented existence in many locations throughout Mexico and the United States, where 'one doesn't have tranquility' for over 20 years before his deportation from New York in 1997. Fear of detection led to an immediate escape back through Mexico, the United States, and on to Canada. JOSÉ told me:

> I suffered greatly when they deported me, because they treated me like a criminal. I didn't deserve that since I had been in the United States many years and respected the law … I arrived with fear … The same day I arrived in Guatemala, I abandoned Guatemala and I went to the border between Guatemala and Mexico and there I passed to the other side … I got myself out of there, in the airport, I went running to leave … more running and walking until I arrived in a crowd. I came across a bus that took me to the border.

On the other hand, many respondents suggested that they follow news of Guatemala closely and envision an ultimate return when political stability is evident. MIGUEL remembers the statements he made at his refugee hearing in the early 1980s and stands by them today:

> But to be honest with you, my dream is to go back to Guatemala. Listen, I never thought I'm going come to *El Norte* [he laughs] … And we said, "Well, OH, I'm going to be in Canada only maybe two or three years," you know. And we're talking 20 years later. So and I said, "I would like to make a final statement. I didn't come to Canada for economic reasons. I came to Canada because it's an alternative for me to save my life." And I said, "Well, I promise to the government of Canada and the people of Canada, I'm going to leave this country at the moment that the causes that forced me to come, to leave my country, the causes disappear I'm going to go back to my country." As you may know, 20 years has passed and the situation didn't change and that was the situation.

Canadian immigration programs, therefore, accepted government, police, and military members to escape to Canada in addition to opposition group members and those searching for a path from poverty. According to all participants, this broad spectrum of accepted applicants is the critical reason for the lack of supportive environment found among Guatemalans in Canada. As MIGUEL expressed, the range of experiences that led Guatemalans to Canada from all sides of the political spectrum, usually individually or in family units, works against the development of close primary social relations at any single scale, but rather weak and unstable ties and internal divisions. Even the sutures offered by friendship with fellow Guatemalans in close proximity rely on keeping half secrets and telling partial truths. The past is rarely discussed so that friendships and relationships in Canada are able to flourish. But, this half measure is not always possible as political lines continue to divide political, social, and solidarity groups. All too predictably, hostilities and fears are reproduced in new spaces of asylum and settlement in Canada.

Varying legal status (undocumented, new refugee claimant, ministerial permit holder, Convention refugee, landed immigrant, and citizen), the continuing instability, impunity, and insecurity associated with living conditions in Guatemala, low income levels (in both countries) leading to lack of communication, and the physical distance between the two countries that inhibits regular travel, all work to create transnational ruptures rather than transnational flows. Rather, their lives are primarily local, 'punctuated with infrequent transnational events' (Mahler 1998) such as receiving a phone call or cassette in the mail; receiving a visitor from Guatemala; and for some, making a first return to the country.

For MIGUEL and JOSÉ limited communication was an early security measure that remains a feature of life today. MIGUEL explains the need for pseudonyms and elaborate arrangements required for family communication:

> Ya, for many years, I'm going to tell you something … we learn from the experience … once at the National Confederation of Workers I make a phone call, right? And somebody answered on the other end, "*Palacio Nacional* Communications." You know? So that, at that moment, I understood that our phone was tapped, you know? … All the international communication were checked in Guatemala. So what I said, well the other thing is, "I am out of the country, but they are going to harass my family." So in order to avoid any kind of problems for my family, I was writing them, using another name, sending my letters to other addresses, other friends were giving my letters to my family … so I couldn't use the phone. No, no. First of all because they didn't have a phone, right? [he laughs] But on the other hand, a friend of mine … arranged to give me the chance to talk to my family on the phone … so what I do is I call my family once in a while … through some of my friends' houses and I write them now and … I feel more comfortable to communicate with them by writing and sometimes phone calls, but writing is my best way to communicate with them, ya.

It is critical to understand that refugees and other force migrants thrown into transnational realities, often against their will, are 'differentially situated and positioned' (Nyberg Sørensen 1998, 264) than migrants and immigrants. 'Refugee transnationalism' encompasses a host of motivations, influences, desires, and imperatives quite distinct from voluntary migrants. Canadian refugee and (im)migrant narratives, for instance, lack a distinct 'return ideology' found by House (1999) and researchers focusing on the Guatemala - USA connection. House argues that migrants from Nueva Unión Maya, Huehuetenango travel to the United

States with two- or three-year work plans, certain of their return and, therefore, are motivated to remit in order to guarantee family survival. Results are mixed from the participants in southwestern Ontario regarding plans of return. Many of those who fled to Canada for survival reasons, such as JOSÉ, hold no illusions of return, while MIGUEL remains optimistic. For others, a return ideology is evident but illusory; one day they are sure of their ultimate return and the next they have no desire to take up where their lives left off in Guatemala. Fresh from a visit to Guatemala, 36 year-old JUAN, puts it this way:

> You know something, it comes and goes … just coming out of … from Guatemala … it was paradise and we came here and I told my girlfriend, "You know, five years from now we'll have to move there." And she said, "NNNNO. No. No. No [laughs]. I go to visit and not to live." But I think that you go through emotions. Just coming from there … having that feeling that that's where you want to be but once you come back and go back to your routine and everything … reality sinks in … then you say to yourself, "Well, it was a nice trip, but it was a TRIP and I hope to go back again but not to live." I don't know … it's hard, it's hard to say. I don't know what's going to happen.

Most participants agree that semi-regular communication with family in Guatemala enables a sense of connectedness and a desire to visit once economically manageable and possibly return if conditions improve. JUANA, now 24, arrived to SUMMERLAND with her brothers as a teenager after bravely traveling illegally overland through Mexico and the United States to join her parents who came as refugees two years previously after her father's union activity at a glass factory in Guatemala City forced his quick departure. Unlike most participants, JUANA has returned to her hometown three times since her departure in 1993 and uses these visits to renew relations with family and friends:

> Um, that's a hard one. I cannot speak for my brothers 'cause they've grown up here – probably they're going to stay here, but my parents, they would LOVE to go back again … Ya, because they don't speak the language, not very good [in Canada]. To them it's hard. It's so hard to say "Yes, at the moment, yes." But once you're there you want to be here. It is SO hard. It's hard, I don't know. Either my answer … if I said, "Yes," or "No," I'd be lying. Because right now, sometimes I want to go back, like so bad, and sometimes I don't wanna go back. So, time will tell.

ISAIAH, a former student activist and PGT member now in THOMASBURG, kept a low profile upon his first return from Mexico. ISAIAH's wife, LILLIAN, remembers ISAIAH's fear of going into the street and how the two days over Christmas 'were really scary.' Participants also recount the need for family to visit Canada rather than return to Guatemala themselves. LILLIAN's mother, for example, was able to obtain a visitor's visa and travels at least once per year. The requirement of a visitor's visa for Guatemalans interested in travel to Canada, though, serves as more often than not to reinforce the ruptures of family than facilitate transnational flows. Of all participants who received visitors from Guatemala, only mothers and fathers were able to obtain visas and only if they traveled separately.[2] No siblings, particularly single males, were able to obtain a visitor's visa for Canada.

ANTONIO, a 65-year old Maya refugee claimant, fled to Chiapas from Guatemala in 1978 and is experiencing a second forced displacement to Canada.[3] The circumstances of his departure are such that he feels return is not an option and wants to remain in Canada:

> I do not want to return because if I return … at any rate, they will kill me. I am not able to arrive in Chiapas … in March was when they killed my wife … well then, to Guatemala, yes, I am able to return but I have nothing. Everything is in Chiapas.

ANTONIO describes a phone call he received on the morning of our meeting that reinforces the rupture of exile and of the high price paid for Canada's offer of security:

> Today in the morning they called me of the death of a family member. But, I'm not able to do anything. I'm not able to go … she died in the capital of Guatemala and I don't know … they have to bury in SAN SEBASTIAN … in the morning they advised me, yes. I'm not able to do anything, I'm not able to go because I do not have … if I had papers I would go by plane the next day. But I don't have, I'm not able to go. It's a problem.

The closest parallels that I have identified to the Guatemalan Canadian context are seen in Mahler's (1998) findings with undocumented Salvadorans on Long Island. We both stress that the interview participants do not live in transnational 'circuits,' but live rather more permanently in the 'adopted' country due to a host of circumstances. Unlike the lively transnationality documented in recent studies in an immigration context, Guatemalans in southwestern Ontario, as with Salvadorans on Long Island, find that refugee transnationalism operates sporadically and poses greater challenges for maintaining significant connections. I agree with Mahler (1998, 81), who argues that it is critical to examine the relationship between mobility and identity. I suggest that the question of political violence and volatile home country socio-political circumstances as a determining factor to mobility remains a highly under-questioned and under-theorized area of study in transnational research.

---

2 The visa issue was a prominent discussion with most families we met with in Guatemala. In SAN JUAN, with ANA's family, the conventional wisdom is that the visa division of the Canadian and American Embassies is a business as visa application fees cost Q340 or $55 U.S. while most applications are denied. American Embassy officials confirmed to Pérez (2000) a 50 per cent visa denial rate. Denials seemed more frequent for the families we spoke with. The Canadian Embassy refused my request (in person and by Email) to release both the number of visa requests per year as well as the Embassy's acceptance rate (Emails, Peter Taylor, First Secretary, Canadian Embassy in Guatemala, 16 May 2000 and 6 October 2000; Nesta Scott, Immigration Division, Canadian Embassy in Guatemala, 15 October 2000).

3 See Appendix Six for testimony of ANTONIO's escape from Chiapas, Mexico first to Los Angeles, California and later to BEVERLY and SUMMERLAND, Ontario.

Paradoxical Spaces, Contradictory Spaces

In this section, I examine circumstances of paradoxical or contradictory space that emerge out of the experience of living in freedom without power. Once in Canada, interview participants indicate that new social positions as refugees and (im)migrants often disable or impede many individuals and families from overcoming the confines of Canadian refugee and (im)migrant spaces. Relatively few Guatemalans scattered throughout the region with widely varying experiences in Guatemala impede the development of 'ethnic solidarity' or strong social networks on which to draw for social and occupational support. After reviewing the interview conversations, I come away with a clear sense that the majority feels imprisoned by the transnational rupture and face a major class shift – admittedly a positive shift for some – though negatively perceived by most.

Using 1991 economic data, Kazemipur and Halli's (2000, 83) study on poverty among ethnic and immigrant groups in Canada indicates that, among arrivals between 1981 and 1991, the highest level of poverty was found among Central and South Americans at 41.1 per cent, compared to 39.4 per cent for those of Arab origins and 35.1 per cent for Vietnamese. Of course, poverty levels vary by city for Central and South Americans as with all ethnic and immigrant groups. The percentage of Central and South Americans below the poverty line in my study area ranged between 20 per cent 42.9 per cent while the average city poverty rates for this same area ranged between 11.7 per cent and 14.8 per cent. The refugee narratives that follow reveal some of the barriers and opportunities of refugee and (im)migrant spaces in Canada and how external factors shape the social relations with those in Guatemala and Canada. In many ways, marginality in Canada encourages strong familial bonds in both countries and restricts the development of local 'ties.'

Freedom without Power? Freedom as Power? Or Barriers and Opportunities

Though refuge and migration to Canada offer the possibility of freedom often unimaginable in Guatemala, and some refugees such as MIGUEL and JUANA eventually develop points of attachment and connectedness in Canada, there are myriad barriers to success and adaptation. As JUAN states, 'you gotta understand that although you want to fit in the society that is new to you, you don't have the same … same ideas, same customs.' A minority of interview participants recounted feelings of connectedness and comfort with their present situation in Canada. More often than not, however, participants reflect on the barriers to successful integration and lack of support by fellow Guatemalans.

The gendered narratives of Canadian refugee social spaces can be reduced to one phrase: freedom without power. The barriers and opportunities for Guatemalan refugees and (im)migrants are evident in all of our interview conversations, though issues of struggle are far more prominent at this stage of their settlement experiences. Both men and women shared the many challenges of exile and forced migration and the costs of freedom and security. Women's narratives, though, convey a sense of drowning in isolation, of yearning for something more, of deserving something more. As Mahler (1995, 106) found with undocumented Salvadorans in the United States, I grew to understand ELENA, CARMEN, LILLIAN, CONCHA, and the other women's desire for contact, inclusion, fulfilling employment, and greater contact with their families in Guatemala 'through their language of exclusion.'

There are four recurrent themes to my discussion with the female participants: (1) no choice in the departure decision, as did the men, but it was usually the problematic activities of the male partners that sparked the need for immediate departure; (2) lack of English-language acquisition that would enable greater socialization and more fulfilling employment; (3) the high price paid for 'security' and feelings of being useless due to under- and unemployment; and (4) weak ties to fellow Guatemalans through compromises and half-truths in addition to weak ties to neighbours in their 'local' settings. The narratives of women and men that follow pick up on these themes, revealing the limiting factors to fulfillment of their potential.

When the choice is not their own 'We are a generation of babysitters,' LILLIAN exclaims in exasperation. The former PGT member and dentist talks of 'going crazy staying at home' with her children in THOMASBURG. As mentioned in CARMEN's transnational ethnography, women connect the circumstances of their flight, the shock of isolation, and feelings of not being useful in the spaces of settlement in Canada. ELENA put it this way:

> But in Guatemala, I was paid well in my job, I worked with people who I loved very much, and I felt good. I worked and my mother looked after the kids. When I came here, I came without a *centavo* in my purse. I left with nothing … the change for me was very difficult … I love my country very much, I YEARN to return there but I think it is better for the children here. I have lots of regret … I looked out the window and I CRIED … how sad it is here. For perhaps two years I was crying every day. All I want is to go and visit my mom.

Women refugees and (im)migrants forced to leave Guatemala in order to hold the family together find the transition particularly difficult and isolating. MATEO speaks of his wife's isolation in THOMASBURG as *triste* [sad], *duro* [difficult], and *cuesta* [a burden]. MATEO connects her inability to speak English to the shock of the family's immediate departure from Guatemala, only 24 hours after MATEO met with the Canadian Ambassador. ELENA joined her husband two years after his forced departure in 1991 in order to keep her young family together:

> He belonged to the union and he had a lot of problems because he defended the poor people when they didn't pay their salaries, well, so he began to receive calls and he decided that it was best that he leave. Well … he told me "I am going because I have this problem, if I stay here I run the risk that they will kill me or that they want to do something to me"… I never thought that I would have to go to Canada! [we both laugh] But I called my husband [already in Canada] and we talked and he said "it is very difficult and I don't know when I will be able to return to Guatemala…." More than anything, it is important for the family

to be together for the kids … and I said to my mom, "Well I believe that here there isn't much to choose."

Language, employment, and isolation Issues of identity and language are central to the whole transnational experience. Rushdie (1991) identifies the (im)migrant and refugee dilemma of living not only an out-of-country but also an out-of-language experience. Ninety per cent of those I spoke with indicated that they did not have knowledge of English before their departure from Guatemala and 16 per cent (women and men) still do not speak English five years after arrival in Canada. Both women and men relate their inability to learn English immediately to depression, shock, and lack of social support. CARMEN responds to my question of when she learned English:

> Oh, after five years I think…. [That's a long time, isn't it?] Yes, but during that time like I told you before I didn't get the chance to go to school like ... and first because I was depressed I didn't want to learn English. I was like I had a closed mind and "I don't know ... I don't want to learn English ... I don't want to stay here ... I don't want to raise my children here. It's all different" ... I was upset.

There is a bitter irony to seeking exile in Canada for CARLOS, who feels he has been swallowed up by the very powers he fought against. Five years after arriving in Canada, CARLOS states that he 'hate[s] the English language, hate[s] using this language' because for him it is a language of domination and oppression. Though he distinguishes between Canada and the United States in this regard, he sees both countries as power structures that explicitly supported state violence, turned a blind eye, or kept objections to a whisper.

Morton Beiser's (1999) study of South Asian refugees who arrived in Canada between 1979 and 1981 – the same time period as early Guatemalan refugees – stresses that 'no matter what their situation, newcomers need to find work and to master the language of their adopted country. Without these minimal tools, successful integration will always remain elusive.' CONSTANCIA and ELENA contribute two common experiences with language acquisition:

> CONSTANCIA: It's hard, you know, but after some time I felt, it was not my country but I felt good and part of the place. But I think it was maybe when I started learning the language and everything because at first I didn't like … people were talking and I didn't know what to say … I felt bad.

> ELENA:I know a person who has been in Canada for many more years and he is the same as me that we don't know how to express ourselves. It is true sometimes, in many opportunities I have felt badly because sometimes I want to be friendly with people and I don't know how to express [myself], so they think ... that they are going to say how badly mannered [badly educated] I am, but I don't know how to say it so I arrive there, "Ay I have to learn, I have to learn."

Both women attribute the feelings of discomfort and lack of integration to their inability to speak English, though CONSTANCIA's high school experience offered immersion and eventually a sense of belonging while ELENA's home-based child-rearing duties reinforced her social isolation and feelings of inadequacy.

Work and language-acquisition are two key points in the gendered narratives of Canadian social spaces. The barriers of spatial and social isolation, particularly of women and single refugees, are reinforced through the lack of language acquisition and widespread underemployment and unemployment, both of which, according to Beiser (1999), constitute a mental health risk. MIGUEL puts it this way:

> The reality as new immigrants that they come do the lower quote unquote jobs, you know, and sometimes they come with doctors' papers, engineers, or accountants … but because the language and Canadian experience, they have to go over there [underemployment].

CARMEN's experience is illustrative of the language-work dimension:

> I ask in interview with my social worker and I talked to her about my situation and I said, "Look I have my Master's degree in Social Worker and I need help. Like I wanna study English ... to improve my English" and I give, gave her all my papers and she said, "I'm sorry I can't help you ... because you have your Master's degree in Social Worker and you have to find a job." [we both laugh] And I said, "Yes, I have my papers here, look, but I can't speak English!"

Tied to language acquisition and employment issues is the critical, though not immediately evident, role of active contact networks to advancement and achievement. As discussed earlier, the broad spectrum of Guatemalans in Canada – the radically different reasons for leaving Guatemala – does not allow for any depth to 'ethnic solidarity,' communities of association and support, nor contacts that might facilitate employment. ELENA puzzles over the lack of 'community' or social support among fellow Guatemalans. 'I don't know what happens between the Hispanics,' she says. 'Normally it is as if they feel jealous of the people. They don't help among themselves.'

JUAN picks up on the lack of 'ethnic solidarity' and employment contacts that reflects many interview conversations:

> I had a girlfriend that has gone through a lot. I think that a lot of people like her that are here, they are professionals in their countries and they arrive here and they can't find a way to work in their field. I mean, she has gone through EVERYTHING! She's a civil engineer … but she's been here for at least 10 years working at housekeeping in hotels and greenhouses … I mean, she's done it all … she's done it all. And NOTHING, I mean frustrating. She took English – ESL. She went to [local] College and took some geographic something-or-other … NOTHING. And I think that, again like we said, you don't have that network … contacts to help you out … I didn't have the connections and I think that was one of the reasons why I was laid off.

ROBERTO speaks with great frustration of the limited support offered by, and lack of trust felt among, Guatemalans in southwestern Ontario that limit employment contacts:

> But here even to find a job it's difficult if you don't have contacts – you have to find some help, you have to ask because if you don't ask they are going to tell you, "Oh, I'm sorry we don't have anything." But if you have somebody to help you it's better ... it's helpful for you.

ROBERTO's and ANTONIO's experiences are much the same as those of JUAN's friend, since language acquisition and employment are factors for both women and men. Seasonal agricultural employment is available to those such as ANTONIO who do not speak English:

> The obstacle I have here is not knowing English. If I knew English, well, I'd get work swiftly. But like I still don't know much English, then I'm going to work in the countryside. Knowing English, I don't go to [work in] the countryside but in an office. But for now in the countryside. I arrived in the summer and there was work in the countryside … picking peaches, pears, apples … with Guatemalans, Mexicans, Hondurans, and residents of other places such as Bosnia. The salary is $7 paid in cash. But at the moment I'm not working because of the cold … now we say it is like being in jail.

But unlike the male participants who, when employed, work in jobs that offered some opportunities for group interaction – such as farm, factory, and restaurant work -- female participants are more frequently unemployed, remaining at home with their children. Additionally, when women find work outside the home, employment tends to be restricted to socially isolating environments – such as night-shift office cleaning and hotel cleaning – that do not require English language skills nor assist in the learning of English.

The high price to pay for tranquility and safety Another frequent theme among female participants is the high price paid for living in tranquility and safety. Though all women and men indicate greater feelings of shelter and security in Canada, women spoke much more passionately about the accompanying sacrifices. Men responded much like PEDRO to the possibilities and opportunities that refuge in Canada presents to newcomers:

> I don't come looking for money. I come looking for location. Somewhere to stay, somewhere to be in peace, right? I am going to school, I am going to have a job in the evening and take a course during the day … maybe soon I could even be an English teacher, one never knows…. Here I feel good. I feel free. I feel supported because I have opportunities to advance … to have a title and a job. I feel sheltered.

The majority of female respondents, though, struggle with feelings of uselessness, loneliness, and separation from primary social relations. While CONCHA is making our coffee, ISAIAH – who introduced us – brings my attention to a framed photograph of a student demonstration hanging on the living room wall. ISAIAH recounts the fate of all the men in the photograph, including CONCHA's husband, all student activists of the late 1970s and early 1980s. Assassinated. Disappeared. Gunned down. CONCHA later says she now feels 'external peace' but does not 'feel good inside' anymore. With little choice in the matter of her departure and no opportunity to return, CONCHA says she wants to 'live in peace now' but 'sometimes you can't feel good anywhere.' Forgetting about her youth was the high price she paid for tranquility and safety; settlement in THOMASBURG made her feel like she was 'losing something' rather than gaining a new chance at life. CONCHA drew strength from the strong Guatemalan community in Mexico City but now in Canada she is 'tired of fighting, tired of participating, tired of everything.'

Like CONCHA, CARMEN speaks of lost youth and the many stresses of life in 'freedom.' When asked to express her sense of identity in Canada, CARMEN responds:

> And how I feel? I feel OLD. YES, I feel old. I feel like since I came to Canada many years ... many years has come to me. When I see my face in the mirror, I say "I'm old, I'm too old." I feel too old and my husband too ... we watch each other! [she laughs] "Oh my God, look at us!" Ya, ya. Ya, but I think it is too much stress...

ELENA, too, feels the price she is paying for human security in SUMMERLAND is far too high:

> Like I say, I like it here for the tranquility but in Guatemala I felt more useful, I felt more useful in Guatemala, I had work where I developed better. Here I have been depressed a lot, I am very nervous, thinking that there my family has problems, that they need things, that I can not even call them … everyday. I sometimes say, "Ay, I wish that they would knock at the door and that my mom would come or my brother or some family member to visit," but no one ever comes. I feel there is a high price paid for the tranquility that one has here because being far from your family is very difficult.

Religion as a weak tie If language and childcare concerns limit employment opportunities, religious participation is a common point of reflection on new attachments that offer the possibility of social relations with other Spanish-speaking residents in the area. Unfortunately, this avenue for collectivity, too, is problematic. Religious affiliation often changes in Canada as a necessary compromise for attachment, connection, and group affiliation. ANA describes her conversion from Catholicism to a Pentecostal faith with her husband as a search for 'community.' When I asked if she spends much time with other Guatemalans or Central Americans, however, ANA replies:

> Only at church. Until I find MARCO, I met MARCO and we went to that church … Christian … Spanish language … everybody has Spanish there, ya. The pastor is from Salvador … Like, I don't know any of my people. No. I think I wasn't interested in that. Even now, I don't know. I don't have time for that. I have to be honest with you, you know.

ALBA LUZ, though, discusses her religious participation outside the Catholic Church as an opportunity to meet other Guatemalans:

> Cati, my religion is Catholic. But we all want to change religion to be good with oneself here in this place because, one doesn't have family to visit, to offer one something, a mutual support, *pues*, one needs a close relationship and for that one needs to seek other churches where Hispanics meet … And I don't feel good in evangelism. But I do it so that there is more communication, so that there are more friendships and I can get out of all this ... To be far from one's country … one wants to be more in the Hispanic family. For this, one changes the religion, simply for chance to chat with more people and have friendships.

JUAN joined the local Baptist church through intense pressure from converted friends but after attending he identified the socialization aspects to membership:

> So at this time, our [Guatemalan] friends … this couple with the girl … they were attending a church, obviously not a Catholic church … this was a Protestant [Baptist] church. And we came to visit them and they invited us to church and we didn't want to go but we saw that we needed something to help us at this time. So, finally they convinced us … I attended for while and then it got too much for me. But my family are dedicated … my sister went back home [to Guatemala] … after she had 2 ½ years of Christian education, they call it. But she got married … back home. And their life revolves around the church.

Upon returning to Guatemala, CONSTANCIA agreed that 'the church, I think, was my biggest experience' in Canada and encouraged her parents and siblings to join the upstart church in Guatemala City. JOSÉ recalls the transformative role of the Mormon faith during his exile though in personal terms and of the possibilities of avoiding other Guatemalans:

> I think that I struggled on my own … [but] with faith in God everything came out well. When one does not have anything, God listens even more. For this, I say that the day that they baptized me into the church, this day, my life changed because I felt that I returned a different person. I pray to God everyday, each moment … I have nobody here, the only family is my faith in God and that is all. [Of fellow Guatemalans] … I don't want anything to do with them nor to talk with them … because there were painful things that happened to me and I don't want to remember them.

Women particularly, then, come to rely on immediate family in Canada and Guatemala as their primary relations while only weak ties develop with others in their workplace (if employed), neighbourhood, and fellow Guatemalans. CARMEN voices a widespread reliance on multi-scale family relations and limited development of ties beyond a circle of confidence. 'Now THIS is our family,' she told me. 'And here we are alone … we don't have family … our family is my husband, my children and me … that's it … Family for us is first, second and third [she laughs]. Yes, it's everything and it's very important.'

All of these actions, silences, and hostilities are reinforced by the uncertainty of return and the limbo status of many refugees who feel lost in Canada. For many Guatemalans in Canada, insecurity limits place making practices, such as transforming weak ties to strong ties, and their impermanence destabilizes existing relationships and discourages the creation of new ones.

Remittances in Reverse: Understanding American – Canadian Distinctions

Questions of remittance commitment and sending began as the centrepiece of my examination into Guatemala – Canada connections. Based on the 'remittance landscapes' I observed in rural Guatemala, in addition to studies by CEPAL (1991) and Stanley (1993) that document the powerful economic impact of remittance money from Guatemalans abroad, I expected to follow through on the role of remittances sent from Guatemalans in Canada to their families or home communities in Guatemala. More recent studies by the Inter-American Dialogue Task Force on Remittances (2004), de la Garza et al. (1997), and Lowell and de la Garza (2000), confirm the intensified flow of remittance money throughout Latin America, while CONGCOOP (1997) and Jonas (1996a) highlight Guatemala's growing reliance on the estimated half-billion dollars from remittance flows. Finer scale 'remittance landscape' analysis by House (1999), House and Lovell (1999), Martinéz Rodas (1999), and Piedrasanta Herrera (1999) demonstrate the geographical variation and local reliance on money sent from relatives in the USA.

Until I spoke with Guatemalans in Canada, though, I little understood the differing migration experiences between those who fled to the USA and those who made their way to Canada. National context plays a major role here as the majority of participants in Ontario indicated their inability, the 'impossibility,' really, of sending remittances to their family in Guatemala from Canada. Due to the prevalence of remittance money from the USA, Guatemalans in Canada face three challenges: (1) extended family expectations to send money; (2) the loss of dignity when forced to accept money and gifts from parents in Guatemala; and (3) the need to 'adapt' to exile in Canada which requires a significant financial commitment. In many ways, the Canadian refugee context creates a reverse remittance phenomena wherein money and communication flows *from* Guatemala *to* Canada and forces a choice between family survival in Canada and meeting family obligations in Guatemala. CARMEN, ELENA, and ALBA LUZ, respectively, explain the challenges this way:

> … and it's difficult because they sometimes they ask you to send some money, we can't do that. Because if we send … like right now only ROBERTO is working a part-time job, he has a part-time job ... we can't do that ... $15 for us ... is $15 for meat and food … Like in my case, my mother didn't ask me anything ... she helps me sometimes [little laugh]. *Pues*, perhaps it's necessary but we are not able [nervous laugh]. Here we, *pues*, with what we earn, we know what we have to buy and pay … I would like to send … more than anything, perhaps for my mother's medicine … because she is very sick.

> It's impossible, it's impossible, Catherine, it's impossible, it's difficult, very difficult … yes, Catherine, my mom calls me, she calls me one time a month, ya, it is very expensive … ya she pays. One time a month to say hello, to know how I'm doing in this situation, right?

Mentioned in ALBA LUZ's final comment is a distinguishing feature of the Canadian context: the inability of many Guatemalans to initiate contact or send remittance money to family in Guatemala. In conversation after conversation, participants revealed how family members (usually parents) actually send goods and monetary assistance to Canada. While CARMEN notes that remittance sending to Guatemala simply is not a financial possibility, her mother, ENCARNACIÓN, talks of paying extra for her overflowing suitcases full of clothing and *recuerdos* for CARMEN and the children on one of her visits to Canada. ENCARNACIÓN says she is always bringing things for CARMEN – eight *trajes* for her folkloric group – and 30 dresses for her granddaughter on her last trip. ENCARNACIÓN, too, initiates phone calls from her home in Guatemala once a week. As CARMEN says, 'Ya, and this year, ya usually … she usually phone me a lot [we both laugh].'

ELENA repeats an oft-stated feeling of pressure to initiate some telephone calls even when finances do not allow for this expense:

> One time a month or so I'm able to [talk] because the whole family there wants to talk to one here and then the bill comes … very high, and so in this way I'm walking around with bad nerves.

ANA also faces a financial burden to initiate or receive collect calls twice per year:

> I don't like they call me very often because the calls are very expensive in the first place and when they talk, they talk too much [laughs] … They go to Guatel to call me and they ask me if I accept this call. You know, I pay almost $60 for one call, you know, too much.

Guatemalans who found first refuge in the USA note most explicitly the shift in their remittance sending commitments and abilities once in Canada. JUAN, for example, perhaps best articulates the contrast between his lack of remittance sending abilities and family expectations:

> I was trying to get my dad to understand that they have this perception that all North Americans make American money and we don't and it becomes difficult at times … Well, that's the thing that relatives … and I'm not talking about my family in particular, but some relatives don't appreciate some of their relatives being in North America … they don't realize those efforts … just because you're here they think you are making all this money to distribute … It's all in how you want to live. I mean, I've seen the two systems … I lived there [in USA] and I know that it matters what you want to do in the future. I mean it seems like over there it is just for the day and eventually you're going to go back and you want to send all this money so that you have enough money to live … So, I was trying to kind of talk about that with my dad and I said here in Canada we have more expenses like you do in the States, too. But, you live in a different way. It's a different

> standard of living in Canada … so … I think that because your goal in the States is just to make money. Your goal here is to live, to make a living, to make this your home…

But the remittance mentality is firmly in place in Guatemala and those in Canada are faced with the need to clarify the American–Canadian distinction in addition to accepting assistance from family in Guatemala. As CARMEN explains:

> We have to explain and even they don't believe us … like we have to explain first Canadian dollars are not the same [laughs] … when they hear "Oh, I'm working and I am getting $8 per hour" they change the Quetzal from dollars … "OH, you're getting good money!" and you say "No, that's no good money 'cause you have to pay rent, we have to pay electricity, we have to pay phone, we have to pay cable, we have to pay food, expenses … and clothes are very expensive, shoes are very expensive, and $1000 for a family is nothing." Yes, people ask us "Could you please send me…?" or "My brother is gonna have an operation and need some money, can you send me something?" It's difficult.

Upon discussing the flow of money, gifts, and communication with family in Guatemala, it is clear that some families understand the American - Canadian distinction, and initiate calls and send small support to relatives in Canada. CARMEN's sister ELSI told me, 'There is plenty communication, we call her to chat … for me it's easier to call by phone … I have a phone and call her once or twice a month.'

Others, like JUAN's parents, are concerned that remittance money is not usually a feature of Canadian exile as it was in the American context. When asked of their communication with JUAN, his mother replied that 'he calls once every month or two. He doesn't send things or money at all,' though JUAN stated he remitted money every two months, 'Well, I make it a point to send … but I'm due … you just reminded me! [laughs] Every other month … a certain amount for my parents. It's not much but they appreciate it, you know.'

ANA's mother, OTULIA, too, seemed surprised that ANA did not send gifts or money with us for our trip to their home in SAN JUAN, Zacapa. OTULIA informed us that ANA used to send photos and money while she worked in California before fleeing to Canada but that she is unable to make the same contributions now. ANA explains:

> Ya, we didn't have nothing, you know, how you come here when you are refugees … I have to start from beginning again. That's the problem, you know what I mean? Oh ya, especially when you come from United States it's more difficult for you ... ya because you were working there, you got jobs ... and now you know the difference between American and Canadian ... I regret at that time to come to Canada … I didn't have ANYTHING, even bed, NOTHING, NOTHING, just my clothes. So it was very hard for me.

ANA's two brothers and a sister remained in California after she left for Canada and make regular contributions to the family purse. The differing remittance experience came into clear focus during our last afternoon with the family. OTULIA's two sisters also have children in '*El Norte*' – EDWINA's three sons and one daughter are in exile in SUMMERLAND, Ontario while SOFIA's two sons are undocumented in Los

Angeles. While we spoke on the open patio, a letter from King Express – a major courier company used by Guatemalans to send remittances – arrived at the door. The package contained two round-trip airline tickets for travel from Guatemala to Los Angeles ($600 U.S. each), letters from OTULIA and SOFIA's children in Los Angeles, a $100 U.S. money order (pocket money for the trip), $50 U.S. from another son, and $20 for an aunt who was unable to obtain a travel visa. So while ANA talks of her time on social assistance and great suffering, her siblings in California are able to send for their mother for a month-long vacation.

Factors of Immobile Transnationalism

So in many ways, Guatemalans in Canada are obviously transnational, forging and maintaining important social relations, and yet they are not necessarily able to move across borders. The necessity to account for the mobility (or lack of mobility) of transnational lives and social relations is articulated in the recent work of Vertovec (2003, 11), Mahler (1998; 2001), Levitt (2001a, 2001b) and Waters (2002), among others, all of whom emphasize the need to 'look at the nature of transnational migrants' "lived reality".' In terms of the Guatemalan population in Canada, I argue that several factors – including Guatemalan political violence, Canadian foreign and immigration policies, immigration status, socio-economic circumstances, and spatial concentration or dispersal of settlement – all factor into the development of a more individual, immobile form of transnationalism.

By recognizing the consequences of political violence for Guatemalans in Canada (such as the inability or unwillingness to return to Guatemala) and those left behind (such as the inability to receive a travel visa to journey to Canada), I suggest that, for refugees and forced migrants in particular, a kind of *psychological transnationalism*, or the desire and yearning for connections in both the home and adopted countries, underlies the narratives of Guatemalan experiences in Canada. A more *concrete transnationalism*, or processes that facilitate remittance-sending, on-going communication, and return – recognized as central to immigrant transnationalism (FOCAL 2004; Goldring 2003; Levitt 1998) – only develop in later stages of place making, if at all.

Monzón and Tudakovic's (2004, 12) recent report for CIC indicates that official remittance estimates are not prepared by the Canadian government and that their initial investigation reveals that "for Canada, the amount of remittances outflows is small in relation to its economy." In our interview conversations, Guatemalans indicated that the practice of sending remittance to one's family in Guatemala is not as significant with Guatemalan Canadians as with those living in the USA. I began this research project thinking that the issue of remittances might be a significant aspect of the research; in fact it was significant by its absence. The agency of refugees and (im)migrants to negotiate Canadian and American labour landscapes is curtailed in different ways and, in the end, restricts remittance sending from Canada and facilitates the practice from the USA. Interviewees identified several related reasons for low levels of remittance sending including the high cost of living in Canada, the low-income situation of their lives, and the high cost associated with sending remittances.

Immigrant status is another important factor in the transnational possibilities for Guatemalans in Canada. As noted in Chapter 4, CIC and IRB data were examined for the 17, 380 Guatemalans who arrived in Canada during the years 1980 to 2004 to determine the proportion of refugees, family class immigrants, and independent immigrants.[4 5] Overall, 59 per cent arrived in the refugee/refugee-like categories, while 28 per cent arrived in immigrant categories, and only 13 per cent arrived as independent immigrants.[6]

Given that the majority of Guatemalans in Canada arrived as refugees, it is necessary to note the recent work by DeVoretz et al. (2004), Lochhead (2003), Picot and Hou (2003), and others who highlight: (1) the persistent and growing income gap between immigrants (refugees in particular) and Canadian born residents; (2) the above average levels of poverty for recent immigrants; (3) the above average levels of unemployment; and (4) the under-representation in well-paid jobs in conjunction with over-representation in the low-income sector. Each of these points is relevant for (im)migrants and refugees in general, but of heightened concern for Latin Americans in particular.

Lochhead (2003, 1) argues that the transition period, or the 'period of time in which they must establish self-sufficiency' is 'better known as a "transition penalty".' For example, the unemployment rate for recent immigrants – or those living in Canada for less than five years – was 12.7 per cent in 2001 compared with the lower rate of 7.1 per cent in 1981, while unemployment rates among Canadian-born were 7.9 per cent in 1981 and 7.4 per cent in 2001. According to Statistics Canada (2004c) data, Latin Americans experienced higher unemployment rates than immigrants in general, rates which rose from 8.4 per cent in the 1980 to 1990 period to 14 per cent in the 1996 to 2001 period.

---

4 Using CIC categories, 'refugees' are those who are listed in the following categories: Convention Refugee, Designated Classes, PDRCC, Deferred Removals, Source Country and Asylum Country, and CR8 Dependents. 'Immigrants' are those listed as Family Class and Assisted Relatives, while 'Independent Immigrants' arrive in Canada as Entrepreneurs, Investors, Self-Employed, Life-in-Caregivers, Retired, and Other Immigrants (skilled labour).

5 Statistical data obtained from Citizenship and Immigration (CIC) in Ottawa and the Immigration and Refugee Board (IRB) in Toronto. According to the IRB Documentation Centre, specific country refugee data, at least of the sort I was looking for, are not available prior to 1989.

6 The International Organization for Migration (IOM) (2003, 3) recently initiated a pilot project to 'select and transfer to Canada' 195 Guatemalan agricultural workers (79.2 per cent men and 20.8 per cent women). The successful project evaluation suggests this program will increase the Independent Immigrant (skilled labour) category in the years to come.

In addition to unemployment rates, rising low-income rates among immigrants in the past two decades are identified by Picot and Hou (2003, 24) while rates among the Canadian-born population are falling. DeVoretz et al. (2004, 27) argue that 'lower average wage earnings are consigning ever-greater proportions of refugees to the poverty ranks of Canadian society.' Specifically, Picot and Hou (2003, 24) highlight low-income rates of 40.6 per cent for Central and South Americans in 1990, a situation which slightly improved to 29.9 per cent in 2000. Given these economic circumstances, remittance sending and transnational mobility is highly curtailed for Guatemalans in Canada.

Geographic concerns at both ends of the spectrum are key factors as well. Though no official records are available to indicate from which location in Guatemala a refugee or (im)migrant arrives, the vast majority of people I spoke with came from larger cities or the Guatemalan capital while only 16 per cent are from smaller, rural communities. These places of origin findings offer a very different migration portrait than that found among Guatemalans in the USA (Burns 1993; Fink 2003; Foxen 2002; and Hagan 1994) who tend to arrive from rural and remote regions of Guatemala.

Geographic concentration and/or dispersal in Canada are significant factors in terms of the lack of development of deep social relations within the Guatemalan population in Canada. According to the most recent Canadian census of 2001, Guatemalan permanent residents number 14,095 (13,680 permanent and 415 non-permanent residents) (Statistics Canada 2004a). Though the 'gateway cities' of Montréal (4,015), Toronto (3,525), and Vancouver (1,360) serve as primary destinations for Guatemalans, as with most refugee and immigrant populations in Canada, thousands live scattered across the country in small- and mid-sized cities and towns (Statistics Canada 2003a).

Documenting the spatial distribution in rural and urban Canada, though, is a challenge for researchers who cannot accurately capture the reality of much rural and small town immigrant settlement. For reasons of confidentiality, census data values are randomly rounded either up or down to a multiple of five or 10 and much information is suppressed for areas with populations of less than 40 (Statistics Canada 2003b; 2003c). Researchers find similar challenges documenting most, if not all, Latin American populations in Canada beyond the gateway cities of Vancouver, Toronto, and Montréal.

Summing Up

By examining the consequences of political violence for Guatemalans in Canada and those left behind, I argue that, for refugees in particular, psychological transnationalism, or the desire and yearning for connections in both the home and adopted countries, underlies the narratives of Guatemalan refugee identity, while concrete transnationalism, or processes that facilitate remittance-sending, on-going communication, and return – recognized as central to immigrant transnationalism –

only develop in later stages of place making, if at all. Political violence and government policies are central to the understanding of the formation of transnational circuits as well as the ruptures of refugee transnationalism. Researchers of 'deterritorialized nation states,' such as the Philippines, the Dominican Republic, and Haiti, tend to interpret the role of government policies of both home and adopted nations, as one of facilitator of transnational flow of capital through remittance sending and tax incentive programs. But, in the case of the Guatemala – Canada connection, government policies of both countries must be seen as major stumbling blocks to the development of robust transnational flows and concrete transnationalism.

Spaces are mediated by unequal power relations that define who belongs and who may be excluded (or eliminated, in the Guatemalan case). Places and spaces are maintained and altered by boundaries that are both spatial and social (McDowell 1999, 4). Because of this arrangement, it is critical that issues of political violence and immigration policies are brought into the discussion of the creation of new refugee 'social spaces.' Many Guatemalans in Canada have been denied their 'place' in Guatemala by physical removal, threats, and poverty. They have been deterritorialized in a physical sense, but their identities and social relations have not so much been deterritorialized as differently territorialized. They bring to their 'place' in Canada new, layered, multiple aspects of their identities that reflect exile, removal, displacement and also refuge, tentative social relations, remembrance, and imagining – a psychological transnationalism.

Rather than the development of new 'communities' of association, I argue that Guatemalan refugees and (im)migrants forge primary social relations within and across multiple scales. Political violence and immigration policies, then, are central to the politics of multi-scaled social spaces characterized by the social costs of ruptures and the opportunities of sutures. Guatemalan experiences in Canada reveal the ways in which primary social relations shift from face-to-face experiences of proximity to relations that stretch across borders.

PART IV
Conclusion

Chapter 7

Refugee Transnationalism

> [T]he underside of culture is blood, torture, death and horror.
> Fredric Jameson (1984, 57)

Scene I: In the evening of a warm day in June 1996, JOSÉ RECINOS told our Central America solidarity group of Kingston how, in 1982, he came to be a refugee in Canada. He revealed his torture in a clandestine Guatemalan jail, his escape across the border into Mexico, his acceptance into Canada, and of the fire that burns inside of him to tell his story so that the horror would no longer be silenced. He told us:

> The silence of the international community allows the Guatemalan government to do what it wants. The killings, the torture, the clandestine jails, the corruption, the pollution. The government can get away with all this as long as the rest of the world looks the other way. I want to let the Canadian government know what's going on in my country.

Scene II: In March 1997, I attended a Canadian Foundation for the Americas (FOCAL 1997) conference in Ottawa organized to discuss the economic implications of the Peace Accords signed in Guatemala only a few months earlier. Though Guatemala is a country with an indigenous population that, according to one of the statistics cited by Lovell and Lutz (1996), composes approximately 60 per cent of the total population, the highest percentage of any country in the Americas apart from Bolivia, the indigenous representation at the conference was closer to six per cent. Aside from Manuela Alvarado López, who participated as a new Deputy of the Guatemalan Congress, the Maya representation came from a handful of refugees in Canada, who sat scattered around the room, listening in the company of some Ladinos. After much discussion on the Peace Accords, a former journalist now in Canadian exile spoke:

> When you suffer in exile you realize that peace is something on paper. What about those of us who were silenced? We call for a real process, not just words blown away in the wind ... just blown away in the wind.

The preceding words of two Guatemalan refugees in Canada for me illustrate the level of frustration felt by many refugees at the silencing they have undergone throughout what Carmack (1988) calls Guatemala's 'harvest of violence' and, subsequently, during their years of exile in Canada. A great number of Guatemalans choose a quiet life in exile while others are standing up to be heard. JOSÉ chose to walk across Canada in an organized campaign to bring awareness of human rights violations in Guatemala. He could not walk 'home,' but could walk the same distance east to west across Canada and use the opportunities afforded to him by refuge in Canada to assist in his healing and recovery. Through his cross-country trek, JOSÉ dealt with his ruptured sense of self and began a process of spiritual and identity renewal. JOSÉ's walk served to spatialize his Maya identity within a Canadian refugee context, and offer the possibilities for returning to Guatemala to participate in the process of social reconstruction.

I conclude this book with their words as a way of completing the circle, for theirs were some of the first Guatemalan refugee testimonies I heard articulate an urgent sense of refugee transnationality. Through their actions and words, JOSÉ and the Guatemalan journalist, like others I spoke with, conveyed a sense of the simultaneity and extensions of events and possibilities that influence transnational existence. These include: (1) complex articulations of ruptures and sutures of identity; (2) the Guatemalan and Canadian national contexts of displacement and refuge; and (3) the dynamic of internal differentiation among Guatemalans in Canada and Guatemala. For them and other Guatemalans, multiple spatial and temporal contexts – here, there, and the journey in between – are brought into a single field of transnational reality.

My research provided an opportunity to examine Guatemalan political violence, refugee response, and Canadian immigration dimensions from a variety of perspectives and through myriad sources. I attempted to avoid perpetuating the silence of Guatemalans in Canada through 'studied silence' (Green 1998) and have employed multi-sited, transnational ethnography, recounted in Chapter Two, to capture the complexity of experiences of political violence, displacement, and lived realities of community and identity. Here I build on the research by Burns (1999) and Montejo (1999b) on transnationalism and refugees in the Americas context as well as limited methodological work on transnational interviewing and multi-site, cross-border research.

Three major themes are addressed: (1) the destruction of communities of association and physical communities through political violence in Guatemala, leading to a forging of primary transnational social relations and weak local ties; (2) the spatialization of refugee movement and settlement in Canada in response to policy change; and (3) gendered narrations of rupture and suture that speak of the obstacles and barriers of identity transformation.

Two key points emerged from my interview conversations that informed a major conceptual shift from 'transnationalism' – typically of immigrants – to 'refugee transnationalism.' First, refugee transnationalism incorporates a conceptual shift from a focus on 'connections' to 'ruptures and sutures' of identity and sense of belonging. Second, as examined in Chapter 2, refugee transnationalism necessitates a shift of focus from 'community identity' to 'transnational social fields' and multi-scaled social relations. By incorporating experiences of political violence into the burgeoning concept of immigrant transnationalism, a differentiated sense of refugee transnationalism emerges that is infused by the effects of political violence and forced displacement. Transnationalism, as a conceptual tool and methodological framework, offers the possibility to grapple, in a critically analytical way, with the entanglements of refugee actions and narrations as well as with government declarations and policy changes.

Through a transnational lens, I draw attention to the spatialization of Guatemalan refugee and immigrant settlement in Canada and draw on the recent work of Mahler (1998; 2001), Vertovec (2003), and Waters (2002) to highlight, as they do, the relatively local and immobile lives, yet highly transnational social relations, that often characterize immigrant and refugee experiences. Most transnational studies concentrate on the fluidity of movement, while my work uncovers the rupture of displacement. Whereas the American- and Mexican-destination research highlights mobility and connections, the Canadian experience I encountered highlights immobility and rupture.

Though mobility is identified as a key feature of transnationalism, it must be recognized that the agency and life choices of the world's refugees are quite different from those of (im)migrants and the social processes that bind the two contexts when physical presence is impossible in the home country. As with all people on the move, refugees undoubtedly maintain a 'double consciousness,' but the transnational social fields they forge and maintain are decidedly different from those created by labour migrants, international entrepreneurs, and transnational political activists. For refugees, physical mobility is often short-term, one-way, and violence-induced. Quick decisions and rapid movement is often required, leaving refugees stuck 'out-of-place' for much longer than expected. As with transmigrants, refugee processes are not new phenomena. By bringing in a newer optic, however, researchers are better equipped to examine the complex experience in ways not possible with conventional research practices.

The roles of the Guatemalan and Canadian states are of immense importance in perpetuating ruptures rather than facilitating transnational flows. This process is an on-the-ground reality discussed in Chapters 3 and 4. Refugees and (im)migrants are 'bound' by the political, social, and national contexts of both (if not more) countries, even if they are able to cross borders with ease. The cross-trajectories of Guatemalan refugee arrivals in the 1980s, together with Canadian immigration and refugee policy reversals, stand as critical moments of policy change and refugee response that created changed geographies of movement and settlement. First, the imposition of a travel visa requirement cut off the possibility for refugees to fly to Canada to request asylum and forced refugees into the much more difficult and potentially dangerous overland route through the USA in order to make their claims at border crossings. This crisis stands as the first time in which the Canadian-American border became a contested zone of refuge. Second, by making direct claims for political asylum, Guatemalan (and Salvadoran) refugees inscribed their presence at the border where they could not be turned away. The Canadian government responded to these acts of desperation with the criminalization of refugee assistance and attempts to deter refugee claims being made.

Though perhaps living intensely local lives with limited communication with family and friends in Guatemala, there is much to be said for how social lives are imagined to encapsulate more than is local, visible, and immediate. The punctuation of transnational events and practices contribute to a deeper sense of identity and encourages a more flexible examination of social and cultural expressions. Physical mobility is perhaps restricted in the refugee context, but imaginative, multiple, hybrid, situated identity and social expression metaphorically work to suture the many fragments of identity and social relations in the process of reconstructing shattered lives.

My research brings into focus the issues of cultural change, population movement and settlement, and the policy implications of the current period of dynamic negotiations of identities. A transnational approach to identity and community transformation offers an embodied and material grounding to abstract notions of globalization and population dynamics. Three *transnational ethnographies* complemented by voices of other participants in Chapters 5 and 6 reveal the ways in which political violence, refugee exodus, and immigration policies engender a shift in primary social relations from face-to-face experiences of proximity that are associated with 'communities' to those that stretch across borders. Weak ties, on the other hand, play a prominent role in the face-to-face experiences confronted in new refugee spaces in Canada.

Internal differentiation among Guatemalans is the critical reason for the lack of supportive environment found among Guatemalans in Canada. The range of experiences that led Guatemalans to Canada from all sides of the political spectrum works against the development of close primary social relations at any single scale; rather, weak and unstable ties and internal divisions are fostered. Varying legal status, the continuing instability, impunity, and insecurity associated with living conditions in Guatemala, low income levels (in both countries) leading to lack of communication, and the physical distance between the two countries inhibiting regular travel, all work to create transnational ruptures rather than transnational flows.

Transnational social fields include new refugee and (im)migrant spaces in Canada, primary social relations in Guatemala and Canada, as well as social relations among those who remain in Guatemala. Identity is constantly redefined and recreated by transnational refugees and (im)migrants with the passing of time and the shifting of place. Neither loss nor reinvention capture adequately the multiplicity of viewpoints and experiences expressed by participants and external entities, such as the Canadian Embassy and the IRB, which exert great influence over new imaginings of identity in Canada. Canadian immigration and refugee policies create shifting social realities given the political climate and visions of the role of (im)migrants and refugees in shaping the country's future. These processes, competing as they are, reinforce each other and continually challenge the meaning of identities to reflect both self-definition and the perceptions and power of others. One conclusion to draw from my research is that transnational processes do not erode state policies or challenge the concept of the nation-state, as many theorists suggest, but much the opposite. In the experience of those with whom I spoke, government immigration and foreign policies function to shape the formation of transnational ruptures.

An exploration of the gendered experiences of forced migration from Guatemala and refugee settlement in Canada has allowed new perspectives to emerge from a wide variety of data. Through their relatively immobile transnational lives, Guatemalan women and men, Maya and Ladino, are placed within Canadian space in particular ways that challenge the centrality of mobility to notions of transnationalism. Through their words and voices, some of the multi-scaled reality of refugee transnationalism (from the fine scale spaces of individual bodies to global flows of forced migrants and refugees) comes to the fore and provides future researchers and policy makers the challenge to work towards the facilitation of transnational flows and reconnections.

Bibliography

Abu-Lughod, Lila (1991) Writing against culture. In *Recapturing Anthropology: Working in the Present*, ed. R.G. Fox, pp. 137-162. Santa Fe, NM: School of American Research Press.

Alonso, Ana María (1994) The politics of space, time, and substance: State formation, nationalism, and ethnicity. *Annual Review of Anthropology* 23, 379-405.

American Friends Service Committee (1988) *In the Shadow of Liberty: Central American Refugees in the United States*. Philadelphia, PA: AFSC Latin America/ Caribbean Peace Education Program.

Amnesty International (2003) *Legitimacy on the Line: Human Rights and the 2003 Guatemalan Elections*. London, UK: Amnesty International. AI INDEX: AMR 34/051/2003 (19 September). Accessed at: http://web.amnesty.org/library/index/ engamr340512003.

Anderson, Benedict (1991) *Imagined Communities: Reflections on the Origin and Spread of Nationalism*. Rev. ed. London, UK and New York, NY: Verso.

Anderson, Kathryn (2003) *Weaving Relationships: Canada-Guatemala Solidarity*. Waterloo, ON: Wilfrid Laurier University Press.

Appadurai, Arjun (1986) Theory in anthropology: Center and periphery. *Comparative Studies in Society and History* 28, 356-361.

Appadurai, Arjun (1990) Disjuncture and difference in the global cultural economy. *Public Culture* 2 (2), 1-24.

Appadurai, Arjun (1991) Global ethnoscapes: Notes and queries for a transnational anthropology. In *Recapturing Anthropology: Working in the Present*, ed. R.G. Fox, pp. 191-210. Santa Fe, NM: School of American Research Press.

Appadurai, Arjun (1996) *Modernity at Large: Cultural Dimensions of Globalization*. Minneapolis, MN: University of Minnesota Press.

Arellano, Pavel (2000a) Familia Portillo se va por temor a Los Pasaco: Inseguridad: Madre, hermana, cuñado y sobrinos temen a criminales, *Prensa Libre* (Guatemala), 21 de junio. Accessed at: http://www.prensalibre.com/pl/2000/junio/21/46203. html.

Arellano, Pavel (2000b) Cumbre: Buscarán unificación de región centroamericana y Canadá, Prensa Libre (Guatemala), 28 de septiembre. Accessed at: http://www. prensalibre.com/pl/2000/septiembre/28/64362.html.

Arellano, Pavel and Miguel González Moraga (2000) Complejo control militar de civiles: Encuentran en la SAE, 650,428 fichados en archivo militar, Prensa Libre (Guatemala), 8 de mayo. Accessed at: http://www.prensalibre.com/pl/2000/ mayo/08/40734.html.

Arensberg, Conrad M. (1954) The community-study method. *The American Journal of Sociology* 60, 109-124.

Aron, Adrianne (1989) Torture, trauma, and terror: Psychotherapy with Central American refugees. *Presentation to the Torture Survivors Network, 5 June.* Accessed at: http:///www.pacinfo.com/eugene/tsnet/Aronpaper.html.

Bailey, Adrian J. (2001) Turning transnational: Notes on the theorisation of international migration. *International Journal of Population Geography* 7 (6) November/December, 413-428.

Bailey, Adrian J. and Joshua G. Hane (1995) Population in motion: Salvadorean refugees and circulation migration. *Bulletin of Latin American Research* 14 (2) May, 171-200.

Bailey, Adrian J., Richard A. Wright, Ines Miyares, and Alison Mountz (2002) (Re)producing Salvadoran transnational geographies. *Annals of the Association of American Geographers* 92 (1) March, 125-144.

Bailey, Cathy, Catherine White and Rachel Pain (1999) Evaluating qualitative research: Dealing with the tension between 'science' and 'creativity.' *Area* 31 (2) June, 169-178.

Bakan, Abigail and Daiva Stasiulis, eds. (1997) *Not One of the Family: Foreign Domestic Workers in Canada.* Toronto, ON: University of Toronto Press.

Balibar, Etienne and Immanuel Wallerstein (1991) *Race, Nation, Class: Ambiguous Identities.* London and New York: Verso.

Ball, Patrick, Paul Kobrak, and Herbert F. Spirer (1999) *State Violence in Guatemala, 1960 - 1996: A Quantitative Reflection.* Report for the American Association for the Advancement of Science (AAAS) and the International Centre for Human Rights Investigations (CIIDH), Washington, DC. Accessed at:http://shr.aaas.org/guatemala/ciidh/qr/english/qrtitle.html.

Barrios, Lucy (1999) Ríos Montt: 'Jamás ordené una masacre,' *Prensa Libre* (Guatemala), 28 de febrero. Accessed at: http://www.prensalibre.com (Noticias Nacionales).

Basch, Linda, Nina Glick Schiller, and Cristina Szanton Blanc (1994) *Nations Unbound: Transnational Projects, Postcolonial Predicaments, and Deterritorialized Nation-States.* Langhorne, PA: Gordon and Breach.

Bastos, Santiago and Manuela Camus (1994) *Sombras de una batalla : Los desplazados por la violencia en la ciudad de Guatemala.* Guatemala City: FLACSO.

Baxter, Jamie and John Eyles (1997) Evaluating qualitative research in social geography: Establishing 'rigour' in interview analysis. *Transactions of the Institute of British Geographers* 22 (4) December, 505-525.

Baxter, Jamie and John Eyles (1999) Prescription for research practice? Grounded theory in qualitative evaluation. *Area* 31 (2) June, 179-181.

Behar, Ruth (1996) *The Vulnerable Observer: Anthropology that Breaks Your Heart.* Boston, MA: Beacon Press.

Beiser, Morton (1999) *Strangers at the Gate: The 'Boat People's First Ten Years in Canada.* Toronto, ON: University of Toronto Press.

Berger, John (1998) How to live with stones: A letter to Subcomandante Marcos in the mountains of Southeast Mexico. *Brick: A Literary Journal* 58 (Winter), 12-15.

Beristain, Carlos Martín (1998) The value of memory. *Forced Migration Review* 2 (August), 24-26.

Bernhard, Judith (1997) Supporting parental involvement in schools: An ethnographic study of the Toronto Latino Parent Support Group. *CERIS Metropolis Research Report* (Toronto). Accessed at: http://ceris.metropolis.net/frameset_e.html.

Bernhard, Judith K., Marlinda Freire, Veronica Pacini-Ketchabaw and Virginia Villanueva (1998) A Latin-American parents' group participates in their children's schooling: Parent involvement reconsidered. *Canadian Ethnic Studies* 30 (3) Fall, 77-99.

Bernhard, Judith K., Luin Goldring, and Patricia Landolt (2005) Latin American Research Group – LARG. Accessed at: http://www.yorku.ca/cohesion/LARG/html/largindex2.htm

Bhabha, Homi (1990) Introduction: Narrating the nation. In *Nation and Narration*, H. Bhabha, pp. 1-7. New York, NY and London, UK: Routledge.

Bhabha, Homi (1994) *The Location of Culture.* New York, NY and London, UK: Routledge.

Bibby, Reginald W. (1990) *Mosaic Madness: The Poverty and Potential of Life in Canada*. Toronto, ON: Stoddart.

Black, Richard (1991) Refugees and displaced persons: Geographical perspectives and research directions. *Progress in Human Geography* 15 (3), 281-298.

Black, Richard (1993) Geography and refugees: Current issues. In *Geography and Refugees: Patterns and Processes of Change*, eds. R. Black and V. Robinson, pp. 1-13. London, UK and New York, NY: Belhaven Press.

Black, Richard, Khalid Koser, Nadje Al-Ali (2000) The mobilization and participation of transnational exile communities in post-conflict reconstruction: A comparison of Bosnia and Eritrea. *Research Briefing #1*, Transnational Communities: An ESRC Research Program, pp. 4. http://www.transcomm.ox.ac.uk/briefings/brief1.pdf.

Bondi, Liz (1993) Locating identity politics. In *Place and the Politics of Identity*, eds. M. Keith and S. Pile, pp. 84-101. New York, NY: Routledge.

Bottinelli, María Cristina, Ignacio Maldonado, Estela Troya, Pablo Herrera, and Carlos Rodríguez (1990) *Psychological Impact of Exile: Salvadoran and Guatemalan Families in Mexico.* Washington, DC: Hemispheric Migration Project, Centre for Immigration Policy and Refugee Assistance at Georgetown University.

Boyd, Monica (1986) Immigrant women in Canada. In *International Migration: The Female Experience*. eds. R.J. Simon and C. Brettell, pp. 45-61. Towota, NJ: Rowman and Allenheld.

Boyd, Monica (1994) Canada's refugee flows: Gender inequality. *Canadian Social Trends* (32) Spring, 7-12.

Brazao, Dale (1987) Bewildered refugees huddled in Buffalos heartbreak house, *Toronto Star*, 24 February, A11.

Breckenridge, Carol and Arjun Appadurai (1989) On moving targets. *Public Culture* 2 (1), i-iv.

Brown, Cathy (1997) 'It's my culture and my history; I have to know it': A journey to Chiapas: Part II. *TESL Contact: Newsletter of the Association of Teachers of English as a Second Language of Ontario* 23 (1), 4-8.

Burns, Allan F. (1989a) Internal and external identity among Kanjobal Mayan refugees in Florida. In *Conflict, Migration, and the Expression of Ethnicity*, eds. N.L. Gonzalez and C.S. McCommon, pp. 46-59. Boulder, CO: Westview Press.

Burns, Allan F. (1989b) Immigration, ethnicity, and work in Indiantown, Florida. *Paper Number 8, Published for the Center for Latin American Studies.* Gainesville, FL: University of Florida.

Burns, Allan F. (1989c) The Maya in Florida. *Migration World* 17, 20-26.

Burns, Allan F. (1993) *Maya in Exile: Guatemalans in Florida*. Philadelphia, PA: Temple University Press.

Burns, Allan F. (1999) Identities in the diaspora: Mayan culture and community today. In *Identities on the Move: Transnational Processes in North America and the Caribbean Basin*, ed. L.R. Goldin, pp. 135-150. Albany, NY: Institute for Mesoamerican Studies, University of Albany. Distributed by University of Texas Press.

Calhoun, Craig (1992) The infrastructure of modernity: Indirect social relationships, information technology, and social integration. In *Social Change and Modernity*, eds. H. Haferkamp and N.J. Smelser, pp. 205-236. Berkeley, CA: University of California Press.

Calhoun, Craig (1995) *Critical Social Theory.* Oxford, UK and Cambridge, USA: Blackwell.

Carmack, Robert, ed. (1988) *Harvest of Violence: The Maya Indians and the Guatemalan Crisis.* Norman, OK: University of Oklahoma Press.

Carrasco, Pia, Damaris Rose, and Johanne Charbonneau (1999) The constitution of weak ties: A bridge for the adaptation of Central American immigrant mothers of young children in Montréal. *Canadian Ethnic Studies* 31 (1), 73-91.

Casillas, Rodolfo (1995) Central American migration to Mexico in the era of NAFTA. In *Central American Migration to Mexico and the United States: A Post-NAFTA Prognosis*, Pew Monograph Series #1. Washington, DC: Hemispheric Migration Project at Georgetown University.

Casillas, Rodolfo and Miguel Ángel Castillo (1994) *Los flujos migratorios internacionales en la frontera sur de México*. México, DF: Secretaría del Trabajo y Previsión Social, Consejo Nacional de Población.

Castillo Priego, Eddy (2005) Crímenes contra mujeres aumentaron en enero. *el Periódico* (Guatemala), 31 de enero. Accessed at: http://www.elperiodico.com.gt/ (Actualidad Nacionales).

Castles, Stephen (2002) Migration and community formation under conditions of globalization. *International Migration Review* 36 (4), 1143-1168.

Castles, Stephen and Mark J. Miller (1993) *The Age of Migration: International Population Movements in the Modern World.* London, UK: MacMillan.

CBC WebPost (2000) Guatemalan president's family flee to Canada, 21 June. Accessed at: http://www.cbcnews.cbc.ca.

CCR, Canadian Council for Refugees (2004) News Release: Safe third country agreement closes the doors on refugees, 1 December. Montréal: CCR.

Chambers, Erve J. and Philip D. Young (1979) Mesoamerican community studies: The past decade. *Annual Review of Anthropology* 8, 45-69.

Chavez, Leo R. (1994) The power of the imagined community: The settlement of undocumented Mexicans and Central Americans in the United States. *American Anthropologist* 96 (1), 52-73.

Chavez, Leo R. (1997) Immigration reform and nativism: The nationalist response to the transnationalist challenge. In *Immigrants Out!: The New Nativism and the Anti-Immigrant Impulse in the United States*, ed. J.F. Perea, pp. 61-77. New York, NY: New York University Press.

Chavez, Leo R. (1998) *Shadowed Lives: Undocumented Immigrants in American Society*, 2nd. ed. Fort Worth, TX and New York, NY: Harcourt Brace Jovanovich College Publishers.

Chinchilla, Norma, Nora Hamilton, and James Loucky (1993) Central Americans in Los Angeles: An immigrant community in transition. In *In the Barrios: Latinos and the Underclass Debate*, eds. J. Moore and R. Pinderhughes, pp. 51-78. New York, NY: Russell Sage Foundation.

CIC, Citizenship and Immigration Canada (2004a) *Facts and Figures 2004: Immigration Overview: Permanent and Temporary Residents*. Ottawa, ON: CIC. Accessed at: http://www.cic.gc.ca/english/pdf/pub/facts2004.pdf.

CIC (2004b) *Data runs for Guatemalans in Canada, 1980 to 2004*, 1980 to 1998 data obtained in March 1999; 1999 to 2004 data obtained in February 2005.

CIC (2004c) *Enforcement Manual (ENF) Manual ENF10: Removals* (October). Ottawa, ON: CIC. Accessed at: http://www.cic.gc.ca/manuals-guides/english/enf/enf10e.pdf.

CIC (2005) *Overseas Processing (OP) Manual OP20: Temporary Resident Permits* (April). Ottawa, ON: CIC. Accessed at: http://www.cic.gc.ca/manuals-guides/english/op/op20e.pdf.

Cleroux, Richard (1987) Churches not exempt from laws, Bouchard warns, *Globe and Mail*, 13 August, A3.

Clifford, James (1988) *The Predicament of Culture.* Cambridge, MA: Harvard University Press.

Clifford, James (1997) *Routes: Travel and Translation in the Late Twentieth Century.* Cambridge, MA and London, UK: Harvard University Press.

Cohen, Robin (1995) *The Cambridge Survey of Migration.* Cambridge, UK: Cambridge University Press.

Collins, Jock and Francis Henry (1994) Racism, ethnicity, and immigration. In *Immigration and Refugee Policy: Australia and Canada Compared, Vol. 2*, eds. Howard Adelman, Allan Borowski, Meyer Burstein, and Lois Foster, pp. 515-548. Toronto, ON: University of Toronto Press.

Comisión Económica para América Latina y el Caribe (CEPAL) (1991) *Remesas y económica familiar en El Salvador, Guatemala, y Nicaragua*. Guatemala: CEPAL.

Comisión para el Esclarecimiento Histórico (CEH) (1999a) *Guatemala: Memoria del Silencio (Tz'inil na 'tab'al)*. Guatemala: Comisión para el Esclarecimiento Histórico (Spanish language). Accessed at: http://hrdata.aaas.org/ceh/mds/spanish/.

Commission for Historical Clarification (CEH) (1999b) *Guatemala: Memory of Silence (Tz'inil na 'tab'al). Report of the Commission for Historical Clarification Conclusions and Recommendations*. Executive Summary (English language). Accessed at: http://hrdata.aaas.org/ceh/report/english/.

Commission for Historical Clarification Canada (CEH Canada) (1998) *Final Report: Project to collect testimonies in Canada from Guatemalans who feel they were affected by the armed conflict of Guatemala*. Final Report to the Department of Foreign Affairs and International Trade (DFAIT) unpublished report, December.

CONGCOOP (Coordinación de ONGs y Cooperativas) (1997) *El impacto de las migraciones de Guatemaltecos al exterior: Reflexiones y datos iniciales*. Memoria de un Taller. Guatemala: CONCOOP.

Córdova, C. (1996) Central American migration to San Francisco: One hundred years of building a community. In *Central Americans in California: Transnational Communities, Economies and Cultures*. Los Angeles, CA: Occasional Papers Series, The Center for Multiethnic and Transnational Studies, University of Southern California.

Corter, Carl (1998) Parent participation in elementary schools: The experience of Hispanic immigrants. *CERIS Metropolis Research Report* (Toronto). Accessed at: http://ceris.metropolis.net/frameset_e.html.

Coutin, Susan Bibler (1993) *The Culture of Protest: Religious Activism and the U.S. Sanctuary Movement.* Boulder, CO: Westview Press.

Coutin, Susan Bibler (2000) *Legalizing Moves: Salvadoran Immigrants' Struggle for U.S. Residency.* Chicago, IL: University of Michigan Press.

Coutin, Susan Bibler (2004) The odyssey of Salvadoran asylum seekers. *NACLA Report on the Americas* 37 (6), 38-41.

CP, Canadian Press (1984) Church officials offer sanctuary to Guatemalans, *Globe and Mail*, January.

Crang, Mike (2002) Qualitative methods: The new orthodoxy? *Progress in Human Geography* 26 (5), 647–655.

Creese, Gillian (1992) The politics of refugees in Canada. In *Deconstructing a Nation: Immigration, Multiculturalism, and Racism in '90s Canada*, ed. V. Satzewich, pp. 123-143. Halifax, NS and Saskatoon, SK: Fernwood Books and the Social Research Unit.

Creese, Gillian and Robyn Dowling (2001) Gendering immigration: The experience of women. *Progress in Planning* 55 (Part 3), 153-162.

Creese, Gillian, Isabel Dyck and Arlene McLaren (1999) Reconstituting the family: Negotiation immigration and settlement. *RIIM Metropolis Working Paper Series #99-10,* March. Accessed at: http://www.riim.metropolis.net/frameset_e.html.

Crisp, Jeff (1999) 'Who has counted the refugees?' UNHCR and the politics of numbers. *UNHCR New Issues in Refugee Research Working Paper Series no. 12*, June. Accessed at: http://www.unhcr.ch/cgi-bin/texis/vtx/doclist?page=research&id=3b8a11284.

Crittenden, Ann (1988) *Sanctuary: A Story of American Conscience and the Law in Collision.* New York, NY: Weidenfeld & Nicolson.

Crush, Jonathan and David McDonald (2000) Transnationalism, African immigration and new migrant spaces in South Africa. *Canadian Journal of African Studies* 34, 1-19. Special Issue: Transnationalism, African Immigration, and New Refugee Spaces in South Africa.

Cullather, Nick (1999) *Secret History: The CIA's Classified Account of its Operations in Guatemala, 1952-1954.* Stanford, CA: Stanford University Press.

Cunningham, Hilary (1995) *God and Caesar at the Rio Grande: Sanctuary and the Politics of Religion.* Minneapolis, MN: University of Minnesota Press.

Cunningham, Hilary (2000) The ethnography of transnational social activism: Understanding the global as local practice. *American Ethnologist* 26 (3), 583-604.

Dafoe, Chris (1999) The role of her life: Despite death threats, Guatemalan actress Wendy Mendez has taken her questions about her 'disappeared' mother home, *The Globe and Mail*, 8 December, R1-R2.

de la Garza, Rodolfo, Manuel Orozco, and Miguel Maraona (1997) *Binational Impact of Latino Remittances*. Policy Brief. Claremont, CA: Tomás Rivera Policy Institute.

de Villa, Gonzalo and W. George Lovell (1999) Land and peace: Two points of view. In *Journeys of Fear: Refugee Return and National Transformation in Guatemala*, eds. L. North and A. Simmons, pp. 40-54. Montréal and Kingston: McGill-Queen's University Press.

Defense Intelligence Agency (DIA) (1979) Military Intelligence Summary (MIS), Vol. VIII, Latin America (U), November. Declassified Secret Summary downloaded from *The Guatemalan Military: What the U.S. Files Reveal, Volume II: Documents* (June 2000). Washington, DC: National Security Archive. Accessed at: http://www.gwu.edu/%7Ensarchiv/NSAEBB/NSAEBB32/16-01.htm.

Desbiens, Caroline (1999) Feminism 'in' geography: Elsewhere, beyond and the politics of paradoxical space. *Gender, Place and Culture: A Journal of Feminist Geography* 6 (2) June, 179-185.

DeVoretz, Don J., Sergiy Pivnenko, and Morton Beiser (2004) Economic experiences of refugees in Canada. *RIIM Metropolis Working Paper Series #04-04,* February. Accessed at: http://www.riim.metropolis.net/frameset_e.html.

Dirks, Gerald E. (1995) *Controversy and Complexity: Canadian Immigration Policy during the 1980s.* Montréal and Kingston: McGill-Queen's University Press.

Diskin, Martin (1995) Anthropological fieldwork in Mesoamerica: Focus on the field. *Latin American Research Review* 30 (1), 163-175.

Doyle, Kate (2000) The Guatemalan Military: What the U.S. Files Reveal. *National Security Archive Electronic Briefing Book No. 32.* Washington, DC: National

Security Archive. Accessed at: http://www2.gwu.edu/~nsarchiv/NSAEBB/NSAEBB32/index.html.

Duany, Jorge (1996) Imagining the Puerto Rican nation: Recent works on cultural identity. *Latin American Research Review* 31 (3), 248-267.

Dunn, Samuel (2000) *'Keeping the Pain': Health, Belonging and Resilience among Guatemalan Immigrant Men*, Unpublished MA Thesis, Graduate Programme in Social Anthropology, York University, Toronto, ON, Canada.

Dyck, Isabel and Arlene Tigar McLaren (2004) Telling it like it is? Constructing accounts of settlement with immigrant and refugee women in Canada. *Gender, Place and Culture: A Journal of Feminist Geography* 11 (4) December, 513-534.

Dyck, Isabel (2005) Suzanne Mackenzie Memorial Lecture: Feminist geography, the 'everyday,' and local–global relations: Hidden spaces of place-making. *The Canadian Geographer* 49 (3), 233-243.

El Periódico (1999) La víctima número 73, 15 años después, *el Periódico* (Guatemala), 13 de agosto, 4. Accessed at: http://www.prensalibre.com (Noticias Nacionales).

Elbow, Gary E. (1992) The overground railroad: Central American refugee flows to Canada. In *Geographical Snapshots of North America*, ed. D.G. Janelle, pp. 57-61. New York, NY and London, UK: Guilford Press.

England, Kim (1994) Getting personal: Reflexivity, positionality, and feminist research. *The Professional Geographer*, Special Issue: Women in the Field 46 (1) February, 80-89.

Evans, Dabney and Brandon Kohrt (2004) No refuge for persecuted neighbors: Human rights and asylum in the Americas. *AmericQuest* 1 (1), 1-21. Accessed at: http://ejournals.library.vanderbilt.edu/ameriquests/viewarticle.php?id=12&layout=abstract.

Falla, Ricardo (1994) *Massacres in the Jungle: Ixcán, Guatemala, 1975-1982*. Trans. Julia Howland. Boulder, CO: Westview Press.

Featherstone, Mike (1995) *Undoing Culture: Globalization, Postmodernism and Identity*. Thousand Oaks, CA: Sage Publications.

Feitlowitz, Marguerite (1998) *A Lexicon of Terror: Argentina and the Legacies of Torture*. New York, NY and Oxford, UK: Oxford University Press.

Ferguson, Jonathan (1985) Helping hand reaches out for Salvadoran refugees, *Toronto Star*, 13 July, B5.

Filóchofo (2000) Political Cartoon: El Presidente informó que sacará del país a su familia … por la inseguridad existente, *Prensa Libre* (Guatemala), 21 de junio. Accessed at: http://www.prensalibre.com/pl/2000/junio/21/46105.html (Opinión).

Fincher, Ruth (1993) Gender relations and the geography of migration. *Environment and Planning A* 25 (12), 1703-1705.

Fincher, Ruth (1997) Gender, age, and ethnicity in immigration for an Australian nation. *Environment and Planning A* 29 (2), 217-236.

Fink, Leon (2003) *The Maya of Morganton: Work and Community in the Nuevo New South*. Chapel Hill, NC: University of North Carolina Press.

Fink, Leon and Alvis Dunn (2000) The Maya of Morganton: Exploring worker identity within the global marketplace. In *The Maya Diaspora: Guatemalan Roots, New American Lives,* eds. J. Loucky and M. Moors, pp. 175-196. Philadelphia, PA: Temple University Press.

Fischer, Edward (1996) *The Pan-Maya Movement in Global and Local Context.* Ph.D. dissertation, Department of Anthropology, Tulane University, New Orleans, LA

FOCAL, Canadian Foundation for the Americas (1997) Conference Report: *Managing the Peace: Building Consensus on Economic Reforms in Guatemala,* 20-21 March. Ottawa, ON: FOCAL.

FOCAL (2004) Final Report: *Hemispheric Integration and Transnationalism in the Americas,* Canadian Embassy (Guatemala City), 16-17 February. Ottawa, ON: FOCAL. Accessed at: http://www.focal.ca/images/pdf/migration_report.pdf.

Fouron, Georges and Nina Glick Schiller (2001) All in the family: Gender, transnational migration, and the nation-state. *Identities. Global Studies in Culture and Power* 7 (4) January, 539-582.

Fox, Richard G., ed. (1990) *Nationalist Ideologies and the Production of National Culture.* Washington, DC: American Anthropological Association.

Foxen, Patricia (2000) Cacophony of voices: A K'iche' Mayan narrative of remembrance and forgetting. *Transcultural Psychiatry* 37 (3), 355-381.

Foxen, Patricia (2002) *K'iche' Maya in a Re-imagined World: Transnational Perspectives on Identity.* Unpublished Ph.D. dissertation, Department of Anthropology, McGill University, Montréal, QC, Canada.

Friedland, Joan and Jesus Rodriguez y Rodriguez (1987) *Seeking Safe Ground: The Legal Situation of Central American Refugees in Mexico.* San Diego, CA and Mexico, DF: Mexico-U.S. Law Institute, University of San Diego Law School and Instituto de Investigaciones Jurídicas, Universidad Nacional Autónoma de México.

Fuentes, Carlos (1985) *Latin America at War with the Past.* CBC Massey Lecture Series, Montréal, QC and London, UK: CBC Enterprises.

Galeano, Eduardo (1992) *We Say No: Chronicles 1963-1991.* Trans. Mark Fried. New York, NY: W.W. Norton and Company.

Gardner, Katy (1995) *Global Migrants, Local Lives: Travel and Transformation in Rural Bangladesh.* Oxford, UK: Clarendon Press.

Garrard Burnett, Virginia (1998) *Protestantism in Guatemala: Living in the New Jerusalem.* Austin, TX: University of Texas Press.

GCSN, Guatemala Canada Solidarity Network (2000) *Situational Analysis.* Unpublished report, Guatemala, February.

Geertz, Clifford (1973) Thick description: Toward an interpretive theory of culture. In *The Interpretation of Culture*, pp. 3-30. New York, NY: Basic Books.

Geertz, Clifford (1988) *Works and Lives: The Anthropologist as Author.* Stanford, CA: Stanford University Press.

Gerardi, Juan (1998) *Speech Made By Monseñor Juan Gerardi On The Occasion Of The Presentation Of The REMHI Report* / Discurso de *Monseñor Juan Gerardi con ocasión de la presentación del informe REMHI* (Guatemala City,

Metropolitan Cathedral), 24 April. Accessed at: http://www.odhag.org.gt/Discurso%20M%20Gerardi/Discurso%20Mon%20Gerardi.htm.

Gidley, Ruth M., Cynthia Kee, and Reggie Norton, eds. (1999) *Guatemala: Thinking About the Unthinkable: Reflections and Responses to the Recovery of Historical Memory (REMHI) and Historical Clarification Commission (CEH) Reports*. London, UK: Association of Artists for Guatemala.

Gillin, John (1945) Parallel cultures and the inhibitions to acculturation in a Guatemalan community. *Social Forces* 24, 1-14.

Gillin, John (1948) 'Race' relations without conflict: A Guatemalan town. *American Journal of Sociology* 53, 337-343.

Gillin, John (1951) *The Culture of Security in San Carlos: A Study of a Guatemalan Community of Indians and Ladinos*. Middle American Research Institute Publication no. 16. New Orleans, LA: Tulane University.

Glaister, Dan (2004) Murderers target Guatemala's young women: Hundreds killed in executions reminiscent of those during civil war. *The Guardian*, 18 September. Accessed at: http://www.guardian.co.uk/international/story/0,,1307280,00.html.

Glick Schiller, Nina (1997) The situation of transnational studies. *Identities: Global Studies in Culture and Power* 4 (2) December, 155-166.

Glick Schiller, Nina, Linda Basch, and Cristina Blanc-Szanton, eds. (1992a) *Towards a Transnational Perspective on Migration: Race, Class, Ethnicity, and Nationalism Reconsidered*. Annals of the New York Academy of Sciences. New York, NY: The New York Academy of Sciences.

Glick Schiller, Nina, Linda Basch, and Cristina Blanc-Szanton (1992b) Transnationalism: A new analytic framework for understanding migration. In *Towards a Transnational Perspective on Migration: Race, Class, Ethnicity, and Nationalism Reconsidered*. Annals of the New York Academy of Sciences, ed. N. Glick Schiller, L. Basch, and C. Blanc-Szanton, pp. 1-24. New York, NY: The New York Academy of Sciences.

Glick Schiller, Nina, Linda Basch, and Cristina Blanc-Szanton (1995) From immigrant to transmigrant: Theorizing transnational migration. *Anthropological Quarterly* 68 (1) January, 48-63.

Goldin, Liliana R., ed. (1999a) *Identities on the Move: Transnational Processes in North America and the Caribbean Basin*. Albany, NY: Institute for Mesoamerican Studies, University of Albany. Distributed by University of Texas Press.

Goldin, Liliana R. (1999b) Transnational identities: The search for analytic tools. In *Identities on the Move: Transnational Processes in North America and the Caribbean Basin*, ed. L.R. Goldin, pp. 1-11. Albany, NY: Institute for Mesoamerican Studies, University of Albany. Distributed by University of Texas Press.

Goldman, Francisco (1999) Murder comes for the bishop. *The New Yorker*, 15 March, 60-77.

Goldring, Luin (1998) The power of status in transnational social fields. In *Transnationalism from Below*, eds. M.P. Smith and L.E. Guarnizo, pp. 165-195. New Brunswick, NJ and London, UK: Transaction Publishers.

Goldring, Luin (2001) The gender and geography of citizenship in Mexico-U.S. transnational spaces. *Identities: Global Studies in Culture and Power* 7 (4) January, 501-537.

Goldring, Luin (2003) Rethinking remittances: Social and political dimensions of individual and collective remittances. *CERLAC Working Paper Series* (February). Toronto, ON: Centre for Research on Latin America and the Caribbean (CERLAC) and York University.

Goldring, Luin and Judith Adler Hellman, eds. (2004) *Canadian Journal of Latin American and Caribbean Studies*. Guest-edited Special Issue: International Migration in the Americas, 29 (57-58) Spring/Fall.

Grandin, Greg (2000) *The Blood of Guatemala: A History of Race and Nation*. Durham, NC and London, UK: Duke University Press.

Grandin, Greg (2004) An interview with Greg Grandin, author of *The Last Colonial Massacre: Latin America in the Cold War* (2004). *University of Chicago Press Online*. Accessed at: http://www.press.uchicago.edu/Misc/Chicago/305724in.html.

Green, Linda (1994) Fear as a way of life. *Cultural Anthropology* 9 (2) May, 227-256.

Green, Linda (1995) Living in a state of fear. In *Fieldwork Under Fire: Contemporary Studies of Violence and Survival*, eds. C. Nordstrom and A.C.G.M. Robben, pp. 105-127. Berkeley, CA: University of California Press.

Green, Linda (1998) Lived lives and social suffering: Problems and concerns in medical anthropology. *Medical Anthropology Quarterly* 12, 3-7.

Green, Linda (1999) *Fear as a Way of Life: Mayan Widows in Rural Guatemala*. New York, NY: Columbia University Press.

Gregory, Derek (2004) *The Colonial Present: Afghanistan, Palestine, Iraq*. London, UK: Blackwell.

Guarnizo, Luis Eduardo and Michael Peter Smith (1998) The locations of transnationalism. In *Transnationalism from Below*, ed. M.P. Smith and L.E. Guarnizo, pp. 3-34. New Brunswick, NJ and London, UK: Transaction Publishers.

Guarnizo, Luis Eduardo, Alejandro Portes and William Haller (2003) Assimilation and transnationalism: Determinants of transnational political action among contemporary migrants. *American Journal of Sociology* 108 (6), 1211-1248.

Guarnizo, Luis Eduardo, Arturo I. Sanchez and Elizabeth M. Roach (1999) Mistrust, fragmented solidarity, and transnational migration: Colombians in New York City and Los Angeles. *Ethnic and Racial Studies*, Special Issue: Transnational Communities 22 (2), 367-396.

Guatemalan Military Archive, 1983-1985. A secret military intelligence dossier published by the National Security Archive in Washington, DC in 1999. Accessed at: http://www.gwu.edu/~nsarchiv/latin_america/guatemala.html.

Guba, E.G. (1990) Subjectivity and objectivity. In *Qualitative Inquiry in Education: The Continuing Debate*, ed. E.W. Eisner and A. Peshkin, pp. 74-91. New York, NY: Columbia University, Teacher's College Press.

Gurr, Ted (2000) *Peoples versus States: Minorities at Risk in the New Century.* Washington, DC: Institute of Peace Press.

Gupta, Akhil and James Ferguson (1992) Beyond 'culture': Space, identity, and the politics of difference. *Cultural Anthropology* 7 (1) February, 6-23.

Gupta, Akhil and James Ferguson, eds. (1997a) *Anthropological Locations: Boundaries and Grounds of a Field Science.* Berkeley, CA: University of California Press.

Gupta, Akhil and James Ferguson, eds. (1997b) *Culture, Power, Place: Explorations in Critical Anthropology.* Durham, NC and London, UK: Duke University Press.

Hagan, Jacqueline Maria (1994) *Deciding to be Legal: A Maya Community in Houston.* Philadelphia, PA: Temple University Press.

Halfacree, Keith H. and Paul J. Boyle (1993) The challenge facing migration research: The case for a biographical approach. *Progress in Human Geography* 17 (3), 333-348.

Hall, Stuart (1989) Imaginary identification and Politics, transcript of talk given at Institute of Contemporary Arts, cited in Watts (1991).

Hamilton, Nora and Norma Stoltz Chinchilla (1991) Central American migration: A framework for analysis. *Latin American Research Review* 26 (1), 75-110.

Hamilton, Nora and Norma Stoltz Chinchilla (1996) Global economic restructuring and international migration: Some observations based on the Mexican and Central American experience. *International Migration* 34 (2), 195-231.

Hamilton, Nora and Norma Stoltz Chinchilla (2001) *Seeking Community in a Global City: Guatemalans and Salvadorans in Los Angeles*. Philadelphia, PA: Temple University Press.

Hanks, William (1990) *Referential Practice: Language and Lived Space among the Maya*. Chicago, IL: University of Chicago Press.

Hannerz, Ulf (1996) *Transnational Connections: Culture, People, Places*. London, UK and New York, NY: Routledge.

Harvey, David (1973) *Social Justice and the City*. London, UK: Edward Arnold.

Harvey, David (1989) *The Condition of Postmodernity.* Oxford, UK: Basil Blackwell.

Hawkins, Freda (1994) *The Asylum-Seekers.* Behind the Headlines, vol. 52, ed. G. Fraser. Toronto, ON: Canadian Institute of International Affairs.

Hawkins, John (1983) Robert Redfield's culture concept and Mesoamerican anthropology. In *Heritage of Conquest: Thirty Years Later,* eds. C. Kendall, J. Hawkins, and L. Bossen, pp. 299-336. Albuquerque, NM: University of New Mexico Press.

Hess, Henry (1987) Refugees find doors to Canada quickly closing, *Globe and Mail*, 23 February, A1.

Hiebert, Daniel and David Ley (2003) Characteristics of immigrant transnationalism in Vancouver. *RIIM Metropolis Working Paper Series #03-15*, October. Accessed at: http://www.riim.metropolis.net/frameset_e.html.

Hilbert, Sarah (1997) For whom the nation? Internationalization, Zapatismo, and the struggle over Mexican modernity. *Antipode: A Journal of Radical Geography*, Special Issue: Geography and Transnational Discourse, 29 (2), 115-148.

Hobsbawm, Eric (1990) *Nations and Nationalism since 1780: Programme, Myth, Reality.* Cambridge, UK: Cambridge University Press.

Hodgson, Dorothy (1999) Critical interventions: Dilemmas of accountability in contemporary ethnographic research. *Identities: Global Studies in Culture and Power* 6 (2-3) July, 201-224.

House, Krista (1999) *'Absent Ones Who Are Always Present': Migration, Remittances, and Household Survival Strategies in Guatemala.* Unpublished MA Thesis, Department of Geography, Queen's University at Kingston, Canada.

House, Krista and W. George Lovell (1999) Transmigrant labour and the impact of foreign remittances in rural Guatemala: The case of Nueva Unión Maya. Paper presented at the *International Seminar on the Population of the Central American Isthmus at the End of the Millennium*, Jacó, Costa Rica, 20-22 October.

Hyndman, Jennifer (1997) Border crossings. *Antipode: A Journal of Radical Geography*, Special Issue: Geography and Transnational Discourse, 29 (2), 149-176.

Hyndman, Jennifer (1999a) Gender and Canadian immigration policy: A current snapshot. *Canadian Woman Studies* 19 (3), 6-10.

Hyndman, Jennifer (1999b) A post-Cold War geography of forced migration in Kenya and Somalia. *The Professional Geographer* 51 (1), 104-114.

Hyndman, Jennifer (2000) *Managing Displacement: Refugees and the Politics of Humanitarianism.* Minneapolis, MN: University of Minnesota Press.

Hyndman, Jennifer and Margaret Walton-Roberts (2000) Interrogating borders: A transnational approach to refugee research in Vancouver. *The Canadian Geographer* 44 (3), 244-258.

Inter-American Dialogue Task Force on Remittances (2004) *All in the Family: Latin America's Most Important International Financial Flow.* Washington, DC: Inter-American Dialogue. Accessed at: http://www.iadialog.org/publications/country_studies/remittances/all_family.pdf.

IOM, International Organization for Migration (2003) *Guatemalan Temporary Migration to Canada: Workers and Employers Assessment.* Guatemala: IOM. Accessible at: http://www.oim.org.gt/Informe%20Canada%20(English).pdf.

IOM (2004) *Survey on the Impact of Family Remittances on Guatemalan Homes 2004.* Working Notebooks on Migration no. 19. Guatemala: IOM. Accessed at: http://www.oim.org.gt/Cuaderno%20de%20Trabajo%20No.%2019%20(English).pdf.

IRB, Immigration and Refugee Board – Canada (1999) *Claims Referred and Finalized, 1989 to 1999 (Guatemala and El Salvador)*, IRB Convention Refugee Determination Division data accessed in April 1999.

IRB (2005a) *Claims Referred and Finalized, 1999 to 2004 (Guatemala and El Salvador)*, IRB Refugee Protection Division data accessed in March 2005.

IRB (2005b) *Acts, Rules and Regulations* (June). Accessed at: http://www.irb-cisr.gc.ca/en/about/rules/index_e.htm.

Israelite, Neita Kay (1998) Voices of recent Latina immigrants and refugees: Effects of budget cuts on their settlement experiences. *CERIS Metropolis Research Report* (Toronto). Accessed at: http://ceris.metropolis.net/frameset_e.html.

Jackson, Peter (1987) The ideas of 'race' and the geography of racism. In *Race and Racism: Essays in Social Geography*, ed. P. Jackson, pp. 3-21. Boston, MA: Allen and Unwin.

Jacob, André and Joseph Lévy (1994) The integration of two groups of women refugees: Guatemalans and Bulgarians. *Centre for Refugee Studies Working Paper Series* (York University), Toronto, ON.

Jameson, Fredric (1984) Postmodernism, or the cultural logic of late capitalism. *New Left Review* 146 (July/August), 53-92.

Jessor, Richard, Anne Colby, and Richard A. Shweder, eds. (1996) *Ethnography and Human Development: Context and Meaning in Social Inquiry.* Chicago, IL: University of Chicago Press.

Jonas, Susanne (1996a) Transnational realities and anti-immigrant state policies: Issues raised by the experiences of Central American immigrants and refugees in a trinational region. In *Latin America in the World-Economy*, ed. R. Korzeniewicz and W. Smith, pp. 117-132. Westport, CT: Greenwood.

Jonas, Susanne (1996b) 'National security,' regional development, and citizenship in U.S. immigration policy: Reflections from the case of Central American immigrants and refugees. In *Transnational Realities and Nation-states: Trends in International Migration and Immigration Policy in the Americas*, ed. M. Castro. Miami, FL: North-South Center.

Jones III, John Paul, Heidi J. Nast, and Susan M. Roberts, eds. (1997) *Thresholds in Feminist Geography: Difference, Methodology, Representation.* Lanham, MD and Oxford, UK: Rowman and Littlefield.

Kazemipur, Abdolmahammad and Shiva S. Halli (2000) The colour of poverty: A study of the poverty of ethnic and immigrant groups in Canada, *International Migration*, 38 (1) March, 69-88.

Kearney, Michael (1995) The local and the global: The anthropology of globalization and transnationalism. *Annual Review of Anthropology* 24 (1), 547-565.

Kearney, Michael (1998) Transnationalism in California and Mexico at the end of empire. In *Border Identities: Nation and State at International Frontiers*, eds. T.M. Wilson and H. Donnan, pp. 117-141. Cambridge, UK: Cambridge University Press.

Kearney, Michael (1999) Neither modern nor traditional: Personal identities in global perspective. In *Identities on the Move: Transnational Processes in North America and the Caribbean Basin*, ed. L.R. Goldin, pp. 69-79. Albany, NY: Institute for Mesoamerican Studies, University of Albany. Distributed by University of Texas Press.

Keith, Michael and Steve Pile (1993) *Place and the Politics of Identity*. New York, NY: Routledge.

Kelley, Ninette and Michael Trebilcock (1998) *The Making of the Mosaic: A History of Canadian Immigration Policy.* Toronto, ON: University of Toronto Press.

Kelly, Philip (2003) Canadian-Asian transnationalism. *The Canadian Geographer* 47 (3), 209-218.

Kirby, Sandra and Kate McKenna (1989) *Experience, Research, Social Change: Methods from the Margins.* Toronto, ON: Garamond Press.

Knowles, Valerie (1992) *Strangers at Our Gates: Canadian Immigration and Immigration Policy, 1540-1990.* Toronto, ON and Oxford, UK: Dundurn Press.

Kobayashi, Audrey (1990) Racism and the law in Canada: A geographical perspective. *Urban Geography* 11 (5), 447-473.

Kobayashi, Audrey (1993) Multiculturalism: Representing a Canadian institution. In *Place/Culture/Representation*, eds. J. Duncan and D. Ley, pp. 205-231. London, UK and New York, NY: Routledge.

Kobayashi, Audrey (1994) Coloring the field: Gender, 'race,' and the politics of fieldwork. *The Professional Geographer*, Special Issue: Women in the Field 46 (1) February, 73-80.

Kobayashi, Audrey and Linda Peake (1994) Unnatural discourse: 'Race' and gender in geography. *Gender, Place and Culture: A Journal of Feminist Geography* 1 (2), 225-243.

Kobayashi, Audrey and Linda Peake (2000) Racism out of place: Thoughts on whiteness and an anti-racist Geography in the new millennium. *Annals of the Association of American Geographers* 90 (2) June, 392-403.

Kobayashi, Audrey and Myer Siemiatycki (1999) *Transnationalism and the Transformation of Citizenship among Hong Kong Immigrants to Canada*, A Metropolis research project. Accessed at: http://canada.metropolis.net.

Kobrak, Paul (1999a) *Organizing and Repression in the University of San Carlos, Guatemala, 1944 to 1996.* Washington, DC: American Association for the Advancement of Science (AAAS) and Centro Internacional para Investigaciones en Derechos Humanos (CIIDH). Accessible at: http://shr.aaas.org/guatemala/ciidh/org_rep/.

Kobrak, Paul (1999b) *Draining the Sea: An Analysis of State Terror in Three Rural Communities in Guatemala (1980-1984).* Washington, DC: American Association for the Advancement of Science (AAAS) and the International Centre for Human Rights Investigations (CIIDH), Washington, DC. Accessed at: http://shr.aaas.org/guatemala/ciidh/dts/.

Kofman, Elinor and Kim England (1997) Citizenship and international migration: Taking account of gender, sexuality, and 'race.' *Environment and Planning A* 29 (2), 191-194.

Kohpahl, Gabriele (1995) *Guatemalan Women in Los Angeles: New Directions for the Understanding of Female Transnational Migration.* Ph.D. Dissertation, University of California, Los Angeles, CA.

Kymlicka, Will (1998) *Finding our Way: Rethinking Ethnocultural Relations in Canada.* Toronto, ON and Oxford, UK: Oxford University Press.

Kymlicka, Will (2004) Culturally Responsive Policies: Background paper for HDR 2004, *Human Development Report Office, Occasional Paper.* New York, NY: United Nations Development Programme. Accessed at:http://hdr.undp.org/docs/publications/background_papers/2004/HDR2004_Will_Kymlicka.pdf.

La Farge, Oliver (1947) *Santa Eulalia: The Religion of a Cuchumatán Indian Town.* Chicago, IL: University of Chicago Press.

Laguerre, Michel S. (1998) *Diasporic Citizenship: Haitian Americans in Transnational America.* New York, NY: St. Martins Press.

Landolt, Patricia, Lilian Autler, and Sonia Baires (1999) From *hermano lejano* to *hermano mayor*: The dialectics of Salvadoran transnationalism. *Ethnic and Racial Studies,* Special Issue: Transnational Communities 22 (2) March, 290-315.

Laurie, Nina (1997) Negotiating femininity: Women and representation in emergency employment in Peru. *Gender, Place and Culture: A Journal of Feminist Geography* 4 (2) July, 235-251.

Lavie, Smadar and Ted Swedenburg, eds. (1996) *Displacement, Diaspora, and Geographies of Identity.* Durham, NC: Duke University Press.

Lawson, Victoria (1998) Hierarchical households and gendered migration in Latin America: Feminist extensions to migration research. *Progress in Human Geography* 22 (1) March, 39-53.

Lawson, Victoria (2000) Arguments within geographies of movement: The theoretical potential of migrants' stories. *Progress in Human Geography* 24 (2) June, 173-189.

Leddy, Mary Jo (1997) *At the Border Called Hope: Where Refugees are Neighbours.* Toronto, ON: HarperCollins.

Leddy, Mary Jo (2004) Speech: Sanctuary is a movement that can only be stopped by justice, 4 August. Accessed on 9 August via CCR (Canadian Council for Refugees) Listserv.

Lefebvre, Henri (1991) *The Production of Space*, Trans. D. Nicholson-Smith. Oxford, UK: Blackwell.

Lemco, Jonathan (1986) Canadian foreign policy interests in Central America: Some current issues. *Journal of Interamerican Studies and World Affairs* 28 (Summer), 119-146.

Lemco, Jonathan (1991) *Canada and the Crisis in Central America.* New York, NY: Praeger.

Levenson-Estrada, Deborah (1994) *Trade Unionists against Terror: Guatemala City, 1954-1985.* Chapel Hill, NC and London, UK: University of North Carolina Press.

Levitt, Peggy (1998) Social remittances: Migration driven local-level forms of cultural diffusion. *International Migration Review* 32 (4) Winter, 926-948.

Levitt, Peggy (1999) Towards an understanding of transnational community forms and their impact on immigration incorporation. Paper to be presented at the *Comparative Immigration and Integration Program, Winter Workshop,* University of California at San Diego, 19 February. Accessed at: http://migration.ucdavis.edu/rs/more.php?id=47_0_3_0.

Levitt, Peggy (2001a) *Transnational Villagers.* Berkeley, CA: University of California Press.

Levitt, Peggy (2001b) Transnational migration: Taking stock and future directions. *Global Networks: A Journal of Transnational Affairs* 1 (3) July, 195-216.

Levitt, Peggy and Nina Glick Schiller (2004) Conceptualizing simultaneity: A transnational social field perspective on society. *International Migration Review* 38 (3) Fall, 1002-1039.

Ley, David (2004) Transnational spaces and everyday lives. *Transactions of the Institute of British Geographers* 29 (2) June, 151-164.

Ley, David and Audrey Kobayashi (2005) Back to Hong Kong: Return migration or transnational sojourn? *Global Networks: A Journal of Transnational Affairs* 5 (2), 111-127.

LIDS, Longitudinal Immigration Database LIDS/IMDB – Canada (2004) Country of Birth (Guatemala) by Year of Landing. Distributor: Citizenship and Immigration Canada (CIC). Accessed on 2 February 2004.

Lloyd, Marion (2004) Guatemala activists seek justice as women die. *The Boston Globe*, 14 June. Accessed at: http://www.boston.com/news/globe/.

Lochhead, Clarence (2003) *The Transition Penalty: Unemployment among Recent Immigrants to Canada, CLBC Commentary.* Ottawa: Canadian Labour and Business Centre.

Lockhart, Shannon (1999) Interview, 18 August (ODHAG office, Guatemala City).

Longhurst, Robyn (2004) Situating bodies. In *A Companion to Feminist Geography, eds.* L. Nelson and J. Seager, pp. 337-349. Oxford, UK: Blackwell.

Loucky, James (1988) Rejection, reaffirmation, or redefinition: Changing identity of indigenous Guatemalans in Los Angeles. Paper presented at the *Annual Meetings of the American Anthropological Association,* 17 November.

Loucky, James (1996) Maya Americans: The emergence of a transnational community. In *Central Americans in California: Transnational Communities, Economies, and Cultures*. Los Angeles, CA: Occasional Papers Series, The Center for Multiethnic and Transnational Studies, University of Southern California.

Loucky, James and Marilyn Moors, eds. (2000) *The Maya Diaspora: Guatemalan Roots, New American Lives.* Philadelphia, PA: Temple University Press.

Lovell, W. George (1999) Peace at last? Not so fast, Guatemala, *The Globe and Mail,* 15 November.

Lovell, W. George (2000) *A Beauty That Hurts: Life and Death in Guatemala*, 2nd edition. Austin, TX: University of Texas Press.

Lovell, W. George (2003) Democracy, elections and peace in Guatemala. Unpublished opinion piece sent by author.

Lovell, W. George and Christopher H. Lutz (1996) 'A dark obverse': Maya survival in Guatemala, 1520-1994. *Geographical Review* 86 (3) July, 398-407.

Lowell, B. Lindsay and Rodolfo O. de le Garza (2000) *The Developmental Role of Remittances in US Latino Communities and in Latin American Countries*. Washington, DC and Claremont, CA: Inter-American Dialogue and the Tomás Rivera Policy Institute. Accessed at: http://www.iadialog.org/publications/pdf/lowell.pdf.

Macklin, Audrey (1996) Opening the door to women refugees: A first crack. In *Development and Diaspora.*, eds. W. Giles, H. Moussa, and P. Van Esterik, pp. 118-142. Dundas, ON: Artemis Enterprises.

Macklin, Audrey (2003) Dancing across borders: 'Exotic dancers,' trafficking, and Canadian immigration policy. *International Migration Review* 37 (2) Summer, 464-499.

Mahler, Sarah J. (1995) *American Dreaming: Immigrant Life on the Margins.* Princeton, NJ: Princeton University Press.

Mahler, Sarah J. (1998) Theoretical and empirical contributions toward a research agenda for transnationalism. In *Transnationalism from Below*, eds. M.P. Smith and L.E. Guarnizo, pp. 64-102. New Brunswick, NJ and London, UK: Transaction Publishers.

Mahler, Sarah J. (1999) Engendering transnational migration: A case study of Salvadorans. *American Behavioral Scientist* 42 (4) January, 690-719.

Mahler, Sarah J. (2001) Transnational relationships: The struggle to communicate across borders. *Identities: Global Studies in Culture and Power* 7 (4) January, 583-619.

Mahler, Sarah J. and Patricia R. Pessar (2001) Gendered geographies of power: Analyzing gender across transnational spaces. *Identities: Global Studies in Culture and Power* 7 (4) January, 441-459.

Malkki, Liisa (1990) Context and consciousness: Local conditions for the production of historical and nationalist thought among Hutu refugees in Tanzania. In *Nationalist Ideologies and the Production of National Cultures*, ed. R.G. Fox, pp. 32-62. Washington, DC: American Anthropological Society.

Malkki, Liisa (1992) National Geographic: The rooting of peoples and the territorialization of national identity among scholars and refugees. *Cultural Anthropology* 7 (1) February, 24-44.

Malkki, Liisa (1997) National Geographic: The rooting of peoples and the territorialization of national identity among scholars and refugees. In *Culture, Power, Place: Explorations in Critical Anthropology*, eds. A. Gupta and J. Ferguson, pp. 52-74. Durham, NC and London, UK: Duke University Press.

Manz, Beatriz (1988) *Refugees of a Hidden War: The Aftermath of Counterinsurgency in Guatemala.* Albany, NY: State University of New York Press.

Manz, Beatriz (1995a) Fostering trust in a climate of fear. In *Mistrusting Refugees,* eds. E.V. Daniel and J.C. Knudsen, pp. 151-167. Berkeley, CA and London, UK: University of California Press.

Manz, Beatriz (1995b) Reflections on an *Antropología Comprometida*: Conversations with Ricardo Falla. In *Fieldwork Under Fire: Contemporary Studies of Violence and Survival*, eds. C. Nordstrom and A.C.G.M. Robben, pp. 261-274. Berkeley, CA: University of California Press.

Manz, Beatriz (2004) *Paradise in Ashes: A Guatemalan Journey of Courage, Terror, and Hope.* Los Angeles, CA: University of California Press.

Marden, Peter (1997) Geographies of dissent: Globalization, identity and the nation. *Political Geography* 16 (1) January, 37-64.

Markowitz, Fran (1993) *A Community in Spite of Itself: Soviet Jewish Émigrés in New York.* Washington, DC and London, UK: Smithsonian Institution Press

Martin, Susan F. (2001) Global migration trends and asylum. *UNHCR New Issues in Refugee Research Working Paper Series no. 41*, April. Accessed at: http://www.unhcr.ch/cgi-bin/texis/vtx/doclist?page=research&id=3b8a11284.

Martínez Rodas, Aracely J. (1999) Migración internacional y sus efectos en una comunidad Maya-K'iche'. Paper presented at *Ponencia para el III Congreso de Estudios Mayas*, Universidad Rafael Ladívar (Guatemala), agosto.

Massey, Doreen (1991) A global sense of place. *Marxism Today* June, 24-29. (Also reprinted in *Reading Human Geography*, eds. T. Barnes and D. Gregory, London: Arnold, 1996.)

Massey, Doreen (1994) Double articulation. In *Displacements: Cultural Identities in Question*, ed. A. Bammer, pp. 110-121. Indianapolis, IN: Indianapolis University Press.

Mata, Fernando G. (1994) The Multiculturalism Act and refugee integration in Canada. *Refuge: Canada's Periodical on Refugees* 13 (9) February, 17-20.

McBride, Michael J. (1999) Migrants and asylum seekers: Policy responses in the United States to immigrants and refugees from Central America and the Caribbean. *International Migration* 37 (1) March, 289-317.

McDonald, Brent (2004) *Guatemala: Toward Justice?* University of California, Berkeley, CA: PBS Frontline. Documentary film accessed at: http://www.pbs.org/frontlineworld/fellows/guatemala.

McDowell, Linda (1992) Multiple voices. *Antipode: A Journal of Radical Geography* 24 (1), 56-72.

McDowell, Linda (1999) *Gender, Identity and Place: Understanding Feminist Geographies.* Minneapolis, MN: University of Minnesota Press.

McFarlane, Peter (1989) *Northern Shadows: Canadians and Central America.* Toronto, ON: Between the Lines.

McKendrick, John H. (1999) Multi-method research: An introduction to its application in population geography. *The Professional Geographer*, Focus: Multi-method Research in Population Geography 51 (1), 40-50.

Melgar, Mynor (2000) Impunity intact: Recent arrests in Gerardi case raises hopes, questions. *Report on Guatemala* 21 (1) Spring, 6-9, 11.

Melville, Thomas R. (2005) *Through a Glass Darkly: The U.S. Holocaust in Central America.* Philadelphia, PA: Xlibris.

Méndez Dominguez, A. (1961) *Social Stratification in a Ladino Community, Guatemala*, Ph.D. Dissertation, University of Chicago, Chicago, IL.

Menjívar, Cecilia (1997a) Immigrant kinship networks: Vietnamese, Salvadoreans, and Mexicans in comparative perspective. *Journal of Comparative Family Studies* 28 (1) Spring, 1-24.

Menjívar, Cecilia (1997b) Immigrant kinship networks and the impact of the receiving context: Salvadorans in San Francisco in the early 1990s. *Social Problems* 44 (1), 104-123.

Menjívar, Cecilia (1999) The intersection of work and gender: Central American immigrant women and employment in California. *American Behavioral Scientist* 42 (4) January, 601-627.

Menjívar, Cecilia (2000) *Fragmented Ties: Salvadoran Immigrant Networks in America.* Los Angeles, CA: California University Press.

Menjívar, Cecilia and Néstor P. Rodríguez (2005) *When States Kill: Latin America, the U.S., and Technologies of Terror.* Austin, TX: University of Texas Press.

Meredith, Diane (1992) *Guatemalan Refugees and Their Process of Adjustment in Toronto.* M.A. Thesis, York University, North York, ON.

Metz, Brent (1998) Without nation, without community: The growth of Maya nationalism among Ch'orti's of Eastern Guatemala. *Journal of Anthropological Research* 54 (3) Fall, 325-349.

Migration Policy Institute (2005) *Number of asylum applicants from Guatemala in the United States, 1980 to 2002.* Washington, DC: Migration Policy Institute. Data generated on 1 February 2005 by Catherine Nolin; using Data Tools: http://www.migrationinformation.org/DataTools/asylumresults.cfm.

Miles, Miranda and Jonathan Crush (1993) Personal narratives as interactive texts: Collecting and interpreting migrant life-histories. *The Professional Geographer* 45 (1) February, 95-129.

Mitchell, Don (2000) *Cultural Geography: A Critical Introduction.* Oxford, UK: Blackwell.

Mitchell, Katharyne, ed. (1997a) *Antipode: A Journal of Radical Geography,* Special Issue: Geography and Transnational Discourse 29 (2).

Mitchell, Katharyne (1997b) Transnational discourse: Bringing geography back in. *Antipode: A Journal of Radical Geography,* Special Issue: Geography and Transnational Discourse, 29 (2), 101-114.

Miyares, Ines, Richard Wright, Alison Mountz, Adrian Bailey and Jennifer Jonak (2003) The interrupted circle: Truncated transnationalism and the Salvadoran experience. *Journal of Latin American Geography* 2 (1), 74-86.

Monroy, Henry (1999) Presentation: *Unmasking Impunity in Guatemala: a discussion with Supreme Court Judge, Henry Monroy.* Bloor Street United Church, Toronto, ON, 16 April.

Montejo, Victor (1999a) *Voices from Exile: Violence and Survival in Modern Maya History.* Norman, OK: University of Oklahoma Press.

Montejo, Victor (1999b) Tied to the land: Maya migration, exile, and transnationalism. In *Identities on the Move: Transnational Processes in North America and the Caribbean Basin*, ed. L.R. Goldin, pp. 185-202. Albany, NY: Institute for Mesoamerican Studies, University of Albany. Distributed by University of Texas Press.

Montejo, Victor (2005) *Maya Intellectual Renaissance: Identity, Representation, and Leadership.* Austin, TX: University of Texas Press.

Montgomery, Charlotte (1984) Rules relaxed for Guatemalan visitors: Rights abuse cited in immigration law changes. *Globe and Mail*, 13 March, A4.

Monzón, Luis and Emina Tudakovic (2004) Remesas de fondos: una perspectiva canadiense. Paper prepared for presentation at the *Hemispheric Integration and Transnationalism in the Americas, FOCAL Workshop*, Canadian Embassy,

Guatemala City, 16-17 February. Coordinación de Políticas Internacionales, Ministerio de Cuidadanía e Inmigración de Canadá (CIC). Ottawa: CIC.

Moodley, Kogila (1983) Canadian multiculturalism as ideology. *Ethnic and Racial Studies* 6, 320-331.

Mora, José Eduardo (2004). Guatemala: Women's lives are worth nothing, say anti-violence activists. *IPS (Inter Press Service News Agency)*, 23 December. Accessed at: http://www.ipsnews.net/interna.asp?idnews=26788.

Moran-Taylor, Michelle (2004) Migra landscapes: How migration changes livelihoods in Guatemala's Oriente. Paper presented in the session, 'Migration and Transnationalism I,' at the *Conference of the Latin Americanist Geographers* (CLAG), Antigua, Guatemala, 20 May.

Mountz, Alison and Richard A. Wright (1996) Daily life in the transnational migrant community of San Agustín, Oaxaca and Poughkeepsie, New York. *Diaspora: A Journal of Transnational Studies* 5 (3), 403-428.

Mountz, Alison, Richard Wright, Inez Miyares, and Adrian J. Bailey (2002) Lives in limbo: Temporary Protected Status and immigrant identities. *Global Networks: A Journal of Transnational Affairs* 2 (4) October, 335-356.

NACLA Report on the Americas and Teo Ballvé (2004) Guatemala and Mexico: Brutal murders of women continue. *NACLA Report on the Americas* 37 (4) January/February, 46.

Nagel, Caroline R. and Lynn A. Staeheli (2004) Citizenship, identity and transnational migration: Arab immigrants to the United States. *Space & Polity* 8 (1), 3-23.

Nast, Heidi (1994) Women in the field: Critical feminist methodologies and theoretical perspectives – Opening remarks on 'Women in the field.' *The Professional Geographer,* Special Issue: Women in the Field 46 (1) February, 54-66.

National Security Archive, 1999 Guatemalan Death Squad Dossier (Internal Military Log Reveals Fate of 183 'Disappeared'), May. Accessed at: http://www.gwu.edu/~nsarchiv/NSAEBB/NSAEBB15/01-01.htm.

Nelson, Diane M. (1996) Maya hackers and the cyberspatialized nation-state: Modernity, ethnostalgia, and a lizard queen in Guatemala. *Cultural Anthropology* 11 (3) August, 287-308.

Nelson, Diane M. (1999) *A Finger in the Wound: Body Politics in Quincentennial Guatemala*. Berkeley, CA: University of California Press.

Nolin, Catherine (2002) Transnational ruptures and sutures: Questions of identity and social relations among Guatemalans in Canada. *GeoJournal: An International Journal on Human Geography and Environmental Sciences*, Special Issue: Geography and Refugees, 56 (1), 59-67.

Nolin, Catherine (2004) Spatializing the immobility of Guatemalan transnationalism in Canada. *Canadian Journal of Latin American and Caribbean Studies*, 29 (57 & 58), 267-288.

Nolin, Catherine and Luin Goldring (2002) Gender structures the migration process. In *Policy-Relevant Research on Immigration and Settlement – Relevant for Whom? A Working Document of the Strategic Workshop on Immigrant Women Making 'Place' in Canadian Cities*. Montréal: Urbanisation, Culture et Société,

Institut national de la recherche scientifique, and Immigration et Métropoles. Available at: http://genderimmigration.inrs-ucs.uquebec.ca/index.htm.

Nolin Hanlon, Catherine (1997) Out of place: Displacement and collective return of Maya refugees. In *Mythic History and Symbolic Landscape / Histoire Mythique et Paysage Symbolique*, eds. S. Courville and B. Osborne, pp. 52-58. Montréal and Kingston: McGill-Queen's University Press.

Nolin Hanlon, Catherine (1999) Guatemalan refugees and returnees: Place and Maya identity. In *Journeys of Fear: Refugee Return and National Transformation in Guatemala,* eds. Liisa North and Alan Simmons, pp. 213-234. Montréal and Kingston: McGill-Queen's University Press.

Nolin Hanlon, Catherine and W. George Lovell (1997) Huida, exilio, repatriación y retorno: escenarios de los refugiados guatemaltecos, 1981-1997. *Mesoamérica* 34 (diciembre), 559-582.

Nolin Hanlon, Catherine and W. George Lovell (2000) Flight, exile, repatriation, and return: Guatemalan refugee scenarios, 1981-1998. In *The Maya Diaspora: Guatemalan Roots, New American Lives*, eds. J. Loucky and M. Moors, pp. 35-55. Philadelphia, PA: Temple University Press.

Nolin Hanlon, Catherine and Finola Shankar (2000) Gendered spaces of terror and assault: *Testimonio* of REMHI and the Commission for Historical Clarification for Guatemala. *Gender, Place, and Culture: A Journal of Feminist Geography* 7 (3) September, 265-286.

Nordstrom, Carolyn and Antonius C.G.M. Robben, eds. (1995) *Fieldwork Under Fire: Contemporary Studies of Violence and Survival.* Berkeley, CA: University of California Press.

North, Liisa and CAPA (1990) *Between War and Peace in Central America: Choices for Canada*. Toronto, ON: Between the Lines Press.

North, Liisa L. and Alan B. Simmons (1999) *Journeys of Fear: Refugee Return and National Transformation in Guatemala.* Montréal and Kingston: McGill-Queen's University Press.

Nurse, Keith (2003) Development: Unthinking the past. *NACLA Report on the Americas* 37 (3) November/December, 29-33.

Nutini, Hugo G. (1996) Mesoamerican community organization: Preliminary remarks. *Ethnology* 35 (2) Spring, 81-92.

Nyberg Sørensen, Ninna (1998) Narrating identity across Dominican worlds. In *Transnationalism from Below*, eds. M.P. Smith and L.E. Guarnizo, pp. 241-269. New Brunswick, NJ and London, UK: Transaction Publishers.

Oakes, Maud (1969) *The Two Crosses of Todos Santos: Survivals of Mayan Religious Ritual.* Princeton, NJ: Princeton University Press.

OAS, Organization of American States (1984) *Cartagena Declaration on Refugees.* Annual Report of the Inter-American Commission on Human Rights. Adopted at the 'Coloquio sobre la Protección Internacional de los Refugiados en América Central, México y Panamá: Problemas Jurídicos y Humanitarios,' Cartagena, Colombia, 19-22 November. Accessed at: http://www.asylumlaw.org/docs/international/CentralAmerica.PDF

Ogelsby, J.C.M. (1976) *Essays in the History of Canadian-Latin American Relations, 1866-1968*. Toronto, ON: MacMillan of Canada-MacLean Hunter Press.

Oglesby, Elizabeth (1995) Myrna Mack. In *Fieldwork Under Fire: Contemporary Studies of Violence and Survival*, eds. C. Nordstrom and A.C.G.M. Robben, pp. 254-259. Berkeley, CA: University of California Press.

Opoku-Dapaah, Edward (1994) Integration of landed refugee claimants in Canada: Toward an explanatory model. *Refuge: Canada's Periodical on Refugees* 13 (9) February, 10-15.

Orozco, Manuel (2003) *The Impact of Migration in the Caribbean and Central American Region,* FOCAL Policy Paper 03-03 (March). Ottawa, ON: FOCAL (Canadian Foundation for the Americas). Accessed at: http://www.focal.ca/pdf/migration.pdf.

Ortner, Sherry B. (1997) Fieldwork in the postcommunity. *Anthropology and Humanism* 22 (1) June, 61-80.

Oxman-Martinez, Jacqueline, Andrea Martinez, and Jill Hanley (2001) Trafficking women: Gendered impacts of Canadian immigration policies. *Journal of International Migration and Integration* 2 (3), 297-313.

Palacios, Edwin and Rodolfo Zelada (1999) Testigo clave: confirmó participación de militares, *el Periódico* (Guatemala), 27 de agosto, 2.

Palmer, Howard (1975) Social adjustment. In *Immigration and the Rise of Multiculturalism*, ed. H. Palmer, pp. 112-118. Calgary, AB and Toronto, ON: Copp Clark Publishing.

Peake, Linda and Brian Ray (2001) Racializing the Canadian landscape: Whiteness, uneven geographies and social justice. *The Canadian Geographer* 45 (1) Spring, 180-186.

Pebley, Anne R., Noreen Goldman, and Arodys Robles (2002) Isolation, integration, and ethnic boundaries in rural Guatemala. *California Center for Population Research On-Line Working Paper Series*. Los Angeles, CA. Accessed at: http://repositories.cdlib.org/cgi/viewcontent.cgi?article=1049&context=ccpr.

Perera, Victor (1993) *Unfinished Conquest: The Guatemalan Tragedy*. Berkeley, CA: University of California Press.

Pérez, Leslie (2000) EEUU rechaza la mitad de pedidos de visa. *Prensa Libre* (Guatemala), 28 de septiembre. Accessed at: http://www.prensalibre.com.

Pessar, Patricia R. (1999) Engendering migration studies: The case of new immigrants in the United States. *American Behavioral Scientist* 42 (4) January, 577-600.

Pessar, Patricia R. (2001) Women's political consciousness and empowerment in local, national, and transnational contexts: Guatemalan refugees and returnees. *Identities: Global Studies in Culture and Power* 7 (4) January, 461-500.

Pessar, Patricia R. and Sarah J. Mahler (2003) Transnational migration: Bringing gender in. *International Migration Review* 37 (3) Fall, 812-846.

Picot, Garnett and Feng Hou (2003) The rise in low-income rates among immigrants in Canada. *Analytical Studies Branch Research Paper Series.* Ottawa, ON: Statistics Canada, Business and Labour Market Analysis Division.

Piedrasanta Herrera, Ruth (1999) Apuntes sobre la transmigración y las remesas del norte entre los Chuj de Huehuetenango, Guatemala. Unpublished paper.

Pierson, Christopher (1996) *The Modern State.* New York, NY and London, UK: Routledge.

Pile, Steve and Michael Keith, eds. (1997) *Geographies of Resistance.* London, UK and New York, NY: Routledge.

Plaut, Gunther W. (1995) *Asylum: A Moral Dilemma.* Westport, CN: Praeger.

Pop Barillas, Pedro (1999) Caso Gerardi: fiscal Celvin Galindo al exilio, *Prensa Libre* (Guatemala), 8 de octubre. Accessed at: http://www.prensalibre.com.gt/noticias.

Popkin, Eric (1999) Guatemalan Mayan migration to Los Angeles: Constructing transnational linkages in the context of the settlement process. *Ethnic and Racial Studies,* Special Issue: Transnational Communities 22 (2) March, 267-289.

Popkin, Eric (2003) Transnational migration and development in postwar peripheral states: An examination of Guatemalan and Salvadoran state linkages with their migrant populations in Los Angeles. *Current Sociology* 51 (3/4), 347-374.

Portes, Alejandro (1996a) Transnational communities: Their emergence and significance in the contemporary world-system. In *Transnational Realities and Nation-States: Trends in International Migration and Immigration Policy in the Americas*, ed. M. Castro. Miami, FL: North-South Center.

Portes, Alejandro (1996b) Global villagers: The rise of transnational communities. *The American Prospect* 7 (25) March, 74-77.

Portes, Alejandro, Luis E. Guarnizo, and Patricia Landolt, eds. (1999a) *Racial and Ethnic Studies*. Guest-edited Special Issue: Transnational Communities, 22 (2) March.

Portes, Alejandro, Luis E. Guarnizo, and Patricia Landolt (1999b) Introduction: Pitfalls and promises of an emergent research field. *Ethnic and Racial Studies,* Special Issue: Transnational Communities, 22 (2) March, 217-237.

Power, Marcus (2003) *Rethinking Development Geographies*. London, UK and New York, NY: Routledge.

Pratt, Geraldine (1997) Stereotypes and ambivalence: The construction of domestic workers in Vancouver, British Columbia. *Gender, Place and Culture: A Journal of Feminist Geography* 4 (2) July, 159-176.

Pratt, Geraldine and Susan Hanson (1994) Geography and the construction of difference. *Gender, Place and Culture: A Journal of Feminist Geography* 1 (1), 5-29.

Pratt, Geraldine and Brenda Yeoh (2003) Transnational (counter) topographies. *Gender, Place and Culture: A Journal of Feminist Geography* 10 (2) June, 159-166.

Pred, Allan and Michael J. Watts (1992) *Reworking Modernity: Capitalisms and Symbolic Discontent.* New Brunswick, NJ: Rutgers University Press.

Prensa Libre (2000) Reporte especial: nuestra gente en los EE.UU., 10 de septiembre. Accessed at: http://www.prensalibre.com/pl/2000/septiembre/10/index.html.

Professional Geographer, Special Issue: 'Women in the field.' 46 (1) February.

Radcliffe, Sarah and Nina Laurie (1999) We are all Indians? Ecuadorian and Bolivian Transnational Indigenous Communities. An ESRC Research Project. Accessed at: http://www.transcomm.ox.ac.uk/wwwroot/radcliffe.htm.

Radcliffe, Sarah and Sallie Westwood (1993) *Viva: Women and Popular Protest in Latin America*. London, UK: Routledge.

Radcliffe, Sarah and Sallie Westwood (1996) *Remaking the Nation: Place, Identity and Politics in Latin America*. New York, NY and London, UK: Routledge.

REMHI, Recuperación de la Memoria Histórica - Informe Proyecto Interdiocesano (1998) *Guatemala: Nunca Más*. Guatemala: ODHAG (Oficina de Derechos Humanos del Arzobispado de Guatemala).

Redfield, Robert (1930) *Tepoztlán: A Mexican Village*. Chicago, IL: University of Chicago Press.

Reed, Thomas F. and Karen Brandow (1996) *The Sky Never Changes: Testimonies from the Guatemalan Labor Movement*. Ithaca, NY and London, UK: ILR Press.

Renzetti, Claire M. and Raymond Lee (1993) The problems of researching sensitive topics: An overview and introduction. In *Researching Sensitive Topics,* eds. C.M. Renzetti and R. Lee, pp. 3-13. London, UK: Sage.

Repak, Terry A. (1994) Labour recruitment and the lure of the Capital: Central American migrants in Washington, D.C. *Gender & Society* 8 (4), 507-524.

Repak, Terry A. (1995) *Waiting on Washington: Central American Workers in the Nation's Capital*. Philadelphia, PA: Temple University Press.

Reyes, Belinda I. (1997) *Dynamics of Immigration: Return Migration to Western Mexico*. Prepared for the Public Policy Institute of California, San Francisco, CA. Accessed at: http://www.ppic.org/publications/PPIC102/ppic102.chap3.html.

Ristock, Janice L. and Joan Pennell (1996) *Community Research as Empowerment: Feminist Links, Postmodern Interruptions*. Toronto, ON and Oxford, UK: Oxford University Press.

Robinson, Rudi (2004) *Globalization, Immigrants' Transnational Agency and Economic Development in their Homelands*. FOCAL Policy Paper 04-9. Ottawa, ON: FOCAL (Canadian Foundation for the Americas). Accessed at: http://www.focal.ca/pdf/globalization.pdf.

Rodman Ruiz, Debra (2002) 'Se perdió el mundo' When the Indians migrate: Ethnicity in the transnational sphere. Paper presented at the *Canadian Association for Latin American and Caribbean Studies* (CALACS) meeting, Montréal, QC, 24-26 October.

Rodman Ruiz, Debra (2004) Maya migration north: Transnational indigenous identities. *Cultural Survival Voices*, 3.1 (March). Accessed at: http://www.culturalsurvival.org/publications/voices/.

Rodríguez, Luisa F. (2000) Reporte especial: Nuestra gente en los EE.UU., *Prensa Libre* (Guatemala), 10 de septiembre. Accessed at: http://www.prensalibre.com/pl/2000/septiembre/10/61319.html.

Rodríguez, Néstor P. (1987) Undocumented Central Americans in Houston: Diverse populations. *International Migration Review* 21 (1) Spring, 4-25.

Rodríguez, Néstor P. and Jacqueline Marie Hagan (2000) Maya urban villagers in Houston: The formation of a migrant community from San Cristóbal Totonicanpán. In *The Maya Diaspora: Guatemalan Roots, New American Lives,* eds. J. Loucky and M. Moors, pp. 197-209. Philadelphia, PA: Temple University Press.

Rosaldo, Renato (1989) *Culture and Truth: The Remaking of Social Analysis.* Boston, MA: Beacon Press.

Rose, Charlie (1995) Excerpt 'Guatemala Massacre,' Guests: Rep. Robert Torricelli, Elliot Abrams, and Allan Nairn. *'Charlie Rose' (PBS Program),* 31 March.

Rose, Damaris, Pia Carrasco, and Johanne Charboneau (1998) The role of 'weak ties' in the settlement experiences of immigrant women with young children: The case of Central Americans in Montréal. *CERIS Working Paper Series* #04-1998, December. Accessed at: http://ceris.metropolis.net/frameset_e.html.

Rose, Gillian (1993) *Feminism and Geography: The Limits of Geographical Knowledge*. Cambridge, UK: Cambridge University Press.

Rose, Gillian (1997) Performing inoperative community: The space and the resistance of some community arts projects. In *Geographies of Resistance*, eds. S. Pile and M. Keith, pp. 184-202. London, UK and New York, NY: Routledge.

Roseberry, William and J. O'Brien (1991) Introduction. In *Golden Ages, Dark Ages: Imagining the Past in Anthropology and History*, eds. J. O'Brien and W. Roseberry, pp. 1-18. Berkeley, CA: University of California Press.

Rouse, Roger (1991) Mexican migration and the social space of postmodernism. *Diaspora: A Journal of Transnational Studies* 1 (1) Spring, 8-23.

Rouse, Roger (1992) Making sense of settlement: Class transformation, cultural struggle, and transnationalism among Mexican migrants in the United States. In *Towards a Transnational Perspective on Migration: Race, Class, Ethnicity, and Nationalism Reconsidered*, eds. N. Glick Schiller, L. Basch, and C. Blanc-Szanton, pp. 25-52. New York, NY: The New York Academy of Science.

Rouse, Roger (1995a) Questions of identity: Personhood and collectivity in transnational migration to the United States. *Critique of Anthropology* 15 (4), 351-380.

Rouse, Roger (1995b) Thinking through transnationalism: Notes on the cultural politics of class relations in the contemporary United States. *Public Culture* 7 (2) Spring, 353-402.

Rubinstein, Robert A., ed. (1991) *Fieldwork: The Correspondence of Robert Redfield and Sol Tax.* Boulder, CO: Westview Press.

Rushdie, Salman (1991) *Imaginary Homelands: Essays and Criticism, 1982-1991.* London, UK: Viking.

Ryan, Jan (2002) Chinese women as transnational migrants: Gender and class in global migration narratives. *International Migration* 40 (2), 93-116.

Sack, Robert David (1997) *Homo Geographicus: A Framework for Action, Awareness, and Moral Concern.* Baltimore, MD and London, UK: The Johns Hopkins University Press.

Said, Edward (1979) Zionism from the standpoint of its victims. *Social Text* 1, 7-58.

Salvadó, Luis Raúl (1988) *The Other Refugees: A Study of Non-Recognized Guatemalan Refugees in Chiapas.* Washington, DC: Hemispheric Migration

Project, Center for Immigration Policy and Refugee Assistance at Georgetown University.

Sandoval, Julieta (1999) Protesta: día de luto, no de fiesta, *Prensa Libre* (Guatemala), 1 de julio. Accessed at: http://www.prensalibre.com (Noticias Nacionales).

Sanford, Victoria (2003) *Buried Secrets: Truth and Human Rights in Guatemala.* New York, NY: Palgrave Macmillan.

Satzewich, Vic, ed. (1992) *Deconstructing a Nation: Immigration, Multiculturalism and Racism in '90s Canada.* Halifax, NS and Saskatoon, SK: Fernwood Publishing and the Social Research Unit.

Scheper-Hughes, Nancy (1992) *Death without Weeping: The Violence of Everyday Life in Brazil.* Berkeley, CA: University of California Press.

Scheper-Hughes, Nancy and Philippe Bourgois, eds. (2004) *Violence in War and Peace: An Anthology*. Oxford, UK: Blackwell.

Schirmer, Jennifer (1993) The seeking of truth and the gendering of consciousness: The CoMadres of El Salvador and the CONAVIGUA widows of Guatemala. In *'Viva': Women and Popular Protest in Latin America*, ed. S.A. Radcliffe and S. Westwood, pp. 30-64. London, UK and New York, NY: Routledge.

Schirmer, Jennifer (1999) *The Guatemalan Military Project: A Violence Called Democracy*. Philadelphia, PA: University of Philadelphia Press.

Schlesinger, Stephen, Richard Nuccio, and Jennifer Schirmer (1999) Preserving *Bitter Fruit*: Re-examining US intervention in Guatemala. *Harvard International Review* 21 (4) Fall, 24-29.

Scoffield, Heather (2000) Fox seeks closer North American ties: Mexican leader will request billions in investment as first step toward a common market, *Globe and Mail*, 16 August, A2.

Scotton, Lindsay (1987) Refugees take Overground Railroad: Volunteers put Central Americans on legal route to Canada. *Toronto Star*, 24 January, A2.

Seijo, Lorena (2005) Estado pide perdón después de 23 años: En Plan de Sánchez, Rabinal, fueron asesinadas 268 personas. *Prensa Libre* (Guatemala), 18 de julio. Accessed at: http://www.prensalibre.com/pl/2005/julio/18/119069.html.

Shami, Seteney (1996) Transnationalism and refugee studies: Rethinking forced migration and identity in the Middle East. *Journal of Refugee Studies* 9 (1), 3-26.

Shankar, Finola (1999) *Organic Beans and Ethical Aromas: Small-Scale Coffee Production in Guatemala*, Unpublished MA Thesis, Department of Geography, Queen's University at Kingston, Canada.

Sharp, Jo, Kath Browne, and Deborah Thien, eds. (2004) *Women and Geography Study Group: Gender and Geography Reconsidered.* CD-ROM.

Sherrel, Kathy and Jennifer Hyndman (2004) Sharing the wealth, spreading the burden? The settlement of Kosovar refugees in small B.C. cities. *RIIM Metropolis Working Paper Series #04-06*, February. Accessed at: http://www.riim.metropolis.net/frameset_e.html.

Sibley, David (1995) *Geographies of Exclusion: Society and Difference in the West.* London, UK: Routledge.

Silvey, Rachel (2004) Power, difference and mobility: Feminist advances in migration studies. *Progress in Human Geography* 28 (4) August, 1-17.

Silvey, Rachel and Victoria Lawson (1999) Placing the migrant. *Annals of the Association of American Geographers* 89 (1) March, 121-132.

Simmons, Alan and Jean Turner (1997) Salvadorans and Guatemalans in Toronto (SAGIT) Research Project. Unpublished project description (1997-1999).

Small, Cathy A. (1997) *Voyages: From Tongan Villages to American Suburbs*. Ithaca, NY: Cornell University Press.

Smith, Carol A. (1990a) The origins of the national question in Guatemala: An hypothesis. In *Guatemalan Indians and the State, 1540-1988*, ed. C.A Smith. Austin, TX: University of Texas Press.

Smith, Carol A. (1990b) Failed nationalist movements in 19th century Guatemala: A parable for the third world. In *Nationalist Ideologies and the Production of National Cultures*, ed. R.G. Fox, pp. 148-177. Washington, DC: American Anthropological Society.

Smith, Carol A. (1991) Maya nationalism. *NACLA Report on the Americas* 25 (3) December, 29-33.

Smith, Fiona M. (1996) Problematising language: Limitations and possibilities in 'foreign language' research. *Area* 28, 160-166.

Smith, Michael Peter (1994) Can you imagine? Transnational migration and the globalization of grassroots politics. *Social Text* 39 August, 15-33.

Smith, Michael Peter and J.R. Feagin, eds. (1995) *The Bubbling Cauldron: Race, Ethnicity, and the Urban Crisis*. Minneapolis, MN: University of Minnesota Press.

Smith, Michael Peter and Luis Guarnizo, eds. (1998) *Transnationalism from Below*. New Brunswick, NJ and London, UK: Transaction Publishers.

Smith, Neil (1992) Geography, difference and the politics of scale. In *Postmodernism: The Social Sciences*, eds. J. Doherty, E. Graham, and M. Malek, pp. 57-79. London, UK: Macmillan.

Smith, Neil (1993) Homeless/global: Scaling places. In *Mapping the Futures: Local Cultures, Global Change*, eds. J. Bird, B. Curtis, T. Putnam, G. Robertson and L. Tickner, pp. 87-119. London, UK and New York, NY: Routledge.

Smith, Robert C. (1998) Transnational localities: Community, technology and the politics of membership with the context of Mexico and U.S. migration. In *Transnationalism from Below*, eds. M.P. Smith and L.E. Guarnizo, pp. 196-238. New Brunswick, NJ and London, UK: Transaction Publishers.

Soberanis, Carlos Ajanel (2000) Cumbre presidencial: Buscan signar TLC con Canadá, *Prensa Libre* (Guatemala), 28 de septiembre. Accessed at: http://www.prensalibre.com (Noticias Política).

Soja, Edward (1998) Citizenship and cultural politics of the postmetropolis. Paper presented at 'Rights to the City' conference, York University, Toronto, ON, 26 June.

Stanley, William (1993) Blessing or menace? The security implications of Central American migration. In *International Migration and Security*, ed. M. Weiner, pp. 229-260. Boulder, CO: Westview Press.

Statistics Canada (1996) *The Nations Series*. Accessed at the Queen's University Data Library.

Statistics Canada (2003a) *2001 Census of Population (Topic-based tabulations - selected places of birth (85) for the immigrant population, for Canada, provinces, territories, census metropolitan areas and census agglomerations, 1996 and 2001 censuses – 20 per cent sample data);* generated on 20 November 2003; using ESTAT; http://www.statcan.ca/english/Estat/licence.htm.

Statistics Canada (2003b) Protecting confidentiality, understanding the data, *2001 Community Profiles.* Accessed at:http://www12.statcan.ca/english/profil01/PlaceSearchForm1.cfm.

Statistics Canada (2003c) Appendix B: Data quality, sampling and weighting, confidentiality and random rounding, *2001 Census Dictionary, Internet Version, modified 22 April 2003;* Accessed at: http://www12.statcan.ca/english/census01/Products/Reference/dict/appendices/app002.pdf.

Statistics Canada (2004a) *2001 Census of Population (Topic based tabulations – Selected Places of Birth (85) for the Immigrant Population, for Canada, Provinces, Territories, Census Metropolitan Areas and Census Agglomerations, 2001 Census – 20% sample data,* generated on 1 February 2005; http://www12.statcan.ca/english/census01/Products/Standard/Index.cfm

Statistics Canada (2004b) *2001 Census of Population (Topic-based tabulations – Ethnic Origin (232), Sex (3) and Single and Multiple Responses (3) for Population, for Canada, Provinces, Territories, Census Metropolitan Areas and Census Agglomerations, 2001 Census – 20% Sample Data);* generated on 1 February 2005; http://www12.statcan.ca/english/census01/Products/Standard/Index.cfm.

Statistics Canada (2004c) *2001 Census of Population (Selected Cultural and Labour Force Characteristics, Immigrant Status, and Place of Birth of Respondent),* generated on 20 January 2004; using ESTAT; http://www.statcan.ca/english/Estat/licence.htm.

Status of Women Canada (1998) *Gendering Immigration/Integration: Policy Research Workshop Proceedings and a Selective Review of Policy Research Literature 1987-1996.* Ottawa, ON: Status of Women Canada.

Stephens, Jacqui (2004) Conflicting perspectives: Q'eqchi' communities, land grabs, and a Canadian mining company. Paper presented at the *Congress of the Canadian Association for Latin American and Caribbean Studies* (CALACS), Guelph, ON, 30 October.

Stephens, Jacqui (2005) *Conflicting Perspectives: Neoliberal Resource Development, Indigenous Communities and Modern Canadian Imperialism in Guatemala.* Unpublished MA Thesis, Interdisciplinary Studies, University of Northern British Columbia, Prince George, BC, Canada.

Stepputat, Finn (1989) Self-sufficiency and Exile in Mexico: Report on a field study among relocated Guatemalan refugees in south-east Mexico, August-November 1988. *United Nations Research Institute for Social Development (UNRISD) Discussion Paper 9.*

Stepputat, Finn (1994a) Repatriation and the politics of space: The case of the Mayan diaspora and return movement. *Journal of Refugee Studies* 7 (2/3), 175-185.

Stepputat, Finn (1994b) The imagined return community of Guatemalan refugees. *Refuge: Canada's Periodical on Refugees* 13, 13-15.

Stoll, David (1999) *Rigoberta Menchú and the Story of All Poor Guatemalans.* Boulder, CO: Westview Press.

Stoll, David and Virginia Garrard Burnett, eds. (1993) *Rethinking Protestantism in Latin America.* Philadelphia, PA: Temple University Press.

Stoltz Chinchilla, Norma and Nora Hamilton (1999) Changing networks and alliances in a transnational context: Salvadoran and Guatemalan immigrants in southern California. *Social Justice* 26 (3) Fall, 4-26.

Strategic Workshop on Immigrant Women Making Place in Canadian Cities (2002) *Policy-Relevant Research on Immigration and Settlement – Relevant for Whom? A Working Document.* Montréal: INRS Urbanisation, Culture et Société, Institut national de la recherche scientifique, and Immigration et Métropoles. Available at: http://GenderImmigration.inrs-ucs.uquebec.ca. [Workshop members: D. Rose (coordinator), J. Bernhard, C. Creese, I. Dyck, L. Goldring, A. McLaren, C. Nolin, V. Preston, B. Ray, E. Tastsoglou.]

Sundberg, Juanita (1999) *Conservation Encounters: NGOs, Local People, and Changing Cultural Landscapes*, Ph.D. Dissertation, Department of Geography, University of Texas at Austin.

Sundberg, Juanita (2004) Identities in the making: Conservation, gender and race in the Maya Biosphere Reserve, Guatemala. *Gender, Place and Culture: A Journal of Feminist Geography* 11 (1) March, 43-66.

Suro, Roberto (2002) *Counting the 'Other Hispanics': How Many Colombians, Dominicans, Ecuadorians, Guatemalans, and Salvadorans are There in the United States*, 9 May. Los Angeles, CA: Pew Hispanic Center. Accessed at: http://pewhispanic.org/reports/report.php?ReportID=8.

Tastsoglou, Evangelia, Brian Ray and Valerie Preston (2005) Gender and migration intersections in a Canadian context. *Canadian Issues / Thèmes Canadiens* (Special Issue: Immigration and the Intersections of Diversity) (Spring), 91-93.

Taussig, Michael (1993) *Mimesis and Alterity: A Particular History of the Senses.* New York, NY: Routledge.

Tax, Sol (1937) The *municipios* of the midwestern highlands of Guatemala. *American Anthropologist* 39 (3), 423-444.

Taylor, Clark (1998) *Return of Guatemala's Refugees: Reweaving the Torn.* Philadelphia, PA: Temple University Press.

Taylor, Matthew (2005) Electrifying rural Guatemala: Central policy and rural reality. *Environment and Planning C: Government and Policy* 23 (2), 173-189.

Teather, Elizabeth K. (1999) *Embodied Geographies: Spaces, Bodies, and Rites of Passage.* London: Routledge.

Tedlock, Barbara (1993) Mayans and Mayan studies from 2000 B.C. to A.D. 1992. *Latin American Research Review* 28 (3), 153-173.

Tuckman, Jo (2004) Land where women are killers' prey: Guatemala is a hunting ground for brutal gangs who feel free to rape and murder. *The Observer (UK)*, 6 June. Accessed at: http://observer.guardian.co.uk/international/story/0,,1232412,00.html.

Tumin, Melvin M. (1952) *Caste in a Peasant Society: A Case Study in the Dynamics of Caste*. Princeton, NJ: Princeton University Press.

United Church of Canada (2004) *Sanctuary for Refugees? A Guide for Congregations*, Rev. ed. Toronto, ON: United Church of Canada. Available at: http://www.united-church.ca/migration/pdf/sanctuary.pdf.

UNHCR, United Nations High Commissioner for Refugees (1999) *Refugee Women*. Geneva: UNHRC. Accessed at: http://www.unhcr.ch/cgi-bin/texis/vtx/protect?id=3b83a48d4.

UNHCR (2001) *Women, Children, and Older Refugees: The Sex and Age Distribution of Refugee Populations with a Special Emphasis on UNHCR Policy Priorities*. Population Data Unit (Population and Geographic Data Section). Geneva: UNHCR. Accessed at: http://www.unhcr.ch/cgi-bin/texis/vtx/statistics/opendoc.pdf?tbl=STATISTICS& id=3b9378e518.

UNHCR (2005a) *2004 Global Refugee Trends: Overview of Refugee Populations, New Arrivals, Durable Solutions, Asylum Seekers, Stateless and Other Persons of Concern to the UNHCR*. Population and Geographic Data Section. Geneva: UNHCR. Accessed at: http://www.unhcr.ch/cgi-bin/texis/vtx/statistics/opendoc.pdf?tbl=STATISTICS& id=42b283744.

UNHCR (2005b) *Refugees by Numbers: 2005 Edition*. Geneva: UNHCR. Accessed at :http://www.unhcr.ch/cgi-bin/texis/vtx/basics/opendochtm?tbl=BASICS&id=3b0 28097c.

USCR, US Committee for Refugees and Immigrants (1993) *El Retorno: Guatemala's Risky Repatriation Begins*. Washington, D.C.: USCR.

USCR (2005) *World Refugee Survey 2005*. Washington, DC: USCR. Accessed at: http://www.refugees.org/worldmap.aspx.

US State Department (1986) Guatemala's disappeared, 1977-86. Declassified Secret document downloaded from *The Guatemalan Military: What the U.S. Files Reveal, Volume II: Documents* (June 2000), National Security Archive. Accessed at: http://www.gwu.edu/%7Ensarchiv/NSAEBB/NSAEBB32/index.html.

Valentine, Gill (1998) 'Sticks and stones may break my bones': A personal geography of harassment. *Antipode: A Journal of Radical Geography* 30 (4) October, 305-332.

Valentine, Gill (1999) Doing household research: Interviewing couples together and apart. *Area* 31 (1) March, 67-74.

Valentine, Gill (2001) The body. In *Social Geographies: Space & Society*., pp. 15-62. London, UK: Prentice Hall.

van der Veer, Peter (1997) Review of 'Global Migrants, Local Lives: Travel and Transformation in Rural Bangladesh' (Katy Gardner, 1995) in *American Ethnologist* 24 (1) February, 257.

Vásquez, Claudia and Irving Escobar (2005) Migrantes buscan un millón de firmas. *Prensa Libre* (Guatemala), 19 de febrero. Accessed at: http://www.prensalibre.com/pl/2005/febrero/19/108111.html.

Vásquez, Claudia and Luisa Rodríguez (2005) Promesas van a consulta a EE.UU.: Migrantes opinarán sobre política guatemalteca. *Prensa Libre* (Guatemala), 19 de febrero. Accessed at: http://www.prensalibre.com/pl/2005/febrero/19/108110.html.

Vertovec, Steven (1999) Conceiving and researching transnationalism. *Ethnic and Racial Studies* Special Issue: Transnational Communities, 22 (2), March, 447-462.

Vertovec, Steven (2003) Migrant transnationalism and modes of transformation. *The Center for Migration and Development Working Paper Series #03-09m*, Princeton University. Accessed at: http://cmd.princeton.edu/papers/wp0309m.pdf.

Vlach, Norita (1992) *The Quetzal in Flight: Guatemalan Refugee Families in the United States.* Westport, CT: Praeger.

Walton-Roberts, Margaret (2003) Transnational geographies: Indian immigration to Canada. *The Canadian Geographer* 47 (3), 235-250.

Walton-Roberts, Margaret (2004) Rescaling citizenship: Gendering Canadian immigration policy. *Political Geography* 23 (3) March, 254-281.

Warren, Kay B. (1993) Interpreting *la Violencia* in Guatemala: Shapes of Mayan silence & resistance. In *The Violence Within: Cultural and Political Opposition in Divided Nations*, ed. K.B. Warren, pp. 25-56. Boulder, CO: Westview Press.

Warren, Kay B. (1998) *Indigenous Movements and Their Critics: Pan-Maya Activism in Guatemala.* Princeton, NJ: Princeton University Press.

Watanabe, John M. (1995) Unimagining the Maya: Anthropologists, others, and the inescapable hubris of authorship. *Bulletin of Latin American Research* 14 (1) January, 25-45.

Watanabe, John M. (1996a) Immersion and intellection: Fieldwork and ethnography in a 'folk society.' Paper presented at the *American Anthropological Association* (AAA) meeting, San Francisco, CA, 22 November.

Watanabe, John M. (1996b) Neither as they imagined nor as others intended: Mayas and anthropologists in the highlands of Guatemala since the 1960s. In *Supplement to the Handbook of Middle American Indians*, vol. 6 (Ethnology), eds. J.D. Monaghan and V.R. Bricker, pp. 1-42. Austin, TX: University of Texas Press.

Waters, Johanna L. (2002) Flexible families? 'Astronaut' households and the experience of lone mothers in Vancouver, British Columbia. *Social & Cultural Geography* 3 (2) June, 117-134.

Waters, Johanna L. (2003) Flexible citizens? Transnationalism and citizenship amongst economic immigrants in Vancouver. *The Canadian Geographer* 47 (3) Autumn, 219-234.

Watts, Michael J. (1991) Mapping meaning, denoting difference, imagining identity: Dialectical images and postmodern geographies. *Geografiska Annaler* 73 (1), 7-16.

Watts, Michael J. (1992a) Space for everything (A commentary). *Cultural Anthropology* 7 (1) February, 115-129.

Watts, Michael J. (1992b) Capitalisms, crises, and cultures I: Notes toward a totality of fragments. In *Reworking Modernity: Capitalisms and Symbolic Discontent*, eds. A. Pred and M.J. Watts, pp. 1-19. New Brunswick, NJ: Rutgers University Press.

Watts, Michael J. (1997) Black gold, white heat. In *Geographies of Resistance*, eds. S. Pile and M. Keith, pp. 33-67. London, UK and New York, NY: Routledge.

Wellman, B. (1996) Are personal communities local? A Dumptarian reconsideration. *Social Networks* 18 (4) October, 347-354.

Wellmeier, Nancy (1994) *Rituals of Resettlement: Identity and Resistance among Maya Refugees in the United States*. Ph.D. Dissertation, Arizona State University.

Wellmeier, Nancy (1995) Rituals of resettlement: identity and resistance among Maya refugees. *Journal of Popular Culture* 29 (1) Summer, 43-60.

West, Candace (1996) Ethnography and orthography: A (modest) methodological proposal. *Journal of Contemporary Ethnography* 25, 327-352.

White, Allen (1999) Refugees, asylum-seekers and human geography – some theoretical perspectives. Accessed at: *Critical Geography Forum On-Line*, http://www.mailbase.ac.uk/lists/crit-geog-forum/files/white.htm.

White, Geoffrey, M. (1991) *Identity through History: Living Stories in a Solomon Islands Society*. Cambridge, UK: Cambridge University Press.

Wiles, Janine L., Mark Rosenberg, and Robin A. Kearns (2005) Narrative analysis as a strategy for understanding interview talk in geographic research. *Area*, 37 (1) Marc-h, 89-99.

Wilkinson, Daniel (2003) *Guatemala: A Human Rights Update: Human Rights Testimony given before the United States Congressional Human Rights Caucus*. Washington, DC: Human Rights Watch. Accessed at: http://hrw.org//backgrounder/americas/guatemala101603.htm.

Willis, Katie and Brenda Yeoh, eds. (2000) *Gender and Migration*. Cheltenham, UK: Edward Elgar.

Willson, Margaret E. (1986) Oral history interviews: Some history and practical suggestions. In *Ethnohistory: A Researcher's Guide*, ed. D. Wiedman, pp. 253-273. Williamsburg, VI: Department of Anthropology, College of William and Mary.

Wilson, Deborah (1987a) Aid network for refugees grows as arrivals increase, Special to *Globe and Mail*, 19 February, A9.

Wilson, Deborah (1987b) Illegal aliens flood across border, Special to *Globe and Mail*, 16 February, A1.

Wilson, Richard (1993) Anchored communities: Identity and history of the Maya-Q'eqchi'. *Man* 28, 121-138.

Wilson, Richard (1995a) *Maya Resurgence in Guatemala: Q'eqchi' Experiences*. Norman, OK: University of Oklahoma Press.

Wilson, Richard (1995b) Shifting frontiers: Historical transformations of identities in Latin America. *Bulletin of Latin American Research* 14 (1) January, 1-7.

Wimmer, Andreas and Nina Glick Schiller (2003) Methodological nationalism, the social sciences, and the study of migration: An essay in historical epistemology. *International Migration Review* 37 (3), 576-610.

Winchester, Hilary P.M. (1996) Ethical issues in interviewing as a research method in human geography. *Australian Geographer* 2, 117-131.

WOLA, Washington Office on Latin America (2003) Rights and development: Reframing economic development, promoting a rights-based approach. *A Bulletin of the Washington Office on Latin America*, November.

WOLA (2003) *Hidden Powers in Post-Conflict Guatemala: Illegal Armed Groups and the Forces behind Them*. [Susan C. Peacock and Adriana Beltrán]. Washington, DC: WOLA. December.

Wolcott, Harry (1990) On seeking - and rejecting - validity in qualitative research. In *Qualitative Inquiry in Education: The Continuing Debate,* eds. E.W. Eisner and A. Peshkin, pp. 121-152. New York, NY and London, UK: Teachers College, Columbia University.

Women and Geography Study Group (1997) *Feminist Geographies: Explorations in Diversity and Difference*. London, UK: Longman.

Wong, Madeleine (2003) *Borders that Separate, Blood that Binds: The Transnational Activities of Ghanaian Women in Toronto*, Unpublished PhD dissertation, Department of Geography, York University, Toronto, Canada.

Woodward, Laura L. (1989) *Central Americans in Tucson, Arizona*. MA Thesis, Department of Anthropology, University of Arizona.

Wright, Ronald (1987) Escape to Canada. *Saturday Night* 102, 44-50.

Wright, Ronald (1993) The death-list people. In *Home and Away*, pp. 63-84. Toronto, ON: Knopf Canada.

Yeoh, Brenda, Katie Willis and S.M. Abdul Khader Fakhri (2003) Introduction: Transnationalism and its edges. *Ethnic and Racial Studies* 26 (2), 207-217.

Zelinsky, Wilbur and Barrett A. Lee (1998) Heterolocalism: An alternative model of the sociospatial behaviour of immigrant ethnic communities. *International Journal of Population Geography* 4 (4) December, 281-298.

Zur, Judith (1994) The psychological impact of impunity. *Anthropology Today* 10, 12-16.

Newspapers Consulted

The Globe and Mail (Canada), http://www.theglobeandmail.com/.

Toronto Star (Canada), www.thestar.com.

Prensa Libre (Guatemala), http://www.prensalibre.com.

Siglo XXI (Guatemala), http://www.sigloxxi.com/.

el Periódico (Guatemala), http://www.elperiodico.com.gt.

Appendix One

Glossary of Immigrant Categories and Related Terms

The 1976 *Immigration Act* created multi-stage, complex, new procedures along with four classes of immigrants (refugees, independent immigrants, family class and assisted relatives) whose criteria have been modified many times since. This Act remained in effect until June 27, 2002 when the *Immigration and Refugee Protection Act* (IRPA) came into effect. This glossary serves as a guide to the various classes and criteria discussed throughout the book.

ASSISTED RELATIVES:
This is a pre-IRPA immigration category that includes independent immigrants who receive additional bonus points for having a relative in Canada and who do not qualify as members of the family class. Applicants have elements of family and independent class but might not qualify for either. In 1993, Assisted Relatives were absorbed into 'Independent Immigrant' class and became subject to the bonus points system.

CONVENTION REFUGEE:
Any person, who, by reason of a well-founded fear of persecution for reasons of race, religion, nationality, membership in a particular social group or political opinion,

(i) is outside his or her country of nationality and is unable or, by reason of that fear, is unwilling to avail himself or herself of the protection of that country, or (ii) not having a country of nationality, is outside the country of the person's former habitual residence and is unable, or, by reason of that fear, is unwilling to return to that country.

COUNTRY OF ASYLUM CLASS:
Those persons who are *outside* of their country of citizenship or permanent residence who have been or continue to be seriously and personally affected by civil war or armed conflict, or have suffered massive violations of human rights. Those in this category are in situations where there is no possibility, within a reasonable period of time, of a durable solution. Individuals selected under this class must be privately sponsored or have adequate financial means to support themselves and their dependants.

CR8 DEPENDENTS:

Convention Refugees (CR) and their dependants who are recognized as Convention Refugees in their own right by the IRB. Dependents are issued a visa for arrival into Canada.

DESIGNATED CLASS:

Immigrants who may not necessarily be Convention refugees, but whose admission to Canada would be in accordance with this country's humanitarian tradition toward the displaced and the persecuted. Often this category includes persons sponsored by a group in Canada (DC3).

DEFERRED REMOVALS:

Those persons who do not qualify as Convention refugees or as PDRCC (see p. 224), but still cannot be sent back to the country of origin. In July 1994, Sergio Marchi created this class in order to regularize the immigration status of refused refugee claims from China whom Canada did not want to remove. It eased the regulations of the PDRCC class established in 1993. Persons in the Deferred Removals class living in Canada for longer than three years can apply for Permanent Residency status.

ENTREPRENEUR:

Entrepreneurs are those economic immigrants in the 'business immigrant' category who are selected on the condition that they have managed and controlled a percentage of equity of a qualifying business for at least two years in the period beginning five years before they apply, and that they have a legally obtained net worth of at least $300,000 (Canadian). They must own and manage a qualifying business in Canada for at least one year in the three years following arrival in Canada. This class was introduced after 1978.

FAMILY CLASS:

A class of immigrants made up of close relatives of a permanent resident of Canada who is 18 years of age or over, and sponsored by that person. Close relatives include spouses and partners (i.e., spouse, common-law partner or conjugal partner), dependent (unmarried) children under 21, parents and grandparents, and orphaned sisters, brothers, nieces, nephews, and grandchildren who are orphaned under 18 years of age. Post-IRPA (2002), fiancé(e)s are no longer designated as a component of Family Class.

HUMANITARIAN AND COMPASSIONATE CASES:

Permanent residents in the 'other immigrant' category, including sponsored humanitarian and compassionate cases outside the Family Class, as well as humanitarian and compassionate cases without sponsorship and cases that take into account public policy.

IMMIGRATION AND REFUGEE BOARD (IRB):
The IRB is an independent tribunal established by the Parliament of Canada to make well-reasoned decisions on immigration and refugee matters, efficiently, fairly, and in accordance with the law.

IMMIGRATION AND REFUGEE PROTECTION ACT (IRPA):
Federal legislation respecting immigration to Canada and the granting of refugee protection to people who are displaced, persecuted or in danger. IRPA received royal assent on 1 November 2001, and came into effect on 28 June 2002.

INDEPENDENT CLASS:
The independent immigrant category is a pre-IRPA immigration category which includes skilled workers selected for their labour market skills and business immigrants (self-employed persons, entrepreneurs and investors) selected on the basis of their business experience and other related skills using a set of rated criteria (the points system).

INVESTOR:
Investors are economic immigrants in the 'business immigrant' category who are required to make a substantial investment in Canada that is allocated to participating provinces and territories for economic development and job creation. These immigrants have successfully operated, controlled, or directed a business or commercial undertaking who have made a minimum investment since applying for an immigrant visa and who has a net worth of at least $700,000. Investors are not necessarily interested in the day to day management of a business operation but are willing to invest at least $250,000.

LIVE-IN CAREGIVERS:
Effective 27 April 1992, the Live-In Caregiver Program replaced the Foreign Domestic Movement. This category includes those 'temporary residents' who have been issued a work permit to work in Canada as live-in caregivers or 'economic immigrants' granted permanent resident status after their participation in the Live-in Caregiver Program. The program brings workers to Canada on a temporary basis for certain kinds of live-in work. Program participants are offered the opportunity to apply for permanent resident status within three years of arrival in Canada and after completing two years of employment under the program.

MINISTER'S PERMITS:
Minister's permits are issued when those persons who are a minimal risk to Canadian society have a compelling need to come into or remain in Canada as part of Canada's social and humanitarian commitment, and international obligations towards refugees and displaced persons. Minister's Permits are not routinely issued to Convention Refugees and are usually offered for a short period of time. Since 1995, departures of permit holders are recorded at port of exit.

REFUGEE CLAIMANT:
Refugee claimants are temporary residents in the 'humanitarian population' category who request refugee protection *upon* or *after* arrival in Canada. A refugee claimant receives Canada's protection when he or she is found to be a Convention Refugee as defined by the United Nations 1951 Geneva Convention Relating to the Status of Refugees and its 1967 protocol, or when found to be a person needing protection based on risk to life, risk of cruel and unusual treatment or punishment, or danger of torture as defined in the Convention against Torture. A refugee claimant whose claim is accepted may make an application in Canada for permanent residence. The applicant may include family members in Canada and abroad.

REFUGEE CLAIMANT IN CANADA, POST-DETERMINATION (PDRCC):
Established in 1993, a post-determination refugee claimant in Canada (PDRCC) is someone who has been denied refugee status but faces exposure to serious risk upon return (i.e., threat to their lives, inhuman treatment, and so forth). The risk has to be personal, identifiable and present in every part of the country of return. When a person is identified, permanent residence is granted, otherwise they are removed. Persons not eligible include those who were refused refugee status before 1 February 1993, withdrawn or abandoned claims, claims with no credible basis, and those who have left Canada since their refugee claim decision.

REFUGEE DEPENDENTS:
Refugee dependants are permanent residents in the 'refugee' category who are family members of a refugee landed in Canada, and who were living abroad or in Canada at the time of application. Their applications for permanent residence are considered concurrently with that of the principal applicant in Canada.

REFUGEE, GOVERNMENT-ASSISTED:
Permanent residents in the 'refugee' category who are selected for resettlement in the Convention Refugees abroad class or the Source Country class and who are eligible for government assistance.

REFUGEE LANDED IN CANADA:
Permanent residents in the 'refugee' category who have had their refugee claims accepted and who subsequently applied for and were granted permanent resident status in Canada.

REFUGEE, PRIVATELY SPONSORED:
Permanent residents in the 'refugee' category who are selected for resettlement in the Convention Refugees abroad class, the Source Country class or the Country of Asylum class and who are privately sponsored by organizations, individuals or groups of individuals.

REMOVAL ORDERS (TYPES OF):
If either a senior immigration officer or an immigration adjudicator determines that a person has violated the IRPA (previously the *Immigration Act)*, they may issue one of the following removal orders: (1) Departure Order; (2) Exclusion Order; or (3) Deportation Order.

CONDITIONAL DEPARTURE ORDERS:
The departure order takes effect only if the claimant: (1) withdraws or abandons the claim to be a Convention refugee; (2) is determined not to be a Convention refugee; or (3) despite being a Convention refugee, does not have the right to remain in Canada. The person must leave Canada within 30 days and confirm such departure with CIC. If the person does not leave Canada within 30 days and does not confirm the departure with CIC, the 'departure' order automatically becomes a 'deportation' order.

DEPORTATION ORDER:
The person is permanently barred from returning to Canada unless they receive written permission from the Minister of Citizenship and Immigration. Departure and exclusion orders are usually issued for less serious violations of the IRPA (previously the *Immigration Act*).

EXCLUSION ORDER:
There are two types of exclusion orders: those with a one and two year ban. Exclusion orders with a one year ban require a foreign national to obtain authorization to return to Canada if they wish to return to Canada within one year after their removal order was enforced. Exclusion orders with a two year ban require a foreign national to obtain authorization to return to Canada if they wish to return to Canada within two years after their removal order was enforced.

RETIRED IMMIGRANTS:
This category was discontinued in August 1991. Persons over the age of 55 coming to Canada without the intention of working and with sufficient funds to support themselves. This class was mainly used by those who had once emigrated to Canada, left, and wanted to return.

SELF-EMPLOYED PERSONS:
Economic immigrants who intend and have the ability to establish or purchase a business in Canada that will create employment opportunity for those people, and will make a significant contribution to the economy or the cultural or artistic life of Canada. Entrepreneur and Self-Employed classes introduced after 1978.

SOURCE COUNTRY:
The Source Country Class is open to persons residing *in* their country of citizenship or habitual residence (e.g., those persons selected specifically by Canadian officials for permanent residence while living in refugee camps or refugee camp-like situations). In addition, this category includes those persons who are residing in their country of citizenship or habitual residence who have been and continue to be seriously and personally affected by civil war or armed conflict. In these cases, persons have suffered serious deprivation of their right of freedom of expression, right of dissent or right to engage in trade union activity and have been detained or imprisoned as a consequence and therefore fear persecution and present no possibility of a durable solution. Additionally, this list includes those who reside in a country that appears

on the Source Country Schedule. The 1999 Schedule includes: Bosnia-Herzegovina; Colombia; Croatia; Sudan; Democratic Republic of the Congo (DRC); El Salvador; and Guatemala. The revised 2001 schedule includes Colombia; DRC; El Salvador; Guatemala; Sierra Leone; and Sudan. Individuals selected under this class may be government-assisted, privately sponsored, or have adequate means of supporting themselves.

Sources: CIC (2004a, 2004c, 2005); CIC personal correspondence, 15 June 2000; IRB (2005b); and Kelly and Trebilcock (1998).

Appendix Two

Seeing More Numbers

Table 4.9
Guatemalan Refugee Claims, by Port of Entry and Inland Offices, 1990 to 1999*

Table 4.10
Guatemalan Permanent Residents, by Port of Entry, 1985 to 2004

Table 4.13
Guatemalan Permanent Residents, by Immigrant Class, 1980 to 2004

Table 4.14
Minister's Permits Issued to Guatemalans and Other Central Americans, 1980 to 2004

*Post-1999 data in this category is no longer supplied through the IRB and is currently unavailable through the newly created Canadian Border Services Agency (CBSA).

Table 4.9 Guatemalan Refugee Claims, by Port of Entry and Inland Offices, 1990 to 1999

LOCATIONS	TOTAL
NOVA SCOTIA	**5**
REGIONAL HQ NOVA SCOTIA	2
ALL OTHERS (20	3
NEW BRUNSWICK	**28**
ST. STEPHEN	23
ALL OTHERS (2)	5
QUEBEC	**1613**
BLACKPOOL/LACOLLE	1116
PHILIPSBURGH	153
MONTREAL	137
MONTREAL EST	109
ALL OTHERS (11)	98
ONTARIO	**1301**
FORT ERIE PEACE BRIDGE	511
C&I ETOBICOKE	119
NIAGARA FALLS RAINBOW	112
WINDSOR INT'L TUNNEL	87
ST CATHARINES	66
WINDSOR AMBASSADOR	64
C&I WINDSOR	49
FORT ERIE	43
NIAGARA FALLS-QUEENSTON	33
ALL OTHERS (28)	217
MANITOBA	**86**
EMERSON	68
C&I WINNIPEG	16

Table 4.9 continued

LOCATIONS	TOTAL
ALBERTA	**128**
CARWAY	48
C&I CALGARY	38
COUTTS	32
ALL OTHERS (3)	10
BRITISH COLUMBIA	**525**
DOUGLAS	237
CIC VANCOUVER ADMIN	205
PACIFIC HIGHWAY	29
INQUIRIES & REMOVALS	22
ALL OTHERS (7)	32
YUKON	**2**
WHITEHORSE	2
TOTAL	**3689**

Table 4.10 Guatemalan Permanent Residents, by Points of Entry, 1985 to 2004*

LOCATIONS	TOTAL
NEWFOUNDLAND	**1**
UNIDENTIFIED	1
NOVA SCOTIA	**19**
YARMOUTH	8
ALL OTHERS (4)	11
NEW BRUNSWICK	**42**
SAINT JOHN	22
FREDERICTON	12
ALL OTHERS (3)	8
PEI	**2**
CHARLOTTETOWN	2
QUEBEC	**5017**
MONTREAL: REFUGEE BOARD, MONTREAL EST, MONTREAL	2985
DORVAL	1341
CIC RENE LEVESQUE	358
MONTEREGIE	79
BLACKPOOL/LACOLLE	75
ALL OTHERS (13)	123
UNKNOWN LOCATION	56
MANITOBA	**254**
C&I WINNIPEG	126
WINNIPEG INT'L AIRPORT	77
EMERSON	50
BRANDON	1

Table 4.10 continued

LOCATIONS	TOTAL
SASKATCHEWAN	**14**
NORTH PORTAL	6
REGINA	5
C&I SASKATOON	3
ONTARIO	**8466**
TORONTO: PEARSON INT'L AIRPORT: I.A. #2, I.A. #1, TERMINAL III	4971
TORONTO: CENTRAL, REFUGEE BACKLOG, DETEN JAILS METRO, DETENTION & REMOVALS	749
ETOBICOKE: C & I, 5S	464
MISSISSAUGA: REFUGEE, CITIZENSHIP MISSISSAUGA, CIC, CPO	424
LONDON: C&I, BACKLOG, A/P	215
WINDSOR: C&I, WINDSOR AMBASSADOR, INT'L TUNNEL	208
OTTAWA: CIC, BACKLOG, I/ A/P, INT'L AIRPORT, ADMIN	172
NIAGARA FALLS (NF): POE, NF WHIRLPOOL, NF RAINBOW, NF QUEENSTON	127
C&I HAMILTON	118
FORT ERIE: PEACE BRIDGE, FORT ERIE	93
ST CATHARINES	80
C&I KITCHENER WATERLOO	109
C & I NORTH YORK	47
C&I SCARBOROUGH	64
OTHERS – EAST (5)	35
OTHERS – WEST (5)	53
OTHERS – NORTH (7)	37
UNKNOWN LOCATION	151

Table 4.10 continued

LOCATIONS	TOTAL
ALBERTA	765
CALGARY: C&I, INT'L AIRPORT	422
EDMONTON: INT'L AIRPORT, C&I	175
CARWAY	100
OTHERS – SOUTH (3)	59
OTHERS – NORTH (2)	9
BRITISH COLUMBIA	1452
VANCOUVER: INT'L AIRPORT, CIC ADMIN, REFUGEE, NEW WESTMINSTER, VANCOUVER ADMISSIONS	1251
VANCOUVER ISLAND (2)	48
PACIFIC HIGHWAY	26
BC INTERIOR (7)	69
LOWER MAINLAND (2)	15
UNKNOWN LOCATION	58
NWT	2
YELLOWKNIFE	2
YUKON	1
WHITEHORSE	1
TOTAL	**16035**

Table 4.13 Guatemalan Permanent Residents by Immigrant Class, 1980 to 2004

IMMIGRANT CLASS	1980-1984	1985-1989	1990-1994	1995-1999	2000-2004	TOTAL	% of TOTAL
CONVENTION REFUGEE	633	1460	1625	793	113	4624	27
DESIGNATED CLASSES	46	1201	3112	203	7	4569	26
FAMILY CLASS	434	683	1653	970	617	4357	25
INDEPENDENT (SKILLED WORKERS)	133	1077	733	140	174	2257	13
ASSISTED RELATIVES	115	476	165	33	n/a	789	5
CR8 DEPENDENTS	0	0	21	216	57	294	2
INLAND & BACKLOG	0	0	0	55	189	244	1
OTHER	15	10	21	117	82	246	1
TOTAL	**1376**	**4907**	**7330**	**2527**	**1240**	**17380**	**100**

Table 4.14 Minister's Permits Issued to Guatemalans and Other Central Americans, 1980 to 2004

MINISTER'S PERMITS	GUATEMALANS	OTHER CENTRAL AMERICANS	TOTAL
1980	0	29	29
1981	135	582	717
1982	108	272	380
1983	132	459	591
1984	211	220	431
1985	692	1871	2563
1986	887	2157	3044
1987	1455	4675	6130
1988	1105	3400	4505
1989	1257	3968	5225
1990	150	735	885
1991	212	594	806
1992	135	589	724
1993	82	347	429
1994	68	273	341
1995	37	151	188
1996	29	80	109
1997	34	53	87
1998	14	39	53
1999	41	62	8
2000	10	48	58
2001	25	50	75
2002	38	88	126
2003	55	203	258
2004	25	151	176
TOTAL	**6937**	**21096**	**28033**

Appendix Three

From Asylum to Control: Testimony of a Deported Taxi Driver

SCENE:	GUATEMALA CITY: TAXI RIDE BETWEEN LA AURORA AIRPORT AND LA EMBAJADA DE CANADÁ
DATE:	TUESDAY, 17 AUGUST 1999
TIME:	8:30 A.M. TO 9:30 A.M.

*****

Upon stepping out of the Aurora Airport in Guatemala City I negotiated the cab fare for a lift to the Canadian Embassy. EMILIO, my taxi driver, started talking to me in English once I made my request in Spanish. I ask him where he learned his English and to which he replied, '*Canada.*' 'Canada? NO!' '*Yes,*' he says, '*I lived there from 1984 until 1995 ... in St. John, New Brunswick.*' He said that he was the first Guatemalan in St. John. I explained my interest in his experience as I was in Guatemala doing related research. He seems interested and says his wife was still '*there,*' meaning Canada. My interest was obvious and he offered, '*Well, let me tell you my story.*' Parked in the shadow of the *Edificio Edyma Plaza*, EMILIO shared his experiences of asylum in Canada and his ultimate deportation directly into the hands of the waiting Guatemalan military. Without probing, pushing, or trying to pry, he pours out his story for an hour – interrupted only by a young, English-speaking Guatemalan lawyer who asks for a ride to city centre. I go along and chat with the lawyer in English and then EMILIO and I drive back to the Embassy again. What follows is a narrative account of our unrecorded interview conversation that EMILIO agreed to contribute to my research project under a pseudonym. The visa office of the Canadian Embassy served as a convenient location in which to write this account immediately after I left EMILIO's taxi.

*****

First, in order to get his papers he married a Canadian woman. She knew that the Canadian government was declining his request for asylum, so she agreed to marry him for $800. He said the problem was that '*she fell in love with me.*' When he asked her for a divorce a year later she refused and said if he pushed it, she would make '*big trouble*' for him. He says, '*I went to see a lawyer about this, that I wanted to divorce her and the lawyer said that if they hadn't been living together for a year and a half that it wouldn't be a problem.*' He asked if he needed to sign any papers, what he needed to do. The lawyer repeated his earlier advice and said that it wasn't a problem. He then married another woman … a woman he loved '*very much*' … a Canadian who doesn't speak Spanish.

'*The problem was,*' he said, '*the government found this out and kicked me out.*'

I asked him to clarify, that the government knew he was married to two women and that is why he was deported?

'*Yes,*' he said, '*they said it was illegal, you know? But I didn't know this. The lawyer told me it was no problem. I had my landed immigrant papers and everything, and they kicked me out. First they put me in prison.*'

'Prison?' '*Yes, prison ... for seven, no, three months.*' 'Where?' '*Montréal. For three months I was in prison and then I was put on a plane.*' 'Directly to Guatemala?' '*No. First to Miami. There I had a chance to run and I didn't. I came to Guatemala ... and I'm still in trouble for this.*' 'What kind of trouble?' '*See this taxi I'm driving ... it's owned, the company is owned, by generals, the military ... all them in the military.*' 'What? Just this taxi company? Or others?' '*Oh, MANY others! Ya many. The guys from the military, they were waiting for us at the airport and they took us to this place and asked us many questions.*'

'You and who else?' '*Seven of us ... me and the others deported.*' 'All from Canada?' '*No, from many places.*' 'Canada and Los Estados?' '*Yes, from different places in* Los Estados. *They knew we were arriving and they were waiting for us there. They took us and asked us what we had told other people.*' 'What do you mean?' '*We had been in the military and they wanted to know what we told people while we were gone. They wanted control of us again so they said we must report to this place. That's why I'm driving this taxi ... it's theirs ... they wanted control of my life again.*'

He said, '*People don't know that the military knows everyone who's coming ... they're told ahead of time and they're waiting.*' 'So you WERE in the military before you left?' '*Yes, yes, I was.*' 'You must have been young.' '*Yes, I was 18, 19 ... something like that.*' 'Did you want to be in the army?' '*NO, NO ... I was forced. They made me. I was a driver ... but I was in a special group ... they do different things ... like the FBI.*'

'The G2? You mean the G2?' I asked softly. '*Yes* [he looks surprised that I knew]. *Yes, the G2. They said it was a special unit. They said it was that but no one would say it was real, when some people came to look for it and no one would tell them nothing ... I saw many things, but I was a driver ... I was a driver and studying nursing. They sent me to the Petén because they said they needed someone who could do the things nurses do. I didn't want to go but they said they needed someone like a nurse. They sent our group to a small village ... not like a village ... only three houses. They gave me a gun, a rifle. They said we were supposed to hide here ... the houses were empty. They found four people and they killed them. I saw those things. Two old people ... a baby boy ... a young girl. Parents and their children. First they killed the parent then they killed the boy and raped the girl. They killed her. Then they destroyed the houses.... But you know in Canada they don't believe me. They said those things can't be REAL ... that I read them in a book or saw them in a movie. They were so hard to me ... they push and push and push and say they don't believe me. It was so HARD ... I had so many nightmares in Canada ... I almost killed myself. They didn't believe me.*'

'When you came to Canada, did you come as a refugee claimant?' '*Yes, as a refugee.*'

'You were young?' '*Yes, I was 24. And they didn't believe me; they told me I had to go. I think in Canada it is too good. They can't imagine these things. They can't believe that human beings can do those things. But it's real ... it's still going on. You go to those places and they still do those things. You know, there was another thing ... something happened in this other place. There was this girl, they had her there and she was pregnant ... she gave birth there. Then they took up the BABY BOY like this* [motions like he is picking up from the ground, like he's grabbing something] ... *holding him by his feet ... upside down ... and then they cut them off* ... [motions that the baby fell to the ground]. *I saw those things ... many things. And you know we're having elections now and that guy, that guy … I have it here* [tries to find something in his wallet] … *no I don't have it. That guy who ordered, "You kill these people and these people, and these people" ... he's trying to run again.*

'Yes, Ríos Montt, yes.' '*Yes him ... and if he gets in, it will all be the same again.*'

'Do you think you can get back to Canada?' '*I'd love to ... I want to go back ... I love it there, you know. I took it as my HOME, it was my country.*' 'Where would you like to live? In St. John again?' '*In TORONTO! I'd love to live in that place.*' 'How did you come to live in St. John?' '*At the border near St. John ... in Maine.*'

'How did you leave Guatemala? How did you get away from the military?' '*I escaped, I hid. I got to Mexico and from there to USA.*' 'And then up to Canada? How did you do that, with help?' '*Friends to Friends ... Friends to Friends, lots of groups.*' 'You mean like sanctuary?' '*Yes, exactly. That's another thing that Canada didn't believe ... that friends in Miami help me to get up to Maine.*'

At this point, I thought I should let him carry on working. I asked if he wanted me to check in the Embassy about his situation … not using his name but to ask about the possibility of getting back to Canada. He said, '*Yes, please, if you can.*' He gave me his business card with his full name, company name, and phone number with a direct line to his beeper. I said I could call when I find something out for him. I wrote my name and a fax number in Antigua.

He then said, '*I'm going to find my* historia ... *if I can't find it, I want to write it out for you and fax it to you. I'll send copies of my landed immigrant papers so you can see they are real.*' Again, I said it might take a few days to get back to him, but I hoped the information could help him. Maybe I'd see him in Toronto, I said.

We shook hands and I went into the Embassy. I asked in the visa section on the 6th floor of the Embassy building about his situation. He has to re-apply and supply copies of all documents. If he doesn't hear from them in three months, the answer is NO. Asked what his chances might be: '1 in a 100.'

Appendix Four

'This is What I Want to Deliver': Antonio's Escape to Canada

SCENE: **ANTONIO'S APARTMENT IN SUMMERLAND, ONTARIO**
DATE: **26 FEBRUARY 1999**
TIME: **1:30 P.M. TO 2:30 P.M.**

*****

ANTONIO, a 65-year-old Maya, searches for the written copy of his *historia* so that he can read aloud as a contribution to the research project. The interview conversation followed but through his prepared testimony ANTONIO is able to control the flow of the interview. ANTONIO awaits a ruling on his political asylum case after two years and two months in SUMMERLAND, Ontario. We discuss his plans to stay for the minimum three-month waiting period across the border at CASA VIVE in SULLIVAN if his case is denied. Three short weeks later his case *was* denied and deportation proceedings commenced. Rather than waiting for an official deportation to Chiapas, ANTONIO arranged for a return to family in Guatemala. PEDRO, who befriended ANTONIO, later confirmed their search for a 'contact' to smuggle him into the United States. *You can find anything in HOPE if you look hard enough*, he said.

*****

The 30th of October 1996. At seven at night in the municipality of [name], the state of Chiapas. And say your name right? ANTONIO ... MORALES ... OROSCO [pseudonym]. *I was sitting in the store ... when four men dressed in army fatigues with pistol in hands and they asked me for the doctor [name], and I replied that they could find him in his room resting and after the men entered my house without asking me for permission after a little while they came outside and they brought the doctor with his eyes covered and the threw him behind and threw him in the vehicle. So when I saw this I asked "Ay! Why are you taking the little doctor?" And just because I said that to them they said, "You, too, son of a bitch! Come here!" And they covered my mouth and my eyes and they threw me in the vehicle. I wanted to yell but the doctor said to me, "Be quiet Don ANTONIO because if you scream it will get worse." So for that I kept quiet.*

Okay, after we had walked like four hours ... all of a sudden the vehicle broke down on the edge of a hill and they began to spin around, it broke down ... two behind got

... under the vehicle to figure out what broke down and it was then that the doctor said to me, "Revive yourself Don ANTONIO and we are going to flee." The ravine was like 15 metres in height. When we fell there below the doctor said to me, "Go into those little trees," he said, "and we are going to wait for them to go." But shortly after we looked up and they had already started to come down, two of them, with flashlights in hand and the doctor said to me, "Prepare yourself Don ANTONIO we are going to have to run" or flee, that is how we fled climbing and descending ridges until we reached Tapachula, Chiapas. This took us like two days. Shortly after we arrived there the doctor bought the tickets for us to go to Mexico [City], *DF ... Yes, but after a few days we began to see suspicious people in the two corners, they were men with sunglasses and they were there for many hours so the family ... the doctor began to be afraid and they thought it was best that we come to the United States while they forgot about us.*

Because they ... where I came from they had killed many of countrymen. The bodies of some had been seen, and others were not seen. They made us suffer, they took them away because we are Indians and there the Ladinos or rather the rich have taken us [away] *furthermore because we also studied the bible and because we are a little ignorant we wanted a little and to learn we only went to the church but the church of the poor because there are also churches of the rich. And they think that that is why they came to take us, more for the doctor or maybe because the Zapatistas used to come to my house and buy food and a little* mosh *and sugar from me. That, nothing else, and I used to sell it to them because that was my business. And because they were brothers,* pues, *I did them the favour of selling them their food. And furthermore because the doctor also, there in his house, cured the Zapatistas at night.* Pues, *they always arrived two or three times a week after midnight, this was before like in January or February of 1995 until the date* [we left] *they always had their meetings there with the doctor.* Pues, *the delegates of Marcos, Comandante Marcos, always continued to arrive.* Bueno, *and through all this the doctor always advised me to leave my land and to come to the United States. We arrived in Los Angeles in January the New Year in the early morning the first of January and the doctor left me in a church and the nun received me. And shortly after they told me that it was best if I came to this place of* Canadá, *that maybe here they could leave me while the problem ends there. Because my desire is to return always, that the army of the government will leave the state of Chiapas, I can't return there because they will kill me. Since I left because of the army of the government and that is how they paid my fare for SULLIVAN. After in the bus terminal some men recommended me and because they saw that I was crying they collected me and took me to the nuns' house. After entering Canada, the 30th of January* [1997], *but first I came before an interview and that was the sixth of January but it was only at the border. That is what I want to deliver.*

Index

age 91–3
airports 103
Alba Luz's narrative 160, 172–3
Ana's narrative 159, 160, 174–5
Anglo-conformity 87
anonymity 26
anti-racist feminist research 37
Antonio's narrative 164, 169
Appadurai, Arjun 45, 117
applications for landing 98–102
Archbishop's Office for Human Rights in Guatemala (ODHAG) 65–6
armed conflict 61–5
assault, spaces of 66–9
'astronaut' families 53
asylum seekers
  deportations 75–6, 78
  numbers 75, 97
  see also immigration policies
Axworthy, Lloyd 95–6, 110

barriers and opportunities 165–72
Basch, Linda 48
Behar, Ruth 44
biological differences, race 62
the body 5
border crossings 78, 107, 183
Bouchard, Benoit 107
Bruce's narrative 127–8, 145–6, 155–6

Calhoun, Craig 153
campesinos 41, 96
Canada
  1980s-2000s 74–8
  Guatemalans' contributions 134–5
  multiculturalism 87–90
  remittance landscape 172–6
  social spaces 159–62
Canadian International Development Agency (CIDA) 95
'Canadianness' 146–8
Carlos' narrative 144
Carmen's narrative 121, 135–41, 146, 170, 171–4
categorization
  Maya 89
  transnationals 85–6
causation 86
CEH *see* Commission for Historical Classification
Central America 94–5
  see also Mexico
Chapin, Frederic 68–9
Chavez, Leo 117
children
  'astronaut' families 53
  counterinsurgency 68
  gender ratios 34
  inclusion in research 25
  numbers 93
choice, women's narratives 166–7
church sanctuaries 76
CIDA *see* Canadian International Development Agency
citizenship 9, 146–8
Citizenship and Immigration (CIC) data 84–6
civil patrols 155
class divisions 61–2
  race links 62–3
  social spaces 158–9
Clifford, James 48
Commission for Historical Clarification (CEH) 64–74
communities of association 49, 133–4, 149
communities/community studies 21, 39–45, 149, 152–4, 155–8, 168
Concha's narrative 169–70
concrete transnationalism 175
confidentiality 13, 26
Constancia's narrative 167–8, 171
contextual information 27
contradictions 9, 15
contradictory spaces 155, 165

counterinsurgency 42, 44, 68
critical ethnographic approach 16
cultural boundaries 46
cultural difference 55–6
cultural studies 38
culture of fear 43

Death Squad Dossier 71–4
deaths 69–74, 108, 137
  see also executions
Deconstructing a Nation (Satzewich) 89
departures from Canada 110–12
dependency, research subjects 12–13
deportations 75–6, 78, 110–12
deterritorialization 50
disappearances 67, 69–74, 108
dual citizenship 9

economic factors
  gendered migration 33
  Guatemala–Canada connections 7
El Salvador 35
Elena's narrative 166–8, 170, 172–3
Elsi's narrative 156
employment
  freedom without power 167–9
  gender 34
  immobility 176–7
  interview subjects 124, 138–9
  permanent residents 107–8, 109
ethical issues 12–13, 37
ethnicity
  Canadian multiculturalism 88
  Guatemala's 'two nations' 61–2
  identity 145–6
  social spaces 158
  see also race
ethnographic research 16–18
evangelicals 11–12
everyday relations 52
executions 67
  see also deaths
exile 61–81

Falla, Ricardo 43
family narratives 125
  Carmen and Roberto 135–7, 140
  Lillian 157
  Miguel 131, 132–3
  Pedro 127–30
  religion 171
  visa requirements 163–4
feminist research 36–9
Ferguson, James 45, 55–6
fiancé(e) visas 34
fieldwork methodologies 18–22, 45–6
final destinations, deportees 110–11
freedom without power 165–72
FRG (*Frente Republicano Guatemalteco*) party 68n
Fuentes, Carlos 88–9

gateway cities 177
Geertz, Clifford 17
gender
  Guatemalan permanent residents 91–3
  human rights violations 67
  migration process 5, 32–9
  political violence 141–2
'gendered geographies of power' model 35
genocide 63, 65–74
geographical research 51–5
geographies
  Canada 1980s-2000s 74–8
  immobile transnationalism 177
  of movement 83–117
  official/speculative 29
  of placement 39
  of power 35
  see also spatialization
Gerardi Conedera, Monseñor Juan 66, 79
'get tough' policies 94–5
Glick Schiller, Nina 47
global/local dichotomy 5
globalization 39, 46, 55, 56, 151–2
Green, Linda 37
Guarnizo, Luis Eduardo 143
Guatemala Canada Solidarity Network (GCSN) 10n
Guatemala
  Canadian connections 3–7, 124, 172–6
  returning to 162–3
  'two nations' 61–5
Guatemalan Military Archive see Death Squad Dossier
'Guatemalanness' 146–8
guerrilla forces 67, 135–6
Gupta, Akhil 45, 55–6

Hamilton, Nora 49
Hannerz, Ulf 153, 158
Harvest of Violence (Carmack) 43
Hilbert, Sarah 52
Hong Kong migrants 52–3
household dynamics 35
human rights violations 42, 65–74
hybridity 143
Hyndman, Jennifer 16, 52

identity
  citizenship 146–8
  ethnicity 145–6
  family relations 140
  Miguel's narrative 133, 134
  Pedro's narrative 130
  place 40–1, 55–6
  redefinitions 184
  researcher 10, 14–15
  rupture and renewal 142–5
  spatialization 122–3, 141
  transnationalization 11
'illegal' refugees 76, 97
immigrants
  'refugee' distinction 162–3
  status 176
Immigration Ministers 93–4
immigration policies 74–8, 87–116, 159–62
Immigration Reform and Control Act (IRCA) 97
immobility 149–78
income 176–7
independent immigrant status 176
individual realities 56–7
interviews
  multi-scaled social space 154–75
  procedures 25–8
  questions 27
  transnational ethnographies 17–18, 122–48
  see also testimonios
IRCA *see* Immigration Reform and Control Act
isolation 167–9

John's narrative 128–30, 145–6, 155–6
Jonas, Susanne 97
José's narrative 161, 163
Juan's narrative 156, 163, 171, 173–4
Juana's narrative 163

Kobayashi, Audrey 37, 88
Kobrak, Paul 69
Kohl, Albert 64

labour movement 70
Ladino 62–5
  early research 41
  human rights violations 67
  identity 145–6
language
  Canadian multiculturalism 87
  freedom without power 167–9
  identity 144
  interviews 26
Latin America 35, 38, 95
Laurie, Nina 155
Lawson, Victoria 35
LCP *see* Live-in Caregiver Program
leaders' departures 69–74, 130–3
Lemco, Jonathan 94
Lillian's narrative 157, 160, 163
Live-in Caregiver Program (LCP) 34
Lockhart, Shannon 65–6
loss, spaces of 69–74, 87

McBride, Michael J. 97
McDowell, Linda 36–7
MacEachen, Alan 95–6
McFarlane, Peter 94
MacGuigan, Mark 95
macro-dynamics 150
Mahler, Sarah 8, 35–6, 47, 142, 164
Malkki, Liisa 8
Manz, Beatriz 43, 62
Maya 62–5
  counterinsurgency 68
  deterritorialization 50
  human rights violations 67
  identity 40–1
  official categorization 89
  social fields 20
Melville, Thomas 68
memory 123
Méndez Calderón, Luz Haydee 72–3
mental health 70
Mesoamerica 40
Mexico 96, 98, 100, 108, 126, 152–3

micro-dynamics 150
migrant/refugee distinction 162–3
migratory circuits 51
Miguel's narrative 121, 130–5, 161–3
military patrols 155
military service 126, 160–1
Ministers of External Affairs 93–4
mis-identifications, researcher 10, 14–15
mobility 183
  see also immobility
moral commitments 37
movement, geographies of 83–117
Mulroney, Brian 107
multi-method research 16–17
multi-scaled social space 154–75
multi-sited research 17, 18–19
multiculturalism 87–90
municipio 39, 40

narratives 121–48, 154–75
  see also interviews
nation-states 50, 61–5
national identity 146
nationalism 63, 151
Nations Unbound (Glick Schiller) 47–8
Nelson, Diane 9, 11
network analysis 152, 153
neutrality 37
North Star Railroad 76

O'Brien, J. 46
occupational categories 107–8, 109
ODHAG *see* Archbishop's Office for Human Rights in Guatemala
official geographies 29
Ontario 100, 103
opportunities and barriers 165–72
Ortner, Sherry B. 45–6
Overground Railroad 76, 78, 106
Oxman-Martinez, Jacqueline 34

PA *see* Project Accompaniment
paradoxical spaces 155, 165
participants 22–8
Peace Accords 6–7, 65
Pedro's narrative 125–30
Pereira Vasquez, Julio César 71–2
permanent residents
  categorization 85, 108
  occupational categories 107–8, 109
  POE data 103
  population characteristics 90–3
Pessar, Patricia 35–6
place making 54–7
placement, geographies of 39
policy dynamics 87–116
political factors
  gendered migration 33
  research process 38
political violence
1999-2005 78–81
  communities 42–4, 155–8
  deportations 110–11
  gender 141–2
  identity 143
  research context 4
  social relations 150, 154
  transnational ethnographies 122, 131–3, 135–6
  see also state-sponsored terrorism
politics of scale 5–6, 154–75
population dynamics 87–116
port of entry (POE) data 100–7
Portillo, Alfonso 79–80
poverty study 165
power
  freedom relationship 165–72
  geographies of 35–6
Pratt, Geraldine 34–5
primary social relations 158–64
Project Accompaniment (PA) 10n
pseudonyms 21, 26, 125n, 162
psychological transnationalism 175

qualitative research 127
Quebec 78, 100, 103

race
  identity 145–6
  social constructions 37
  'two nations' 62–3
racialization 89
reciprocity 24–5, 28
recording interviews 26–7
reflexivity 38–9
refuge, spaces of 98, 106, 112, 114–16
refugee transnationalism 7–8, 149–78, 181–5

refugees
  access rights 89, 97
  categorization 85–6, 176
  displacement 61–81
  'migrant' distinction 86
  transnational studies 54
religion 170–2
REMHI findings 65–74
remittances 7n, 50, 172–6
renewal 141–5
research
  approaches 15–22
  contexts 4–7
researchers
  identity 10, 14–15
  participation 37
return migration 32, 33, 162–3
Roberto's narrative 121, 135–41, 169
Roberts, John 96
Rosaldo, Renato 38
Rose, Gillian 155
Roseberry, William 46
rural violence 68, 135
Ryan, Jan 32

'safe spaces' 64–5
safety, living in 169–70
Salovesh, 46
Sanctuary Movement 76, 77–8
Scheper-Hughes, Nancy 43–4
'scorched earth tactics' 68
secondary sources 18
Shami, Seteney 8
Shankar, Finola 127n
Silvey, Rachel 5–6
Singapore 35
Smith, Carol 61–3
Smith, Fiona 26
Smith, Michael Peter 143
Smith, Neil 107
snowball sampling 22
social actors 47
social constructions 37
social relations
  new social spaces 4, 50, 158–64
  political violence 150, 154
  transnational communities 152–4
social spaces
  place making 54–7
  political violence 4
  politics of scale 154–75
  refugee transnationalism 149–78
  research contexts 19–22
  social relations 50, 158–64
  transnationalism 150–2
  see also spatialization
solidarity 10–12, 43–4
Sosa Ramos, Alvaro Rene 73–4
spaces of assault 66–9
spaces of loss 69–74, 87
spaces of refuge 98, 106, 112, 114–16
spatialization 121–48
  see also geographies; social spaces
speculative geographies 29
state-sponsored terrorism 65–74, 155–8
statistical data 16–17, 84–6, 90–3
Stoltz Chinchilla, Norma 49
strategic transnationalism 53
students 69–71, 108
subjectivity 38–9

Temporary Protective Status (TPS) 53
terror/terrorism 43–4, 65–74, 155–8
testimonios 64, 65–7
  see also interviews
thin relations 153
TPS *see* Temporary Protective Status
tranquility, living in 169–70
transcripts 27
transition penalties 176
transnational community studies 44–5
transnational ethnographies 17–18, 121–48
transnationalism
  areas of study 47
  critiques 53–4
  definitions 7–8, 46–8
  geographical research 51–5
  immobility factors 175–7
  macro- and micro-dynamics 150
  social spaces 150–2
Trudeau, Pierre 95
truthfulness 13, 26
'two nations' (Guatemala) 61–5

Underground Railroad 76, 106
unemployment 176
United States
  deportation 111

remittance landscape 172–6
state-sponsored terrorism 68–9, 70–1
through-travel 74–8, 126
transnational communities 44
transnational social relations 152–3
universities 69–71
urban violence 68, 69–74
URNG *(Unidad Revolucionaria Nacional Guatemalteca)* 65

Valentine, Gill 28
validity 17
vengazas 137
violence 4, 41–4
see also political violence
visas 34, 75, 96, 163–4, 183

Waters, Johanna L. 53
Watts, Michael 7
weak ties 149, 153, 158–64, 170–2
Wellman, B. 153
White, Allen 8
women
employment 138–9
freedom without power 165–72
human rights violations 67
numbers and roles 4–5, 33–5
political violence 78–9
see also gender

Yeoh, Brenda 34–5

Zapatistas 52

Gender in a Global/Local World

Also published in the series

Vulnerable Bodies
Gender, the UN and the Global Refugee Crisis
Erin K. Baines
ISBN 0 7546 3734 4

Fashioning Inequality
The Multinational Company and Gendered Employment in a Globalizing World
Juanita Elias
ISBN 0 7546 3698 4

Setting the Agenda for Global Peace
Conflict and Consensus Building
Anna C. Snyder
ISBN 0 7546 1933 8

Un(thinking) Citizenship
Feminist Debates in Contemporary South Africa
Edited by Amanda Gouws
ISBN 0 7546 3878 2